DEEDS NOT WORDS

*A History of the
Swansea General and Eye
Hospital 1817–1948*

DEEDS NOT WORDS

*A History of the
Swansea General and Eye
Hospital 1817–1948*

T. G. DAVIES

With a Foreword by Professor Glanmor Williams

CARDIFF
UNIVERSITY OF WALES PRESS
1988

© T. G. Davies, 1988

British Library Cataloguing in Publication Data
Davies, T. G. [Thomas Gruffydd], *1931–*
   Deeds not words: a history of the Swansea
   General and Eye Hospital 1817–1948.
   1. West Glamorgan. Swansea. Hospitals.
   Swansea General and Eye Hospital, to 1948
   I. Title
   362.1'1'0942982

ISBN 0-7083-1010-9

All rights reserved. No part of this book may be reproduced, stored in a retrieval system, or transmitted, in any form or by any means, electronic, mechanical, photocopying, recording or otherwise, without clearance from the University of Wales Press, 6 Gwennyth Street, Cardiff, CF2 4YD.

Cover design: Cloud Nine Design, Cardiff
Printed in Great Britain by The Bath Press, Avon

Cyflwynir y llyfr hwn i Rosina, Lisa Sioned
ac Iwan Tudur am eu hir amynedd

Contents

List of Illustrations	viii
Foreword by Professor Glanmor Williams	ix
Preface	xi
Acknowledgements	xiii
List of Abbreviations	xv
Chapter One: Early Medicine	1
Chapter Two: The Dispensary	12
Chapter Three: The Infirmary—Early Days	19
Chapter Four: From Infirmary to Hospital	41
Chapter Five: The Swansea Hospital	72
Chapter Six: The Swansea General and Eye Hospital	107
Chapter Seven: Crisis and the War: 1909–1919	147
Chapter Eight: Post-war Developments	163
Chapter Nine: The Depression: 1929–1939	187
Chapter Ten: The Second World War: 1939–1945	208
Chapter Eleven: The Coming of the National Health Service: 1945–1948	223
Appendix I	235
Appendix II	239
Appendix III	241
Appendix IV	242
Appendix V	243
Notes and References	244
Select Bibliography	252
Index	255

Illustrations

	Page
The site of the original Dispensary in College Street	16
The Old Bathing House on the beach, 1791	20
The Infirmary and the House of Industry, 1818	20
Extract from the *Catalogus*, c. 1817	27
Dr G. Gwynne Bird in 1853	54
Head Nurse in the 1880s	95
Dr Jabez Thomas, c. 1880s	95
Mr Frank Thomas	137
Dr Florence Price, the first woman doctor appointed	137
The Hospital, c. 1911	149
Swansea motor ambulance, 1908	149
The medical and nursing staff in 1919	173
Treatment room in the Out-patients Department	179
Domestic staff, 1924	179
Visitor's ticket from 1926	185
Nurse's certificate from 1935	192
Soldiers in a ward during the Second World War	218
Inspecting bomb damage in 1943	218
The nursing staff at Swansea Hospital in 1960	231

Foreword

EMERITUS PROFESSOR GLANMOR WILLIAMS

The unprecedented pace and suddenness of economic and social changes associated with the Industrial Revolution brought in their wake unanticipatedly acute and painful problems, not the least of which was the issue of public health. The rapid rise of industrial conditions of employment was accompanied by a sharp increase in the number and incidence of industrial accidents and diseases. The congestion of thousands of men, women and children in grossly insanitary, overcrowded and squalid circumstances in the swift-growing towns quickly outpaced such efforts as were made to control and cure the spread of ailments and epidemics. Such pre-industrial arrangements as existed in social organization and local government to deal with these dangers were increasingly exposed as unsatisfactory and insufficient. Yet, in this, as in other spheres of public life, the Victorians refused to allow themselves to be daunted by the problems facing them. By a characteristic combination of parliamentary legislation and voluntary effort—with the latter always predominating—they applied themselves with zeal, energy and moral conviction to grapple with their difficulties. One of the more impressive of their successes was the gradual creation of a hospital service to cope with some of the worst threats to health.

As a major port and early metallurgical centre, Swansea was one of the first Welsh towns to experience the impact of modern industry. It also had one of the more impressive records of the development of a municipal hospital provision. Fortunately, the records of that service have been unusually well preserved and have been available for study by those who wished to trace its origins, growth and expansion. No one has been anything like as successful in that respect as Dr Tom Davies, author of this volume. He brings to his task an unusual combination of gifts. A distinguished medical practitioner with long and successful experience of the problems of treating patients inside hospitals, and outside them, he also possesses all the instincts of a gifted historian and for many years has practised the skills associated with the study of history. The result is an account of Swansea Hospital from its origins until the time of its absorption into the NHS. It tells of the unending struggle to raise money, the painful lessons learnt from trial and error, the fostering of a high sense of public duty and responsibility on the part of doctors and nurses, and the tensions aroused from time to time by the conflicting attitudes of medical men and laymen not to mention the occasional disputes among doctors themselves. This experience of the mixture of human devotion and frailty will not be unfamiliar or unexpected to any of us who have come into contact with public effort on a considerable scale. Figures of great and abiding interest were associated with Swansea Hospital; most famous of them being the great Florence Nightingale herself, who embodied more dramatically and persuasively than anyone else the herculean effort needed to raise nursing and hospitals to a worthy status in the last century. The whole history of our local hospital reminds us *in parvo* of what a struggle it has been to achieve worthwhile recognition of the role that modern medicine and the hospital service have to play in our contemporary society. The achievements—and mistakes—of our predecessors need to be taken to heart by our own generation. I sincerely hope that this book will have the large and attentive audience that it richly deserves.

Preface

This work does not represent the first attempt that has been made to record the history of the Swansea General and Eye Hospital. Two small pamphlets were produced many years ago and Mr Geraint Felder's MA thesis on hospital administration, which I have deliberately not yet read, were all concerned with the subject. In 1983, the Swansea Consultants' Medical Staff Committee, aware that the building was to be demolished, invited me to write this book and I am grateful to them for having given me that privilege.

History, according to the Dutch historian, Pieter Geyl, is an argument without end. Those inclined to a cynical point of view might be tempted to suggest that much of the history of Swansea Hospital consisted of one long, endless argument, but they would surely be wrong. To be sure, there were frequent, unavoidable arguments: it took people of sterling qualities to organize and manage such a place at a time when it could never be taken for granted that there would be enough money available to maintain even a minimal level of service and it was often that very strength of character of theirs which made disagreements inevitable.

Be that as it may, it is certain that there will be much to argue about in a book that attempts to tell the story of a hospital whose life history spanned the two most exciting centuries known to medicine. Those who were concerned with it witnessed a series of changes in their styles of working that invaded every sphere of medical practice and transformed the treatment of illness from being a nebulous concept, of interest only to the esoteric and available to a minority, into one of the major concerns of the State. It might not be altogether inappropriate here to make a comparison with Macaulay's tribute to Jeremy Bentham who, he said, 'found Jurisprudence a gibberish and left it a science'.

There are those who mourn the destruction of the building and who still speak with *hiraeth* of its once salubrious asepticity and (often in the same breath) its cockroach-ridden corners. Yet, it must surely be true that the greatest tragedy that could befall the memory of the hospital is not that the building has been demolished but that the work that was done there should be forgotten. If this book, for all its imperfections, should help in any way to ward off that possibility, it may be that the Medical Staff Committee's decision will not have been taken in vain.

T. G. DAVIES

Acknowledgements

It was a great honour for me that Professor Glanmor Williams, with characteristic generosity, agreed to read the manuscript, and I am doubly privileged that he has also written the Foreword. His willingness to give of his time in order to discuss the completed work made my task that much more enjoyable. All the defects that remain are mine.

I am especially grateful to the West Glamorgan Health Authority, its Chairman, Professor W. M. Williams, and its General Manager, Mr J. H. Button, for their generous help with publication costs, and to Mr R. A. Hoyle, the Manager of the Authority's West Unit, for his unfailing co-operation.

I must also thank: Mrs Patricia Moore, the Glamorgan Archivist, for permission to quote from the superb collection of hospital papers and from several other documents housed at the Glamorgan Record Office; Mrs Bennett, the Record Office Archivist at Swansea, for whose kindness I am very grateful; Mr Geoffrey Orrin and Dr Cowley of the Library at University College, Swansea, for helping, as they have done so frequently in the past, by tracing documents; the staff at the National Library of Wales and the Swansea City Archivist's Office for permission to quote from documents in their possession; the Royal Institution of South Wales and the Librarian at the University of Wales College of Medicine for allowing me access to their collections; the editors of the *British Medical Journal* and *The Lancet* for permission to quote from those journals; the Archivist at the London Record Office and St Thomas's Hospital Medical School for allowing me to quote from their comparatively unknown Nightingale St Thomas's Hospital Collection; the Keeper of the Public Record Office for the right to quote from Census and Tithe Map Records; Mr Leighton Evans on behalf of May and Baker Ltd., who made available a microfilm copy of material which would otherwise have been difficult to obtain; Mr Richard Morris of Chalfont St Peter for lending me his transcripts of Lewis Weston Dillwyn's diaries; Mrs Olga Welbourn for permission to quote from those diaries; Mr Brian McKenna of the National Library of Ireland for providing information from the *Dublin Chronicle*; Mr W. Pring, of the Photographic Department at University College, Swansea, and Mr Steve Brown of the Industrial

Therapy Department, Cefn Coed Hospital, for copying some of the photographs; my secretary, Mrs Cynthia Jenkins BA, and her predecessor, Mrs Susan Brace, for their patience and help; Mr John Rhys and Mrs Ceinwen Jones of the University of Wales Press for their co-operation and advice in preparing the book for publication; Dr Beverly Littlepage and his predecessor, Dr David Phillips-Miles, for many kindnesses; and finally, my family whose tolerance in the face of every difficulty tells more of them than any words of mine could and it is to them that I am glad to dedicate this work.

Abbreviations

H   Committee Minutes of the Swansea Hospital Collection (D/DHS 1–257) at the Glamorgan Record Office.

D/DHS   Other documents in the Swansea Hospital Collection at the Glamorgan Record Office, followed by the number of the document.

NLW   National Library of Wales

The unattributed information and quotations in the text are taken from the Swansea Hospital records. As more than 1,200 references are made to that collection, they are not listed individually.

CHAPTER ONE

Early Medicine

'Doctor indeed,' grumbled father, ... 'and where shall she find a doctor as shall know as much as old Betty Perkins of Penclawdd? I do believe that a word from she and a look from her one eye shall do more to cure someone than all the doctors as was ever born, or all the oils as was ever mixed ...'[1]

NOT a great deal is known of the practice of medicine in Swansea and western Glamorganshire before the nineteenth century. In view of the impact that a wide variety of diseases must have made on the local community over the centuries, it is all the more surprising that so little of this impact has been recorded. It is tempting to speculate that this may be connected with the constraints traditionally placed on doctors which, throughout the ages, have prevented their making public the details of their patients' illnesses, although those restrictions were far less rigid at that time than they have since become. Even if the doctors recorded little, other observers of the local medical scene have been equally reticent, and the few scattered observations on the incidence of disease in the locality, at a time when the concept of the official notification of ill-health was unknown, do nothing to provide a coherent account of patterns of illness.

The very first example of disease recorded locally was found, not in humans, but in animal remains that are now known to have belonged to the Palaeolithic Age. When Dean Buckland discovered the so-called 'Red Lady of Paviland' in Goat's Hole, Gower in 1823, he found among the many bones in the cave the lower jaws of two bears which were 'firmly anchelosed' (*sic*) and part of a diseased elephant trunk which he believed had received a severe blow.[2] No other evidence in prehistoric animal skeletons has been found in the district, but examples of bone disorder in bovine remains from Roman times have come to light at Caer-went and Chepstow.

One prehistoric example of human disease was unearthed at Gelligaer in the eastern part of the old county of Glamorgan, in the form of a child's skull (dated as 2000–1500 BC) which showed changes typical of iron-deficiency anaemia. In Roman times, the legionary fortress at Caerleon housed a large military hospital and while it is virtually certain that the Roman forts at Loughor and Neath would also have contained hospitals, their sites have not yet been identified. The only medical instruments known to have been used in that period were disovered at Caer-went.

Little evidence of medical matters in the Swansea area comes to light until the twelfth century, more than a thousand years later. The Cistercian abbey at Neath was founded in 1130, and the name of an adjacent farm, Cwrt y Clafdy, may have survived as a reminder that the monks maintained their own infirmary. Certainly, the abbeys in Wales on the whole provided some form of medical attention for lay people, while it was possible to buy in advance the right to a place there during old age.

During an excavation in 1950, parts of the building that housed the Hospital of the Blessed St David were found on the site of the Cross Keys Inn in Swansea. This St David's Hospital functioned from 1332 to 1550 and, although it was hardly a hospital at all in the modern sense, it was opened to care for 'blind, decrepit or infirm priests and other poor men';[3] with the exception of the abbey infirmary, it was the only charitable institution which provided such residential accommodation in the district for nearly 600 years. Nothing came of Bishop Burgess's wish, expressed in the charge delivered by him to the Chapter of St David's Cathedral in 1811 that this 'long lost charity' should be restored to its former function.[4]

In the sixteenth century a law was passed which decreed that it was obligatory for the bishops to issue licences to physicians and surgeons to allow them to practise. In deciding whether this permission was to be given or not, 'expert persons' were to be asked for their advice if necessary,[5] and, apart from the interregnum of the seventeenth century, this system (together with the licensing of midwives) continued until well into the eighteenth century, after which its use gradually diminished.

In 1665, the Bishop of St David's (whose diocese then included Swansea) knew of only three 'practisers of physick'[6] in the whole diocese and of those, two were clergymen and they all worked in areas far from Swansea. Even though fines could be imposed on anyone who practised illegally, it is certain that there were many who worked as doctors (and especially as surgeons) without the authority of the Anglican Church. No letters of recommendation from western Glamorgan have survived, but in 1705, the Visitation Returns for Swansea record:

> We have none to o^r knowledge that practiseth Phisick Chirurgery or Midwifery wth out License.[7]

The entries for the Gower parishes are typified by that for Oxwich ('... nor any as doo practise Physick or Surgery'[8]) and Penrice ('We know of no Hospital ... nor any ye make a Publick Practice of Physick or Chirurgerie[9]). From his use of the word 'Publick', it may well be that the churchwarden at Penrice was aware that there were unlicensed practitioners working locally but that he had no wish to make that known. At Bishopston, 'an ordinary midwife there is', while at Penard (*sic*), there was reported to be no hospital in the parish though 'ordinary midwives there are'.[10]

It has been possible to trace four doctors who lived in Swansea in the seventeenth century, of whom only one was granted a 'Facility to practise Surgery'. In the next century, of the nineteen doctors listed under Glamorgan in the privately published *Medical Register for the year 1780* (London, 1780), five lived in Neath, three in Swansea and two in Margam. This does not necessarily represent the true distribution of doctors in the district since it has been possible to trace another ten who worked in Swansea alone. Two doctors from western Glamorgan deserve a mention.

The only local physician listed in the *Medical Register for 1780* was Dr Andrew Paterson of Margam. As far back as 1775, he was accepting subscriptions on an annual basis, possibly through the Laudable Society. The sums paid varied from one guinea to ten guineas a year (for a member of the Talbot family). In 1787, Thomas Williams, a Swansea surgeon, born at Palleg in the Swansea Valley, achieved some notoriety by resuscitating eight miners thought to be dead when they were brought to the surface after a colliery explosion at Llansamlet. In a letter to a Mr Hawes of Dublin which was published in *The Dublin Chronicle* (6–8 November 1787), he wrote of:

> the advantages I received from being a pupil to your Course of Lectures on suspended animation ... all [the miners] were brought up apparently lifeless ... The plan recommended by you ... was vigorously pursued for an hour, when we discovered signs of life ...

He was still practising in 1804 when he described himself in an advertisement in *The Cambrian* of 29 September as an:

> apothecary, Man-midwife, Chemist and Druggist [who] has received a large supply of genuine Cow-Pock Matter from a member of the Royal Jennerian Society, and has since inoculated 40 children in this town. Being anxious to contribute to the extirpation of the dreadful malady ... he will inoculate the children of gentlemen and tradesmen at five shillings each and poor people's gratis.

It is possible that this man was related to a Dr Thomas Williams (son of Thomas Williams, Swansea, gentleman) who is known to have graduated in medicine at Oxford in 1743.

In spite of the major advance of inoculation against smallpox, the practice of medicine was still primitive, and when the incumbent vicar of Llan-giwg wrote of his duties in 1733 as largely consisting of 'visiting the sick and preparing them for their departure from this life'[11], there was indeed little more that the doctors of the day could have done for the seriously ill.

In the eighteenth century, and even well into the nineteenth, most non-fatal illnesses and injuries would have remained untreated by the few orthodox medical practitioners. Their services, such as they were, were more readily available to the more wealthy sections of the community and, from time to time, to the needy who suffered from more serious disorders. Later in the nineteenth century, there were notable exceptions to this when an increasing number of local doctors set aside time each day to deal with the poor. From the historical point of view, by far the most striking example of such benevolence by a Swansea man was that provided by Dr Nicol, who was later elected a physician to the Swansea Infirmary. At some indeterminate time before 1835, he visited:

> a poor patient [who being] unable to give him a pecuniary remuneration for his services, begged his acceptance of a small box containing old deeds and papers . . .[12]

In the year 1326, King Edward II had fled from Swansea Castle and in his haste was said to have left behind him some papers which included the contract concerning his marriage to Isobel, daughter of King Philip IV of France. The box given to Dr Nicol contained this marriage contract and he later presented it to the Royal Institution of South Wales.

Alternative medicine, increasingly in vogue today, had not yet gone out of fashion during the nineteenth century. At times of illness, many had, from time immemorial, resorted to visiting holy wells with which the locality was more than adequately endowed. Their water was used in the treatment of skin disease and scurvy and, in the case of St Helen's Well (near the site of the Swansea Hospital), for helping in the healing of wounds and the curing of cancer. If the subject of medical botany was relegated to the level of 'quackery' in Neath when a series of public lectures on the topic was arranged, books on the same theme (in Welsh and in English) by such men as the Reverend Rees Price of Cwmllynfell and Evan Griffiths of Swansea (to cite only those by local authors) could run into several editions and were sold by the thousand, as they promised relief from virtually all known ailments by the ingestion of concoctions made from combinations of the local flora.[13] In addition, medicines of various kinds, for which the most extraordinary claims were made, were advertised in newspapers, and the Swansea paper, *The Cambrian*, and Welsh language journals, such as *Seren Gomer*, followed the course taken by their English contemporaries in publicizing those wares. Of course, the average Swansea resident was too impoverished to be able to afford to buy newspapers, but advertising must have brought a return; of the medicines regularly advertised there, 'Dicey Daffey's Elixir', a mixture of seventeenth-century origin, was still being sold as late as 1910.

Dr Thomas Richards's description of Restoration Wales as having been 'the happy hunting ground of quacks and conjurers' might well have been applied for a considerable time after that.[14] Folk medicine survived, in part at least, because of the poverty of the mass of the population who could not afford to engage the orthodox medical practitioners whose practices were sometimes difficult to distinguish anyway from those of their more amateurish opponents. Little is known of the work of the folk practitioners who worked in the vicinity, but for most of their patients the nineteenth century was a time of great promises rather than a time of great promise. Some of them, such as the bone-setters, were skilled and exploited their natural talents in a way that benefited the community while the alleged expertise of others would have played upon an injudicious mixture of ignorance and superstition. Their success rate was likely to have depended largely on their level of psychological sophistication, a commodity too important ever to be ignored by a healer of any persuasion.

As late as 1861, it was being said (in *The Cambrian* of 3 May):

> for here, even here in the good town of Swansea, the belief in witchcraft has been acknowledged.

This was a reference to a man who believed that his asthma was caused by the influence of *the evil eye*, having been told by a local 'witch-curer' that the source of the evil spell was 'a woman to whom the Gower folks gave credence for powers infernal'. The issue of whether such practitioners believed in the true efficacy of their own treatments (as opposed to using deliberate deceit) is complex, but their treatments have been known to work well in disorders with a psychological overlay, of which bronchial asthma can be one.

The Griffith family of Cadoxton-juxta-Neath are said to have had a great reputation for being able to cure the jaundice (without ever having realized that jaundice can be caused by several quite unrelated disease conditions).[15] They were said to use 'enchantment', and it may be that the spontaneous disappearance of symptoms played a part in enhancing their reputation, or that they had accidentally discovered a treatment which relieved jaundice brought about by one cause. *Torri'r llech* (incising the lobe of the ear as a—totally ineffective—means of curing rickets) was practised occasionally even in this century in the Neath district. In spite of their many deficiencies as healers, it should not be forgotten that the folk practitioners possessed some techniques of great antiquity which had stood the test of time, and that their results in treating at least some disorders cannot have been all that much worse than those of the doctors of the day.

There were, of course, several kinds of unqualified medical practitioners (who, until well into the nineteenth century, included the majority of those practising as surgeons), and *The Lancet* in December 1870 must surely have over-simplified a most complex issue by suggesting that quacks would flourish:

> as long as medical practitioners fail to see the importance of paying attention to the little aches, pains and discomforts to which flesh is heir.

Those words might well be true in the third quarter of the twentieth century, but in a community where fatal infections, a high mortality rate and a short life-span were to be expected, little aches, pains and discomforts would not have loomed large in the minds of most of the populace.

The time had not yet arrived when medicine had a role in improving the quality of human life as well as in preserving it, and many of our present medical services would have been regarded as luxuries in the nineteenth century. The Swansea of those days, however, was not without its luxury medical services. While the government was struggling after a fashion with plans 'to prevent spreading of the plague and other contagious diseases', there were gradually becoming available to the wealthy a variety of provisions which dealt with less serious afflictions. By 1818, there was one surgeon-dentist working in the town and, nearly twenty years later, an optician's advertisement in *The Cambrian* of 2 September 1837 ('To all those who value their sight') testified to the increasing demands for services of that kind. Provision for the affluent was later augmented with the arrival of Mons. Picard, a chiropodist, (who persuaded a senior Swansea physician to allow his name to be included in advertisements as having had a corn removed 'without giving me the slightest pain'.)

Although later on psychiatry came to be regarded (mistakenly) by many as being a luxury service (when prominence was given to treating the lesser serious disorders), this was not the case when Dr Thomas Hobbes set up the first known asylum in Wales, at Swansea. This was a privately run house and he would probably not have taken any interest in (and indeed, might not have been too aware of the existence of) the neurotic disorders, which contribute to such a great extent to the work of the present-day psychiatrist. The fusion between the psychiatric and the other specialist services was not to occur for a considerable time yet.

Preventive medicine as a scientific discipline was unknown at the beginning of the nineteenth century. Yet it was being practised in the late eighteenth century within twenty miles of Swansea by a Unitarian minister, Reverend Thomas Morgan of Blaengwrach. He was the first person in Glamorgan, though not in Wales, known to have practised vaccination. In 1784, when there were no doctors working in that vicinity, he vaccinated more than a hundred children in the Neath valley after a severe epidemic of smallpox.[16] Men of his calibre and foresight were not common in the western parts of Glamorgan in those days.

Traditionally, physicians were men of learning whereas surgeons were less well educated and had a lower status although their standard of practice was often higher because of the more relevant and practical nature of their training. In July 1806, the Royal College of Physicians was sufficiently concerned about the many complaints received by them of 'irregular Practitioners ... who exercise the profession of Physic without authority' that they issued public warnings of the dangers.[17] There was no legal requirement for anyone who styled himself a doctor to be registered by law and many of those who were legitimate practitioners had no formal qualifications. Of the nine doctors known to be practising in the town in 1801, two were physicians, and of the seven surgeons, only two are known to have held any formal qualifications.

Several medical publications by Swansea doctors of that period (all of them interesting but not all of great importance) are known. Seen through twentieth-century eyes, and filtered through the accumulated knowledge and experience of more recent times, these works appear now to be a naïve conglomeration of irrelevancies which testify only to the underdeveloped state of the medical science at that time. Looked at in their proper context, they represent genuine, but often unsuccessful, efforts to solve the most puzzling of health problems using the most primitive of techniques.

Dr William Turton MA, MB (1762–1835), Fellow of the Linnean Society, is better remembered today as a conchologist than for his work in medicine. Nevertheless, his medical writings, including *A Medical Glossary* (1797) and *Some Observations on Consumption* (1813), are of some historical interest. His *Treatise on Hot and Cold Baths* (printed at his own Press in Swansea in 1803), although on the whole an unremarkable document typical of its day, shows how similar were some of the treatments prescribed by the orthodox doctors to those used by the folk practitioners. He put forward 'immersion' almost as a panacea, useful in such different conditions as catarrh, enlarged liver, lumbago and hypochondriasis, while:

> R. P ... an elderly magistrate ... sitting, in the discharge of his official duties, with his feet resting upon cold damp flag stones [developed] pains in the back and bowels, with ... indigestion and flatulence and great depression of spirits ...

had, when all else had failed, improved almost at once on being:

> seated naked on a chair, with his legs in an empty tub; cold water immediately from the sea was dashed ... very plentifully all over his body [and within a few days he was] soon restored to complete health by the gradual use of good food and a few cordials.

Dr Turton's *Letter to ... the Jennerian Society on the introduction ... of COWPOCK in Wales* (1803) is of greater interest. Having been born in Gloucestershire, Turton was already familiar with Jenner's work on vaccination. He had been struck by the simplicity of the technique and when he discovered that nearly 200 people a year were 'swept off' by the disease in Swansea, he went to London in 1799 and brought back with him sufficient lymph to start vaccinating in Swansea. So convinced was he of the effectiveness of Jenner's technique that he started by inoculating his infant daughter. He then:

> exposed her in every way to infection, by taking her into houses where the smallpox raged, putting her into bed with the foulest objects ...

After nearly four years, he was glad to 'see this method universally adopted here ... It is now more than three years since any death has occurred.'

Dr John Charles Collins (1780–1824), in *A Sketch of the Medical Topography of Swansea* (London, 1815), acknowledged his indebtedness to Dr Turton's earlier work with vaccination in Swansea, and explained how he himself had vaccinated more than 5,000 people between 1804 and 1815. He found that, according to the parish registers, from 1796 to 1805 there were 805 deaths from smallpox in the town, whereas in the following ten years only 10 people died from that disease. In spite of the fact that smallpox was the only fatal infectious disorder which was preventable at that time, Collins tends to present a rather idealized picture of the state of public health in Swansea. He claimed that the annual death rate was 1 in 84 of the population as compared with 1 in 73 for Cardiganshire, 1 in 53 for the county of Glamorgan and 1 in 36 for Middlesex. With some intermittent exceptions, fevers, he thought, had been remarkable by their absence over the previous fourteen years, although measles had carried with it a high death rate. Typhus 'mitior' was said to be one of the commoner infections and in the epidemic which had occurred about the year 1806 in (unspecified) neighbouring parishes, washing patients with cold vinegar and water was found to be effective early in the course of the illness, but the usual treatments were bleeding, blistering, emetics, and purgatives.

When infections did affect the 'lower classes of population', they were likely to take the form of erysipelas in his experience. This was known locally as 'blast' as it was generally thought to be brought on by the strong fires which were commonly seen in working-class homes. The miners, who started working underground from six to sixteen years of age, were not thought to be more liable to develop scrofula (tuberculosis of the glands of the neck) or other diseases as a result of their work, and he stressed the important protective effect with which the 'general use of flannel' was associated.

Neither Dr Collins nor William Llewellyn, a surgeon of Baglan who wrote a paper on the treatment of cholera in 1832,[18] seem to have raised the possibility that the great killer diseases of the nineteenth century might have been preventable by improving environmental conditions, although they were both well aware that smallpox could be effectively prevented by vaccination. Great surprise has sometimes been expressed that doctors working at that time should have failed to be aware of the possibility that there might exist a relationship between insanitary conditions and ill-health. It should be remembered that the causes of infectious disorders were not properly elucidated for a considerable time after that. Dr Prestwood Lucas in *A Report on the outbreak of epidemic cholera in Brecon in 1854* (London, 1855) wondered, 'Why in one year typhus, in another malignant scarlatina, and in another cholera, should prevail in the same locality ... science has not yet discovered.'

There followed a gradual change in thinking on the subject, with an increasing emphasis on improving standards of hygiene, and this was reflected in the more pointed criticisms which some of Swansea's medical men made of the state of the town as the century went on.

Dr J. W. G. Gutch, whose *Medical Topography ... of Swansea* was published in 1839, long after the opening of the hospital, raised the possibility that the fatal cases of typhus recently found in the locality:

> may ... have in some measure originated from the imperfect state of the sewerage, the impure condition of the streets and the comparatively small supply of fresh water, all calling sadly for improvement.

'All is darkness and confusion, vague theory and vain speculation', proclaimed *The Lancet* in discussing the causes of infectious and other diseases on 22 October 1853, but before that time the newfangled ideas had started to take hold. In 1849, Mr Evans, a Morriston surgeon, (probably William Price Evans who came to Landore as a surgeon in about 1815) offered evidence to the enquiry conducted by G. T. Clark on behalf of the Board of Health, in which he claimed that the ever-present fever:

> is . . . mainly owing to . . . no drainage . . . The weir situated immediately below Morriston is unquestionably another very fertile source of disease . . . the bulk of the inhabitants drink their tea and beer brewed with this filthy water. It is therefore plain that fever, food and cholera are unremittingly supplied to the lungs and bowels of the inhabitants of Morriston.[19]

Those words were indicative of a new style of thinking, but it was the iconoclastic George Gwynne Bird (who was a member of the Swansea Infirmary's honorary medical staff) who best caught the spirit of the times in a popular lecture at Swansea's Royal Institution in 1847. His talk was aptly titled *Observations on Civic Malaria and the Health of Towns*, (later published in London in 1849), and in discussing public health measures, he eloquently asked:

> Who can expect health—who contentment—who happiness . . . These are not the children of hope, they are the foundlings of despair . . . Is there no skill, industry or power, to be brought to bear to remedy this? . . . Let me assure you charity cannot effectively combat the evils to which I have adverted. You may send clouds of whitewashers, loads of clean bedding, ample supplies of food, medical appliances and medical men and clergymen and schoolmasters too; you may build hospital on hospital; all this has been tried by a benevolent public, and God forbid such a source of succour should ever fail the needy . . . But . . . this benevolence, this munificence on your part, will not suffice to crush the evil. It is legislative enactment only, aided by efficient and good regulations, rigidly enforced by the arm of authority, and supported by law and justice, that can cure this evil . . . Let us all, then, seriously reflect on these subjects . . .

But the new public health system had not yet been properly established in Swansea and it was not until 1853 that W. H. Michael was appointed to be Swansea's first Medical Officer of Health.

James Rogers worked as a surgeon at Ystalyfera at the time of the cholera outbreak of 1866, and although his study on the origin of the epidemic[20] did not reach any important conclusions about the cause of the disease, his paper represents a genuine attempt to apply the scientific method to a large-scale study of illness. By 1873, when he read his paper on sanitary reform[21] at a Poor Law Congress at Swansea, his arguments were much more forcibly put, and he could rightly refer to himself as a 'sanitarian'. By then, the notion of disease prevention was a part of orthodox medical practice.

Back in the earlier years of the century, however, when medicine was practised by a handful of doctors working separately, the most exciting local medical advance of that time occurred when it became obvious that some more highly organized system of providing medical care for the bulk of the population was necessary. That could only be brought about with the creation of a dispensary, and later, an infirmary.

CHAPTER TWO

The Dispensary

> The phlebotomy did me good and the saline draughts did me no harm, which is all I ask of any medicine or medicus.[1]

THOSE stoic words, written by the Earl of Chesterfield, a man 'cold in heart and unamiable in disposition'[2] several decades before the opening of the Swansea Infirmary, might adequately sum up the expectations of the population as a whole with regard to medicine well into the nineteenth century. The eighteenth century had seen very few changes or advances in medical practice; primitive influences were still at work and there were many who would not have disputed commonplace statements like that of James Stonehouse in 1748 that illness arose from God's wish 'to humble and reform his thoughtless, foolish and rebellious children'.[3] By the end of the century, however, there was a growing feeling that some interference in the welfare of the poor was necessary and, increasingly, voluntary hospitals came to be established in many localities. The usual pattern was for a dispensary, with out-patient ('outdoor') facilities only, to be established first. Later, this might be converted into an infirmary which offered both out-patient and in-patient ('indoor') facilities for treating illness in the poor, whose medical needs had previously either been ignored or dealt with ineffectually by the Poor Law system.

There is no universal agreement as to the value of the earlier eighteenth-century infirmaries in the treatment of disease. It has been argued that not only did they fail in their intended purpose of relieving the suffering which was associated with disease but that they actually had a harmful effect on the health of their patients.[4] Other work based on individual hospital records has suggested that during the last quarter of the eighteenth century they may have made a notable contribution to the decline in the death rate.[5] Between 1700 and 1825, 154 dispensaries and infirmaries (with approximately three dispensaries for every one infirmary) had been established in England and Wales. At the end of that period, Swansea had the only infirmary in Wales, although dispensaries had been formed in other Welsh towns at earlier dates.

There are conflicting views as to why the voluntary hospitals should have gained ground at that time. It has been commonly held that their creation was indicative of a new philanthropic attitude which had accompanied the prosperity that came in the wake of the Industrial Revolution. On the other hand, there are those who believe that subscribing towards the provision of health care for industrial workers might have arisen from a sense of religious obligation, or that it was a sound economic investment, or even a means of gaining prestige. Such interpretations tend to assume that morbidity rates and the social structure and conditions in the communities concerned were uniform, and none of them explains satisfactorily all the known facts about the situation as it was in south Wales. In the smaller town of Carmarthen a dispensary had been established as early as 1807. In rural Llandeilo, it was a local landowner who initiated the process, while at Haverfordwest in November 1813, three physicians petitioned the High Sheriff to convene a meeting to establish 'a dispensary for administering advice and medicines to the sick poor'.[6] Moreover, many industrial concerns employed their own surgeons and the provision of extra medical facilities would have been deemed unnecessary by the employers; yet hospitals were formed in such areas. (One notable example of a surgeon being employed by a local industry long after the hospital was opened occurred in the extensive copper and other works on the west side of Swansea where William Price Evans was Medical Superintendent as late as 1854.)

It may be that local needs and the influence exercised by the prime benefactors (both factors of the greatest importance in the establishing of any medical charity) were of paramount importance in first setting up the dispensary in Swansea, while different reasons may have operated at different times elsewhere in the development of voluntary hospitals. It certainly cannot be denied that the fashion of the times might have had some part to play; it happened to be that the opening of new dispensaries was in vogue early in the last century, and the imitation of one locality's charitable activities by others may have accelerated this process. That other great energizing force in Wales, Welsh Nonconformity, was at that time concerned with issues other than the worldly well-being of its followers and had not yet assumed its later more philanthropic attitude. It is impossible to delineate with any accuracy the precise reasons as to why the dispensary at Swansea was first opened but, without doubt, the opening of the Carmarthen Dispensary had drawn attention to the need for such provisions in Swansea.

By the year the dispensary was opened, Swansea was growing rapidly in population. A settlement near the mouth of the river Tawe had been in existence since the ninth or tenth century and the borough itself is of Norman origin. The castle is known to have been built by 1116, and several charters were granted to the town from 1153 onwards, after which it became the administrative centre for the Seigniory of Gower. With a poorly developed road system, the sea provided a natural means of communication with the outside world and the port played an important part in the economic development of the locality. Swansea's rapid growth as an urban centre occurred during the eighteenth and nineteenth centuries, when the town became established as the single most important British centre for the production of non-ferrous metals. With the added advantage of readily-available supplies of coal mined locally, its importance as an industrial centre continued to increase into the second half of the nineteenth century. These industrial developments brought with them a massive increase in population, greater prosperity, but more ill-health, accidents and social problems, all of which in turn called for better medical services.

On 6 January 1810, *The Cambrian* stated that the establishment of a regular packet between Swansea and Ilfracombe had indirectly led to an improvement in the medical services available to the people of Swansea (or more correctly, perhaps, to those who could afford to make the journey) as they were then able to travel more easily to the West of England Infirmary at Exeter. Two years previously, the same newspaper reported that Swansea residents ('emulating the laudable example of the Borough of Carmarthen') had been invited to attend a meeting at the Mackworth Arms on 29 September 1808 to consider establishing a dispensary 'affording advice and Medicine to the Poor, gratis'. Generous subscriptions had been guaranteed before the day of this first meeting.

It has generally been accepted that the prime mover in setting up the dispensary at Swansea was the Swansea-born London barrister, Richard Phillips, who came from a Quaker family of Cornish descent. He was interested in the practice of vaccination, and knew Edward Jenner. During a visit to his sister's home in Rutland Place in the autumn of 1808, a poor, sick woman is said to have called at the house at breakfast time to apply for assistance. His attention was drawn to the lack of medical facilities for such people in the town and before dinner time on the same day, he had collected a 'comparatively handsome sum' for that purpose. He is known to have established a dispensary in Brighton five years later.[7] There has recently appeared other evidence, reported in *The Cambrian* of 24 May 1878, that the Dispensary was first opened by a Dr Sylvester in a room in what later became the Horse and Groom public house in College Street, near the junction between Castle Street and High Street.

Whichever is the true version, (and it is not impossible that the two men collaborated in the venture), Richard Phillips was later (in 1817) made a Life President of the Infirmary in recognition of his services.

The new institution was to be called the Swansea Dispensary, and subscribers of half a guinea a year or donors of five guineas were entitled to nominate one patient at a time for treatment. Calvert Richard Jones of Heathfield was elected President; he came from a wealthy Swansea family whose members were Portreeves on more than one occasion. Those elected as Vice-Presidents were the Portreeve of Swansea (Griffith Jenkins), Sir John Morris of Clasemont, a wealthy industrialist, John Llewelyn of Penllergaer, a county landowner and former High Sheriff (he was the father-in-law of Lewis Weston Dillwyn), and George Jones, possibly the Guardian of the Swansea House of Industry. John Voss, a Swansea draper who later developed an interest in banking, was the first Treasurer.

A committee of six members was proposed, and three physicians and three surgeons were to be elected annually by the subscribers. A physician and surgeon attended the Dispensary daily with the exception of Sundays. Mr Sylvester and Mr Leyshon Rees were the surgeons and when Mr Rees resigned in 1813, Mr John Davies, who had 'long been honoured with the appointment of Auxiliary Surgeon', replaced him and remained as surgeon until 1825. Mr Thomas Prosser was the third surgeon from 1814 to 1817. The ubiquitous Dr Collins, author of *A Sketch of the Medical Topography of Swansea*, who became Portreeve of Swansea in 1821 and later Duke of Beaufort's Coroner, had also offered his services as an occasional surgeon and by 1815, he had joined Dr Elliott and Dr Hobbes as a physician. Dr Thomas Hobbes ($c.1757–1820$) specialized in dealing with the mentally ill.

The Dispensary was opened sometime during October 1808, and in the first three months, according to *The Cambrian* of 18 February 1809, 148 outdoor patients had been admitted, which was only slightly fewer than the total admissions to the Carmarthen Dispensary in the whole of its first year. From the outset, the Dispensary was to play an important part in the field of preventive medicine by offering free inoculation against smallpox. Nearly half the patients dealt with in those first three months came to be inoculated and it was decided that 'Professional Gentlemen residing at a distance may have a supply of Cow Pock on application'. Thereby was established firmly the practice, retained throughout the history of the Dispensary and the Infirmary, that the services offered were open to anyone poor enough to need them. By 14 October 1809, a year later, *The Cambrian* stated that 1,060 patients had been admitted (as out-patients, of course) of whom 576 were discharged as being well or relieved; 390 people were inoculated and 85 remained under treatment at the

The site of the original Dispensary in College Street. (*By kind permission of Glamorgan Record Office.*)

beginning of the second year. (It is to be assumed that the other 9 patients died.)

The first dispenser, who worked for three hours a day, was appointed in 1811, but he died some months afterwards and, as it was he who should have recorded the names of those who attended as patients, the numbers documented for that year were considerably fewer than for the years before and after. When the post was advertised in 1813, the salary was fifty guineas a year and a knowledge of Welsh was desirable.

The subscriptions obtained (£139. 2s. 4½d. in 1811–12) were sufficient for their needs with a medicine bill of £32. 3s. 11d. and a rent of 10 guineas a year.

In January 1812, a meeting of subscribers was called:

> to take into consideration the propriety of incorporating an Infirmary with the present Dispensary for ... admitting patients in desperate cases ... on a scale proportionate to the funds of the charity.[8]

A new committee was formed to solicit donations but the project seems to have failed at that time. As an alternative, in September 1814 a subscription of two guineas a year to the Bristol Infirmary was started so that use could be made of their in-patient facilities. Two years later (in May 1816), contractors interested in building a dispensary (with no mention of an infirmary being made) were asked to view the plans at Mr Voss's draper's shop, but nothing seems to have come of this move and later a somewhat biased witness, Henry Sockett, wrote of:

> a languishing and expiring Dispensary ... supported by a voluntary but decreasing subscription.[9]

Donations were again being invited in October 1816, this time for the adaptation for use as an infirmary of part of the Bathing House, with its facilities for at least sixteen beds. By December of that year an advertisement had been placed in *The Cambrian* for a House Surgeon and Apothecary:

> to superintend a small establishment of In and Out patients, under the direction of the Medical Attendants. It is presumed the situation will peculiarly suit a Medical Gentleman on half-pay of the navy or army. Respectable references will be expected. The situation is on the sea-cost (sic).[10]

Several applications were received, and the subscribers were requested not to commit themselves until the committee had reported on the candidates' qualifications. As was usual in days before doctors had to be registered by law, candidates were allowed, and even expected, to canvass the subscribers by advertising in the local press. Mr Jos. Jones was the only one who did place such an advertisement but, as far as is known, no appointment was made.

A further six months passed before the subscribers met (on 28 June 1817) 'for ... establishing the Rules of the New infirmary'. The Dispensary's medical staff were asked to continue until an election of physicians and surgeons could take place, and an address was to be presented to Princess Charlotte 'imploring her protection as patroness to the establishment of the first charity of the kind in Wales'.[11] The new institution, housed in part of the Bathing House, was to be known as 'The Swansea Infirmary, for warm and cold Seawater bathing, and for the relief of the sick and lame poor from every part of the kingdom'. There were to be sixteen beds in the sick wards, two of which were to be 'reserved for accidents'. The governing of the house was to be vested in the Patroness, Presidents, Vice-Presidents, Governors, two Physicians, two Surgeons, the resident Surgeon and Apothecary, the Treasurer and the Secretary. No patients were to be admitted who could 'pay for their cure', and vagrants and beggars were allowed admission only after serious accidents. A donor of 50 guineas would be a President for life and a subscription of 10 guineas would ensure election to a Presidency for that year. A Life Governorship could be bought for 25 guineas and, even though the Hospital Sunday movement did not come into being for many years afterwards, ministers of religion who preached sermons and made collections for Infirmary funds at places of worship on the Sunday before the annual meeting were to be entitled to recommend patients for treatment.

However great the apathy shown over the previous years had been, on the afternoon of the 18 July 1817, more than fifty gentlemen sat down at the Mackworth Arms for 'an excellent dinner', which cost them half a guinea each inclusive of a bottle of wine; 'prosperity to the new infant charity was drunk with enthusiasm' and that evening a 'Ball and Tea Drinking' concluded what was described as 'a most cheerful evening'.[12] And so it was that, in the town described in 1804 by a traveller as being 'if not an unwholesome, a very disagreeable place of residence',[13] the first infirmary in Wales was opened.

By then, the war against Napoleon was over and that small group of Swansea philanthropists who busied themselves with the affairs of the Infirmary could hardly have known that the battle with which they were concerned was, in the end, to have far more lasting effects than those of the Battle of Waterloo for the working-class people of the locality.

CHAPTER THREE

The Infirmary—Early Days

> There are individuals—doctors and nurses, for example—
> whose very existence is a constant reminder of our frailties, and
> considering the notoriously irritating character of such people,
> I often wonder that the world deals so gently with them.[1]

THE Bathing House on the Burrows (near the South Dock) had originally been used as a small hotel which was kept by Ann Julia Hatton (Sarah Siddons's sister). Part of it was now leased from the Corporation and it was there that the new Infirmary was established, the other part being used by the Poor Law Authority as its House of Industry (known as the 'Poor House'), whose kitchen was to supply food for the Infirmary's in-patients, originally at a cost of three shillings a week for each patient.

The first patients were accepted on 18 July 1817, the day of the opening dinner, and the first weekly meeting of the Board of Governors, or committee, was held four days later, with one of the Vice-Presidents, John Jones, in the chair. (For many years, breakfast-time meetings were held with all the committee members, apart from the Secretary, paying for their own meals.) There were 170 outdoor patients on the books, and the wards were found to be 'perfectly clean'. There was little business to be done on that day although it was resolved that:

> Thomas Harwood number 4 is not a proper subject of this Charity being a man of property.

A box for casual donations was to be made and fixed in a conspicuous place. A week after that, two indoor patients were admitted and the first mention was made of the new House Surgeon and Apothecary, William Edwards, who was born in Cardiganshire and had been working in Swansea until then. Mr Voss, previously Treasurer to the Dispensary, resigned as Secretary and Mr William Stroud took his place.

The Old Bathing House on the beach, 1791.

The Infirmary and the House of Industry, 1818. (*Pictures by kind permission of West Glamorgan Health Authority.*)

Mr Stroud became manager of the Glamorganshire Bank and, according to his obituary notice, he was Treasurer 'of all the leading institutions of the Borough'.

Hardly were the doors opened before the first disagreement between the committee and the medical staff occurred. This concerned the status of the House Surgeon, the only resident medical officer. The Medical Board, as the honorary medical staff were known (they were, in fact, the same honorary physicians and surgeons as had been appointed to the Dispensary), had submitted resolutions suggesting that one physician and one surgeon should be responsible for the patients admitted during any one week and that the two of them should meet at the Infirmary every morning except Sundays at ten o'clock. In the absence of either, the House Surgeon was 'to officiate for them'. It was those words that led to the disagreement. The committee had intended that Mr Edwards should have a status that was equal to that of the honorary surgeons themselves and that he was 'entitled ... to his Professional Rank and equal share of patients'.

In their reply, the honorary staff inferred that, having conceded to the House Surgeon the entire care of the neighbouring Poor House (which must surely have taken a great burden away from them), they *had* somehow already accorded him a level of prestige that was equal to theirs. Although the matter was resolved by Mr Edwards's being allowed to join the honorary staff's rota, it does not seem to have ended in an entirely satisfactory manner. The committee wrote to Drs Collins and Hobbes and to 'Surgeon Williams' (but not to Mr Sylvester):

> lamenting the want of that confidence and unanimity which they hoped would have existed between [blank space] and themselves which are so essential ... [they] feel themselves under the necessity of respectfully declining his further attendance at the Infirmary ...

It is probable that the doctor referred to here is Dr Collins, who in June 1818, published his *Enquiry into the Conduct of the Committee of the Swansea Infirmary*[2] in which he wrote of his:

> unabated anxiety ... on account of [their] extraordinary conduct ... we were dismissed from attendance ... not for any neglect but [through] want of confidence because the Medical Officers would not submit to be placed under the control of the House Surgeon and Apothecary, who receives a handsome salary ...

He wished it to be known that for many years previously he had been 'actively endeavouring' to establish an infirmary. In the event, the subscribers re-elected the whole of the honorary staff but Dr Collins refused to continue as a physician.

There also occurred a more long-standing administrative problem at that early stage. There were defaulters among those who had promised to subscribe, and there was little that could be done to correct this. Although the Charity Box yielded more than its share of widows' mites, with a building that was insured for more than £600, drug bills which sometimes mounted to £5 a month, a House Surgeon's salary at £17. 10s. a quarter and a proportion of subscribers who rarely paid their dues on time, donations from any other sources proved to be readily acceptable.

Clergymen of all denominations were requested to preach charity sermons in aid of the hospital, although in July 1818 these sermons had to be postponed because, for some reason, it was thought that the General Election was likely to bring about a reduction in the amounts collected. Great efforts were made to persuade 'the principal Gentlemen of the County' and local industrialists to subscribe so that their employees could be accepted as patients, especially if it was possible to point out to them that 'all the other ... Companies on the line of the Swansea river' had already become subscribers. Fines levied by courts of law were sometimes passed to the Treasurer, and by far the most unusual donation ever received was brought about as a result of the assault made by Mr Joseph Jones, a Llanelli surgeon (probably the same 'Mr Jos. Jones' who had applied for the House Surgeon's post in 1817), on two of Lewis Weston Dillwyn's maids at Penllergaer. Jones was said to be 'beastly drunk' and was remanded in custody for two days by Dillwyn. He was then released on bail:

> on his paying two guineas to each of my two servant maids, three guineas to the Constable and two guineas to the Dispensary (*sic*).[3]

One worthwhile and profitable means of increasing the skilled help available was for the House Surgeon to take on apprentices. They would work under his supervision, study with his help and virtually all of them from that time onwards would prepare themselves for the examinations of the Royal College of Surgeons (MRCS) and the Society of Apothecaries (LSA), while a few would go on to study medicine at a university. In 1815, the Apothecaries Act, which had such a profound effect on improving medical training and education, became law. Within three years of the passing of that Act and six months after the hospital was opened, Mr Edwards was reporting to the committee on the 'necessity of having an apprentice'.

It was an exciting time to start on a career in medicine. Shortly after the Infirmary's first apprentice started work, Laënnec published his work on the invention and use of the stethoscope and soon more stress would be laid on the importance of accurate diagnosis. Anyone beginning his clinical career at that time might well have lived to witness the many changes that revolutionized medical practice later on in the century. The proper training of doctors had already been given a new impetus and Swansea in 1818 had its own Medico-Chirurgical Society (of which little is known). It was probably the second of its kind in Wales (the first having been the Caernarvon and Anglesey Medical Reading Society, which had been formed in 1813).[4]

In October 1818, Mr Rees Bevan asked for his son Thomas to be apprenticed and it was agreed that fifty guineas should be paid, two-thirds of this sum to the House Surgeon and the remainder to the hospital. A week later, William Rowland became the second apprentice until he was (unwillingly) released in order to continue with his studies at the University of Edinburgh. They soon became valuable members of the hospital's staff:

> whose attention to their duties and general conduct justify the expectation that they will one day be ornaments to the profession which they have entered.[5]

In April 1821, T. B. Powell was allowed to attend for a brief period 'to ascertain how far he would like the profession', and he was allowed to spend the last six months of his apprenticeship studying in London, 'in consequence of his entering into the apprenticeship at the advanced age of seventeen'.

The hospital was fortunate in the choice of its first House Surgeon. William Edwards worked energetically and uncomplainingly to establish not only the limited in-patient services (there were rarely more than six indoor patients at any one time) but to develop the extensive facilites of the outdoor department. Clinics were held every morning on six days in the week and special vaccination sessions were arranged. Those patients unable to attend 'will be visited at their own homes if residing within the Turnpike Gates of the Town'.

The distinction between typhus and typhoid fever was not to be made for several decades yet, but the severe epidemic which occurred in the town in 1817 was thought to have been typhus (or jail fever, as it was often called because of its tendency to occur wherever conditions were overcrowded). Throughout the episode, the new House Surgeon took his duties in the community seriously and from April to September he had visited 109 patients with this condition, of whom only 3 had died. No one suffering from typhus was admitted to hospital (although they were 'admitted' as outdoor patients, of course) but he considered that:

> the progress of the Infection would have been speedily arrested by separating the Diseased in an early stage from the Healthy, and following up the disinfecting system by cleansing and fumigating the infected

> Houses. [He was grateful for] the very human and philanthropic manner in which I was assisted by suitable nourishment, wine, porter and other comforts from several Ladies and Gentlemen's Houses in the vicinity of the disease.[6]

He applied to the parish officers for a nurse to help with caring for the sick. Martha Davies, 'a pauper from the Castle [the old Poor House] was sent'. She caught the infection and, after she was sent back to the Poor House, another pauper there was also infected. The House Surgeon felt that his work was being thwarted by:

> the anxiety of Relatives and friends to see the Sick and the gossiping Women who make a point of meeting at such places under the impression of acting with kindness.

He was able to trace the 'connecting chain' of the infection through the district. Having started in houses that 'have no outlet or window to the rear' and which were in 'a very dirty state', he was certain that the disease, which was no respecter of profession, had been carried back to the Strand area 'by a Sister of Dr Bevan's wife'. He insisted that:

> to enable the disinfecting plan to be carried into full effect ... Patients should be admitted without the least delay ... Houses should be immediately whitewashed and fumigated.

Mr Edwards's attempt to solve the problems created by the epidemic gave rise to a crisis of a different kind. As infected patients could not be admitted to the Infirmary wards, his plea resulted in the passing of a resolution that it was 'highly expedient' that fever wards should be built at the Infirmary, and donations were asked for. A sufficiently large sum was raised for the work to proceed 'without pressing upon the Middle Class of Society'. But eighty-five local residents, including some members of that class and three of the hospital's medical staff requisitioned the town's Portreeve (or Mayor) to call a meeting to prevent this happening because it was unnecessary 'on account of the providential salubrity of the air in Swansea and that it would be expensive and might lead to a feeling of panic'.[7] In a powerful letter in *The Cambrian* of 18 October 1817 Henry Sockett added to the strength of the opposition and asked:

> What Governor of a House of Industry could, in his conscience, force a poor creature to attend as a nurse in a Pest House?

He was, he maintained, 'decidedly in favour of ... Pest Houses' but until the doctors of Swansea put up a strong plan for its creation, he could not support the project, especially as the public were to be misled by the decision to name the Pest House a 'House of Recovery'. Three days after the requisition was published, Lewis Weston Dillwyn recorded in his diary that he had:

> assisted in healing a quarrel which had latterly occupied much of my time, respecting a Fever House, and which threatened to split our neighbourhood into parties.[8]

No record of such a meeting has survived and the isolation wards were not built at that time.

Attempts were made to collect information about the hospital's work as much to satisfy the subscribers that their money was being well spent as for any other reason. Fluctuations occurred in the incidence of the rarely absent ague, while the value of the sea-water baths in curing or relieving rheumatism and scrofula was regularly attested to. This intense belief in the purifying effect of sea water was, as it were, almost written into the hospital's constitution and was maintained for many years. Patients sometimes came from afar to take advantage of what was once referred to as 'the judicious use of this valuable remedy'. It eventually became necessary to buy a carriage to carry water from the sea until a culvert, which was connected to a reservoir in the hospital building at high tide, was built.

There exists a curious variation in the nomenclature used to describe patients' illnesses. Conventional diagnoses such as 'tetanus', 'asthma', 'scrofulous opthalmia (*sic*)' and 'cronic (*sic*) hepatitis' vie with such diagnostic curiosities as 'disease in the head', 'died of a severe nervous disease' and 'sank under a complication of Diseases with a constitution undermined by every species of irregularity'.

A society for providing trusses for the poor formed locally by 'a few Gentlemen' in August 1822 had, in the first six months of its existence, enabled fifty-one people of both sexes who suffered from hernias to continue with their employment:

> which they otherwise could not possibly have done to say nothing of the risk they were hourly in for want of such assistance of having their Disease so aggravated as to place their Lives in imminent danger.[9]

It may be that the 'severe and dangerous operation ... performed without delay' on a lady with a strangulated hernia in May 1824 highlighted the value of the work of this society in a way which led the physicians to appeal to the subscribers to take over the responsibility of providing trusses for those unable to buy them. It was accepted that every annual subscriber of one guinea to the Infirmary would be entitled to recommend one person for the loan of a truss, upon payment of four shillings. Dr Edwards believed, somewhat over-optimistically, as it happened, that this move would 'increase the interest of the public in behalf of the Charity'.

The two amputations of limbs performed in 1824 and 1825, described only by a brief mention in the records, were shortly afterwards overshadowed by an operation of an even more formidable nature which attracted a great deal of attention. The patient suffered from a scrofulous (tuberculous) ulcer in the groin:

> ... in spite of all that could be done to arrest its progress, [it] became so deep as to open the Iliac Artery. The tremendous bleeding which necessarily followed was checked by the Gentlemen then in the Infirmary and within half an hour after the accident took place, all the Medical Officers were assembled to perform the operation which could alone prevent the patient from bleeding to death within a few hours. He recovered perfectly from the operation but was destroyed six months after by the most aggravated form of scrofula.[10]

The dangers associated with surgery, together with the extreme discomfort caused to patients wihout the use of anaesthetics or aseptic, or even antiseptic, precautions, ensured that only the most necessary (usually life-saving) operations were performed. Yet, eye surgery was practised almost from the time of the hospital's opening. In April 1818, Mr Edwards, in preparing for a cataract operation, discovered 'J.E. an Indoor patient . . . to be pregnant and that it would be improper to perform any further operations on her eyes'. Over the next year, at least two other patients had similar operations. Soon, even more sophisticated eye surgery was being successfully practised with an operation 'for artificial pupil'. Successes of this kind were sometimes used as evidence of the hospital's usefulness as when the Parish of Llanelli was invited to subscribe two guineas a year so that D.T. 'who is blind in both eyes might be admitted an Indoor Patient, there being great probability of a cure'.

In-patients who had disorders which were thought to be highly infectious were liable to be discharged at short notice and the understandable obsession with avoiding their spread reached its height in the case of venereal diseases. At times, the reluctance to treat such patients even extended to an objection being made to their being dealt with in the outdoor department unless there were special circumstances (such as 'being the Chief Supporter of an aged Mother').

In the town, the major infectious disorders continued to appear at regular intervals. In the absence of a vigorous public health educational campaign, the population had tended to become more apathetic in its attitude towards protection against the smallpox. The number of people vaccinated at the hospital was often small. From June 1824 to February 1825, there occurred another outbreak including a 'very

Extract from the Catalogus, c. 1817. (By kind permission of Glamorgan Record Office.)

suspicious case' where a child known to have been vaccinated two years previously developed the disease. The total recovery which followed:

> afforded an excellent illustration of the power of the vaccine ... to modify the smallpox and destroy the danger even when it does not prevent its attack.[11]

It is likely that some of the outbreaks of cholera morbus recorded were not examples of true cholera. In 1832, an epidemic did occur when about a half of those who caught the condition died, with 18,000 people being killed throughout England and Wales. By early August, about twenty people had died in Swansea and Lewis Weston Dillwyn 'never saw the streets so deserted on a Market Day'. So frightened were the medical staff that when it appeared in the House of Industry, they decided to discharge the aged in-patients from the Infirmary at once.

The earliest list of drugs compiled for use in the hospital (entitled *Catalogus Simplicium et Compositorum Medicamentorum in Usum Nasaconii Swanseansis...*) contained 188 different preparations, some of which were still in use within living memory.[12] The names of many serve as a grim reminder of the ineffectiveness of much of the treatment that was available. In spite of this, attempts were made to keep abreast of the few advances that did occur in medical practice and in December 1819, the doctors were allowed to buy:

> such Elementary Books as they may deem proper, to the extent of £15 and that they be at liberty to take in periodical Works to the extent of £5 per annum.

To the twentieth-century observer, with his vastly different notions of what medicine can accomplish, the optimistic tone which pervades the earlier Infirmary reports might seem bewildering. Many treatments long since discarded and known now to have been largely ineffective were practised and praised. The cure-rates quoted were, by any standards, high: for example, only 6.9% of indoor patients and 0.34% of outdoor patients were regarded as incurable in 1822. What must be taken into account here is that the whole notion of what constitutes a cure (often a nebulous concept) has altered greatly in the intervening years. (As late as 1875, when a limb was amputated successfully and the patient survived the operation, this was regarded as a cure.) Those who were 'cured' or 'greatly relieved' were asked:

> at their Dismissal whether they are desirous of returning their humble and grateful thanks to Almighty God, for the benefit through his Blessing they have received from the Swansea Infirmary.

They were requested to give permission for their names to be mentioned in the General Thanksgiving at St Mary's Church each week, presumably as a means of attracting more subscriptions.

Already, there was evidence that the Infirmary was serving a wider area than Swansea itself. The vast majority of those who failed to continue to attend in the first weeks lived 'at a distance in the country', and it was assumed that, having not attended again, they must have been cured. By 1821, nearly one in five of the out-patients lived either in distant parts of Glamorgan or in other counties of Wales. Poor Law Guardians from more remote parts, and industrialists such as J. J. Guest and William Crawshay of Merthyr, were soon to realize the advantages that might be gained from becoming subscribers. Although the outside notice board proclaimed that patients were accepted 'from every part of the Kingdom', admission was virtually only available to those bearing a letter from a subscriber (who might have lived in any part of the kingdom). In spite of these constraints, which did not usually apply in the case of severe accidents, it was sometimes possible to find subscribers who were prepared to recommend for admission people other than their own employees.

It certainly seems that applying for help from the Poor Law Guardians was as unpopular then as it became in a later age. In recording the death of two children in February 1822, the Secretary wrote:

> It is to be regretted that the Poor will seldom apply for Medical assistance until all other means have been ineffectual . . .

On the other hand, the committee had already decreed that 'in future no indoor patient be admitted to this Charity who cannot prove his parish'. The certain knowledge that no parish was obliged to provide relief for those who lived outside its boundaries must have been a powerful factor in deterring patients from outside Swansea who might otherwise have sought help at the hospital. If their own authorities were not subscribers to the hospital, the Swansea Poor Law Authority would not consider an application for help from them.

Except in the case of severe accidents, it was the Infirmary committee rather than the medical staff who had the power to accept or refuse patients. They met weekly but had no regular chairman and were themselves elected annually from among the subscribers. They were made up largely of public-spirited business men, with a minority of clergymen and a few of the wealthier members of the community. It was part of their weekly task to visit the wards to assess the patients' conduct and the cleanliness of the wards. This they did with great diligence and possibly without showing too much concern for the patients' comfort. Those who failed to conform to the rules of the house (such as 'H. J., having gone into town without leave and returned in a state of intoxication' and 'J. O., having applied to an irregular practitioner in the town') were a perpetual source of discomfort to the committee. They were frequently discharged and were usually refused readmission. 'Harriet L.' was a rare exception; she 'left the house clandestinely ... expressed contrition ... [was] again received, at the earnest solicitation of her mother'. Sometimes, such offenders would be admonished, as when a male patient read aloud from a book that was considered to be obscene in the male ward. The book was burned in his presence and he was warned that any future lapses would result in his 'instant dismissal'.

With Mr Edwards's marriage towards the end of 1818, he resigned from his post as there were no married quarters available. Being 'so sensible of the very great advantages which the Institution has derived from his work' the committee presented him with an inscribed piece of gold plate valued at £15. A Plate Committee was set up and, on their behalf, the famous Dr Thomas Bowdler (who originated the word 'to bowdlerize'), a keen supporter of the Infirmary, was asked to enquire if the inscription should be in Latin or English, and whether the Parish and the Infirmary were the donors or whether the committee members themselves would donate the money. The gold plate with which Mr Edwards was presented had an English inscription and neither the Parish nor the Infirmary committee members accepted that they themselves should pay for it. It was possible for the Parish to justify paying their part of the subscription:

> in conciquence (*sic*) of the great Exertion that he Manifested towards the Sick Poor ... for which he had had no remuneration.

It was common, if not usual, for vacancies for physicians to be taken up by one of the surgeons on the staff, but in December 1818, Mr Edwards became the only doctor in the hospital's long history to be promoted immediately from being House Surgeon to Honorary Physician.

Finding a new resident surgeon was not difficult. Advertisements in *The Times*, the *Morning Chronicle*, and *The Cambrian* produced forty-six applications. In the reply sent to eight of the candidates it was said that the Infirmary was:

> capable of containing sixteen but has not yet contained above eight or nine Indoor Patients ... The House Surgeon is expected to be of Middle Age and if possible, Single, as accommodation in this House ... viz., a Sitting Room, Bedroom, Kitchen and two Garrets, are not sufficient

for a family of Children ... the Salary is £70 per annum with an Allowance of Coal and candles ... He will not be allowed to enter into private practice ... He will take his rank as one of the Surgeons of the Infirmary but will be expected to prepare the Medicines with the assistance of the Apprentices ... [He] will be expected to superintend the whole arrangement as there is no regular Matron.

Mr John Wasdell of London, a former army surgeon, was considered 'as a very fit and proper person' and was elected with one modification to the terms of his appointment. Lewis Weston Dillwyn, who had frequently asked Mr Edwards to treat members of his own family privately, proposed an amendment which was carried unanimously, as his amendments usually were, that the new resident should be allowed to practise privately 'subject to such restrictions ... as the Committee may think proper'. Much of the new House Surgeon's time was taken up in dealing with the fevers which were 'very rife of late among the poor'. He had non-clinical duties to perform as well. Among them were the supervision of the whitewashing of the wards and bathing room and of the painting of the shower bath and buying 'a suitable grate for the Wash House'. It was these domestic duties which proved to be Mr Wasdell's downfall. He was soon thought to be unsuited for a situation where 'internal management is necessarily combined with professional ability' and, four months after starting his work, he was asked to resign. Had he refused to do so he would have been given notice. In spite of a mild protest on his part that there was 'no specific charge of breach of Duty, or explanation', he left his post. He was allowed to offer himself for re-election on a day when feelings ran sufficiently high for Dr Bowdler to earn a vote of thanks for his 'conciliatory conduct'. There was not sufficient support for Mr Wasdell to be reinstated. A few days later, he published a notice in *The Cambrian* of 21 August 1819 thanking his supporters ('although unsuccessful ... from causes which possibly had now better be consigned to oblivion'). He died at the age of 37 after an illness said to have been of a few days' duration 'brought on, it is feared, by fatigue and anxiety'. Every doctor in Swansea was at his funeral.

His successor was Edward Osler (1798–1863), uncle of the world-famous physician, Sir William Osler. Edward Osler had entered Guy's Hospital as a medical student a year later than John Keats and, although Osler's medical career lasted for longer, he too eventually gave up medicine to devote himself to writing.

For four years after Dr Collins's departure, there had been no serious differences of opinion between the Board of Governors and the unpaid medical staff. Then, possibly because of the Governors' belief that the doctors were over-generous in prescribing for patients, it was resolved:

it appears expedient that no Medical Gentleman attend the Committee excepting their presence be requested by the Committee.

The honorary staff felt that there was no evidence that money was being wasted on the purchase of excessive quantities of drugs but it was decided that the House Surgeon should, in future, be required to prepare all the medicines himself, in addition to his in-patient work and to caring for an average of 98 outdoor patients at any one time.

Meanwhile, the relationship of the Infirmary Board of Governors with the Poor Law authorities was also worsening. The care of the sick poor in the town had long since created great difficulties. In the absence of a body which was solely concerned with that task, and with harsh criteria for distinguishing between the results of poverty and sickness, those who were unfortunate enough to be doubly disadvantaged in this way had inevitably suffered great neglect. The Poor Law Act of 1601 had brought about the appointment of overseers and collectors of the Poor Rate. Since then, the emphasis had been on protecting the town's inhabitants from having to maintain those 'expelled from other places and towns' and whose care might put a permanent burden onto the ratepayers. What little care that there was seems to have been left to private individuals, who were paid small sums of money to look after the more seriously ill in the patients' own homes. The passing of Gilbert's Act in 1782 did nothing to separate the care of the 'sick poor' from the 'idle'. Nor did it help to sharpen the distinction between the two categories except in so far as it allowed for the setting up of workhouses for destitute children, the old and infirm, and the sick, thereby excluding the young healthy poor section of the community. When the 1782 Act was put into effect in Swansea, part of the Castle was used as a Poor House, and the magistrates no longer held their weekly Petty Sessions at the Town Hall where 'crowds of applicants for relief' had attended. The care of the poor was entrusted to an honorary Visitor and a Guardian; the latter was paid £50 a year and elected annually at a parish meeting. Henry Sockett, who had been an early and enthusiastic member of the Infirmary's committee and a Vice-President, became Visitor to the House of Industry in 1818, and devised a scheme whereby the sick and suffering poor of the neighbourhood were not neglected without having to increase the financial burden on the ratepayers. He was a man of some initiative and had taken issue with the Infirmary committee more than once. He had already dissociated himself from the abortive attempt to open a 'Pest House' (fever wards), probably partly because the Infirmary committee had asked him for £100 out of the Poor Rate towards the cost of the building at a time when his reputation for avoiding such excesses of expenditure was at its highest. Any existing ill-feeling was heightened by the dispute between the two sets of officials on the terms on which the Infirmary buildings were originally leased. It was held by the Infirmary that they were entitled to be paid interest on the £350 which they had invested in Parish Bonds when the money was required in order to set up the House of Industry, whereas Sockett believed that they should forego that right in lieu of rent. The controversy was intensified in October 1822 when he and Captain George Jones, the Guardian of the House of Industry wrote:

> Upon the most mature consideration we are of opinion that it is necessary to the Independence and prosperity of the House of Industry that the two Establishments should in future be kept perfectly distinct except of Medical assistance. You will therefore be pleased to consider the necessity of providing for the Indoor Patients [meals] yourselves as soon as convenient—as the Governor has directions to make no further provisions for the Infirmary of any kind after Friday, 26th October.[13]

By April 1823, Sockett had withdrawn the parish subscription (of twenty guineas a year) to the Infirmary, and had arranged for another surgeon, William Harris Long (probably the son of David Long, a Swansea apothecary), who eventually joined the Infirmary's honorary staff, to care for the Poor Law institution. A measure of the degree of Sockett's confusion in his later attitude to the Infirmary can be found in the conflicting remarks which he made in the same report in which he contended:

> [In] the House of Industry ... we scarcely know the existence of disease ... The resident surgeon of the infirmary attends the sick daily ...[14]

A public meeting under the chairmanship of Dr Collins eventually resolved the argument concerning the rent charges by agreeing to continue with the lease of the Infirmary building at a quarterly rent of a peppercorn. By that time, Henry Sockett had declined to take his seat on the Infirmary Board.

With the abrupt withdrawal of the kitchen facilities, the medical staff (obviously back in favour by then) were asked to produce a scheme for feeding the in-patients. Their suggestions were:

> Being as near the plan adopted in Regimental Hospitals ... the Stipendiary Medical Officer [was] to keep an account of the Dietary and washing expenditure [and was] minutely to inspect each article of provision as it comes into the House ... that he may return the same if not of proper quantity and quality ... [He had] also to inspect each meal after being cooked ... and to state to the nurse and one of the convalescent patients what quantity of each article is required for each meal and what quantity of each for every patient. [The nurse and the patient were] to weigh out the proper quantity ... the patient can easily watch the cooking,

that the Nurse may go to any other work, and when cooked both can assist in carrying the same to the Wards.

Three meals a day were to be provided, with breakfast being at 9 a.m., from Michaelmas to Lady Day, but at 8 a.m. for the remainder of the year, and the last meal of the day at 6 p.m.

Almost immediately after these new arrangements were brought about, Margaret Morris was appointed 'to act in the capacity of Matron to this Institution under the control of the Resident Surgeon', for which she was paid four guineas a year. (The title of Housekeeper had previously been used when she was found to be 'rather out of Pocket' having prepared breakfast for a larger number of committee members than actually attended the weekly meetings.)

Since the time of the unfortunate pauper Martha Davies in 1817 the nursing work had been undertaken by women who were often sent from the Poor House. They were never skilled or trained and the most that could be expected from them was that they were able to undertake domestic duties with the help of the fitter patients. For this, they were paid about a shilling a week. The first nurses named are L. A. Pitcher and Sarah Griffiths, 'at this time on the Parish Books'. The need to train nurses for their work had not yet become apparent, but it was indirectly recognized as early as April 1818 when the House Surgeon wrote in despair:

> The two cases of death I attribute to the want of following the orders I gave respecting the Medicines and domestic management &c more than to the malignity of the disease.

Later in the century, that most histrionic of upper-class revolutionaries, Florence Nightingale, was to claim that nursing was usually reserved for women 'who were too old, too weak, too drunken, too dirty, too stolid, or too bad to do anything else'.[15] In Swansea, those depths never seem quite to have been reached, but the supervision of nurses must have severely tested the patience and skills of successive House Surgeons in that internal management which had been found to be so lacking in the case of the late Mr Wasdell. The situation had hardly improved by 1836 when the House Surgeon complained of the 'constant Quarrels between the Matron and the Nurse', which led to the view that 'a final decision should be come to'. Mediocrity among the nursing staff had now been replaced by belligerence.

It was almost inevitable that the conflict between the unpaid medical staff and the committee should have recurred at regular, if infrequent, intervals. Often suspicious of the doctors and always anxious to assert their authority, the committee members were at a disadvantage from knowing that the physicians and surgeons gave of their time more generously than was expected of anyone else who worked there in a voluntary capacity. Yet, when criticism was called for, and sometimes when it was not, the Medical Board's honorary status offered them no protection and episodic attempts were made to assert more control over them. In June 1822, the vote of thanks to the surgeons for their year's work was given, 'at the same time lamenting that they have not found it consistent with their private avocations to afford a more regular attendance at this Institution'.

The medical staff were not averse to disagreeing among themselves from time to time. By 1822, Mr Sylvester held no special status by virtue of his pioneering work in founding the Dispensary and his resignation went almost unnoticed. It was brought about because Dr Edwards had introduced two of his own private pupils to the Infirmary against the rules of the house. Having discovered that this was common practice elsewhere, the rules were changed in Dr Edwards's favour as he had 'obtained a Diploma to act as a Physician at the request of this Institution, and with an expressed understanding that it should not interfere with his practice as a Surgeon'.

When members of the honorary staff resigned or became ill, it was usual for other doctors who already worked in the district to offer their services in the hope that they themselves might later be elected. These posts were much sought after (a fact of which the committee was only too aware) and candidates would advertise freely in the local press in an attempt to attract votes for themselves. Following a severe illness, Dr Edwards resigned in 1831 and a wise choice of a successor was made in Dr Edward Howell, who was to serve as Honorary Physician for nearly twenty-four years. It was most unusual for the medical men of Swansea at that time to have had a university education. The older English universities did not provide an apprenticeship for their physician graduates so that they were often more inexperienced than those who aspired to the lesser rank of surgeon. A native of Neath, Dr Edward Howell was a man with a vastly different background from his predecessor's. He had travelled widely (to London, Paris and Edinburgh) for his medical training and had already established himself in the town as a physician with the publishing of a notice some years previously. In this, he begged:

> respectfully to inform his friends who have kindly honoured him with their confidence, and the Public generally that for the future he purposes confining his Practice to Physic and Midwifery exclusively.

For many years, the House Surgeon, possibly the single most important member of the staff, was required to find himself a locum tenens before being allowed to take a holiday. It was for the committee to decide whether they would refund him the locum's fee or not. In

1817, it had been decided that the resident doctor was to receive instructions only from the committee, which was, in effect, an open acknowledgement that his status was equal to that of the honorary staff. The whole issue was reopened in 1835 with the election of a new House Surgeon. Edward Osler, having resigned from the post in 1824 after four and a half years, virtually invited the committee to appoint him a Visiting Surgeon, which they did a year later. He resigned after two years but in 1835, having recently presented to the hospital library a copy of what was to become his most famous work, *The Life of Admiral Viscount Exmouth*,[16] he reapplied for the resident post, but was not appointed. The fact that he had made the application at that stage of his career was a firm indication of the status that the post could carry, and yet it was possible to get such a post immediately after qualifying as a doctor.

Osler had been replaced as Visiting Surgeon in 1827 by George Gwynne Bird (c. 1800–1863), who had offered himself for the post almost as soon as he had arrived in Swansea. Bird continued as a member of the honorary staff for the following twenty-eight years. Untypically, he seems not to have entered into any great controversies during his first eight years on the staff. Soon after William Bevan had been temporarily appointed House Surgeon, Mr Bird published his *A Letter to the Subscribers to the Swansea Infirmary* ... (Swansea, 1835). This was, in fact, a 36-page printed pamphlet, in which he claimed that the other members of the Medical Board had sought his advice on the need to revise the hospital's rules, particularly those concerning the House Surgeon. Having gone to the trouble to write to eighteen other hospitals to ask for information, he maintained that the House Surgeon should have charge of the 'whole arrangements' of the house and the management of patients, the visiting of the outdoor patients and the supervising of the work of the nursing staff. He should be 'the adjunct and assistant to the physicians and surgeons' instead of being 'entirely beyond their control'. In his typically forthright manner, Bird went on to quote the late Mr Abernethy (a London surgeon) as having said that the House Surgeon is:

> like a nought amongst figures; taken by himself, he is as nothing, but put him after and in addition to his principals, whom he is to assist, he increases their value tenfold.

William Bevan was sufficiently upset by Bird's pamphlet to reply in the correspondence columns of *The Cambrian*.[17] But his superior was not one to leave criticisms made of him unanswered. An embarrassing and fascinating account of the whole affair was made public in the newspaper, to which Edward Osler and Henry Sockett also contributed.[18] Sockett declared, 'I am not the person who has incurred the awful responsibility of disturbing the tranquillity of the excellent institution', and claimed that he had been deprived of his right to discuss and oppose the new rules accepted at the Annual Meeting.

Much was made of the alleged diminution in status of the House Surgeon with the adoption of the new rules, and William Bevan refused to continue to work there. But there were other equally important changes in the conditions of service that originated from that time. In future, the resident doctor would have to promise to accept his post for five years. He was not to absent himself in the course of the week when the visiting staff were in attendance, while the Matron was absent, or without leaving a note 'stating where he may be met with'. Nor was he to stay out after midnight without the permission of the committee.

In future, no 'Capital operations' were to be performed without a previous consultation among the medical staff, for which summonses were to be sent on the previous day. In addition, the surgeons were always to meet at one o'clock on Saturday afternoons to consult on 'all difficult and extraordinary surgical cases', with the help of the physicians if necessary. If there occurred a difference of opinion, a majority vote on the appropriate treatment would be binding. Each surgeon was to be allowed to bring in two of his own pupils to gain experience. They were not to 'obtrude themselves unnecessarily' and were only to perform 'trivial operations of bleeding, extracting teeth &c'. It was also resolved that the stipendiary medical officer would 'not suffer gaming in any part of the house' and 'if any Pupil shall so far forget himself as to appear in the House when in a state of inebriation', he was instantly to be dismissed and could only be reinstated in exceptional circumstances after 'a respectful apology ... expressing contrition for his fault'.

The better diagnostic facilities, the more expensive medicines available to the poor only in hospital, and 'breathing a purer air than can often be enjoyed in the dwellings of the poor' were among the more important benefits thought to arise from the opening of the Infirmary. At first, it was believed by the committee that merely making these advantages known generally would surely 'call forth the most active and benevolent energies' among local people and there seemed to be some grounds for believing this. In 1812, the Dispensary subscriptions had been £139. 2s. 4½d., whereas three years after the opening of the Infirmary they were £328. 0s. 3d. Sufficient had been accumulated in that short space of time for £381. 10s. to be invested. Osler had written in 1824 that he was resigning from the hospital 'at a period when it has surmounted all the difficulties with which it had to contend ... when it has united all parties in its favour'. This was far from being true and it took a considerable time and the apathy of countless would-be subscribers before that early and unjustified optimism gave way to the more realistic attitude of the 1830s. Indeed, the 'low state of the funds' was worsened by the financial crisis of 1825–6, which affected Swansea badly. The affairs of Joseph Gibbins, a local banker who had been the Infirmary's treasurer since 1818, and that of his colleague, Robert Eaton, were badly affected by the monetary situation. At one stage, the possibility of taking legal action against Gibbins was considered as he had difficulty in paying back nearly £400 which he had been holding on the hospital's behalf.

Before the onset of the financial crisis, an attempt to increase the number of beds had failed. It was to be many years before money became available to allow for a larger building that might relieve to a greater extent 'that most dreadful combination of misfortune, illness and poverty'. During the first 10 years, 292 indoor patients and 10,095 outdoor patients were admitted and, with the increasing number of serious accidents occurring in the neighbourhood, together with the greater number of surgical operations being performed, the need for better facilities was becoming increasingly more urgent. As sometimes happened at times of great difficulty, a revision (radical in this case) of the rules concerning the admission of in-patients was accepted. It was proposed that:

> No woman lying with child, no child under seven years of age, no persons disordered in their senses, or suspected to have the smallpox, epilepsy, itch, or any infectious distemper, or who are not clean and free from vermin, nor any who are apprehended to be in a dying or consumptive state, or who are suspected of having the venereal disease, or who may receive equal benefit as Outdoor Patients shall be admitted ...

Doubling the number of beds from 15 to 30, it was estimated in 1830, would have called for an additional income of between £100 and £150 a year after all building costs had been paid, and it seemed likely that this could be achieved within a few years.

In 1832, shortly before his death, Dr Edwards, believing that the Infirmary building was 'much out of Repair and too confined', offered £500 towards a new building if an additional £1,500 could be raised before his money was made available. This was seen as an opportunity not to be missed and committees were formed in each district in the town to organize collections. Books for recording subscriptions were placed at each of the Swansea banks and the office of the local newspaper, the Portreeve was asked to summon a Common Hall, the council of burgesses, to solicit support from the Corporation, and the noblemen and gentlemen of Glamorgan and the adjoining counties were asked for their patronage.

When Dr Edwards died soon after making this offer, he left to the Infirmary most of his valuable collection of books, his library table, cabinet 'and minerals therein', all his surgical, anatomical, philosophical and chemical apparatus, four prints by Havard and Hunter, an 'Electrifying Machine' with an insulating chair, and all his manuscripts, medical, surgical and chemical books and papers, which were to be 'forever kept, in some suitable place, in the said Infirmary for the use of the Medical Gentlemen connected therewith'. After the death of his wife, £1,500 was to be given to build a new hospital providing that another £1,500 was collected before 1840. A management committee consisting of four Members of Parliament, the Vicar of Swansea, the Trustees, the Portreeve and the Medical Board was charged with settling the arrangements for the erection of the new building. Not more than £2,000 were to be spent and the building was to be no larger than the income likely to be subscribed for its support would allow. As a token of respect and gratitude, the main ward in the new hospital was to be called the Edwards Ward and the library, the Edwards Library.

It happened several times in the history of the Infirmary that offers of large sums of money donated for a specific purpose were followed by an upsurge in donations, and this first large donation ever received was no exception. By February 1833, £1,500 had been collected, but Dr Edwards's trustee refused to pay the money from his estate because of a serious legal complication. Many years previously, 'in an unfortunate hour', the young William Edwards had entered into an agreement which meant that by the time of his death, he was responsible for the debts of his former associates, and these debts were sufficiently great to absorb all the available money as long as Mrs Edwards continued to live in the house. The trustee was of the opinion that he would be censured even for offering the library and the instruments to the hospital, but he suggested this in an attempt to persuade the hospital's trustees to release him from any further financial liability towards them. There were protests that it would be impossible to carry out 'the Doctor's good intentions', and the Infirmary's solicitor was instructed to file a Bill of Equity against Dr Edwards's trustee. The matter was not finally settled for a further two years when £250 was accepted together with the library 'with an indemnity for returning the same or paying fair value . . .'

The difficulties over Dr Edwards's will did not prevent the plans for a new building going ahead after the Corporation had provided the additional land nearby, and the new Infirmary was ready to receive patients on 2 November 1835. The old building was to be put into a 'thorough state of repair' after which it would be used as a surgery and sitting room for the resident surgeon.

It is difficult to avoid the conclusion that in those early days the Swansea Infirmary was a badly organized and ill-equipped institution. Yet, in an age when it hardly seems possible that any relief from severe disease could be obtained at all, the Infirmary's scarce resources were ably and fully put to the best possible use. There can be no doubt that the claims of the Medical Board were justified when they declared:

> The System of an Infirmary, which ensures to patients an attention far more constant and regular than could be afforded by the private charity of the most benevolent practitioner ... the command of important auxiliary means, which the poor can only obtain in such Institutions ... will sufficiently explain why many cases are relieved or cured in them, which, under circumstances less favourable, would be absolutely incurable.

CHAPTER FOUR

From Infirmary to Hospital

> The poor man must have his doctor as well as the rich, and care should be taken that he is not driven, by expense, to seek advice from services less competent than such as now supply it to him.[1]

'THE bounty of the Swansea Infirmary', it was proudly said, 'is limited to no locality.'[2] But the provision of a new building brought its attendant problems. Already there was insufficient money to cope with the increasing burden of work, and with the decrease in income brought about by deaths among the subscribers and the failure of others to pay their dues on time, a reduction in the clinical services provided seemed inevitable.

That threat was overshadowed by two events of great significance in the field of health care in Swansea which occurred in the autumn of 1835. In October, a well-attended public meeting considered the possibility of applying to Parliament for an Act for 'supplying the town with spring water from the hills', and in November, the new wards at the Infirmary were to be opened. Eight months later, the new building was not altogether ready for use and the medical staff's optimism regarding the future seemed rather misplaced:

> [They] look[ed] forward with sanguine and confident hopes that at no distant period the charitable disposition and humane liberality of the Public will enable this useful Establishment to relieve the sick poor on a scale commensurate with its capabilities . . .

In spite of the financial constraints, the number of beds permanently occupied did slowly increase from 15 in 1836 to 25 in 1847.

The Poor Law Amendment Act of 1834, which had become law a year before the opening of the new Infirmary building, did little to ease the problems faced by the bulk of the sick poor population. The Act made virtually no satisfactory provision for them and although the services for 'sick outdoor paupers' (the sick poor not in workhouses) were slightly reorganized, this hardly lessened the difficulties faced by the voluntary infirmaries. (Considerably later, the 'hospital branch of the Poor Law administration' came into being and many workhouses were adapted for use as Poor Law infirmaries. In Swansea, this occurred in Tawe Lodge, which was later renamed Mount Pleasant Hospital.)

Locally, the inadequate quality of the care to be found was highlighted when a local philanthropist, Richard Aubrey, before becoming Mayor in 1841 had felt the need to establish a night asylum. This had no medical function and was only meant to act 'as a refuge for the wandering and homeless poor'. The two bodies (represented to some extent by the same people) responsible for caring for the sick poor, the Infirmary Board of Governors and the Poor Law Guardians, continued to function quite independently of each other and often in an opposing manner as though their functions and interests were separate and irreconcilable. Paupers from other districts were never admitted to the Infirmary without payment and a promise that the Poor Law authority concerned should subscribe annually from that time on. To confuse the issue further, from 1834, 'poor persons who have frequent ailments, who are ruptured and are generally of weak constitution' but who earned even minimal sums were regarded as being able-bodied and the only institutional form of treatment available to them was at the voluntary hospitals which were often reluctant to take them unless the Poor Law Guardians accepted the financial responsibility. The Swansea Guardians continued to refuse to subscribe to the Infirmary even when they were sent a letter in March 1841 'begging' them to do so. Four years after that, the Poor Law Commissioners instructed them to start an annual subscription but even then they did not. In the years that followed, although there was no active co-operation between the Guardians and the Infirmary, the tensions eased, but any concessions that were made occurred largely on the Infirmary's side. In 1851, a further act authorized Guardians to subscribe to the voluntary hospitals from the Poor Rate. By 1856, relationships between the two bodies were rather more amicable when there occurred a redistribution of property, with each side giving up part of their land to the other. Even by 1868, when their subscription was increased from ten guineas to fifty pounds a year, the Guardians failed to realize the extent of the impact of the Infirmary's work among the poor.

The contrast between what was meant to be government policy on the one hand and its actual implementation on the other does not seem to have been a cause for concern. Yet there were marked deficiencies and differences between localities. In 1862, the House of Commons Select Committee on Poor Relief recommended that Boards of

Guardians should supply 'expensive medicines such as codliver oil, quinine and opium', but in many cases, that advice was ignored. Seven years later, it was said that, in deciding whether sick people should be given relief or not, the Guardians in Swansea took into consideration the nature of the disease and the patients' suitability to be treated in their own homes.[3] In the same decade, the policy in Gower was that 'being poor people they received no medical attention'.[4] It was this lack of a properly implemented national policy that proved to be one of the major difficulties facing those concerned with organizing the Infirmary's affairs.

Consequently, at times, all enthusiasm seemed to wane. In 1839, means had been sought to ensure a better attendance at the weekly Board meetings by appointing a permanent chairman (Mr W. R. Grove at first and later Mr Lewis Llewelyn Dillwyn). By 1845, it was shown that the Medical Board rarely met. After more detailed enquiry, it was found that of the 156 attendances required of each member of the visiting staff during the year, Dr Howell and Mr Long had attended 106 and 100 times respectively, Mr Bevan had only attended 49 times and Dr Bird 44 times. One of the first of the recurring attempts to increase the numbers of visiting medical staff failed as Dr Howell had summoned enough support among the subscribers to cause the matter to be postponed. Again, in 1853, the idea had to be relinquished, as the Medical Board found it to be 'extremely distasteful [to be treated] as the creatures of a committee'. The medical staff sought the support of the Medico-Ethical Society of South Wales (an organization about which no other information has survived) and the committee had to be content with regretting that offence should have been taken, even though Dr Bird had only been at the Infirmary three times throughout 1851.

A new impetus was given to this quarrel in 1854 at a meeting at which 'charges were made and recriminations indulged in'. Lewis Llewelyn Dillwyn proposed that a House Committee should be formed, three of whom would form a quorum (a sad reflection on the committee's poor attendances) and who would meet once weekly. They were to have the power to regulate the admission and discharge of patients and should appoint a Visiting Committee of Ladies. Dr Bird and Dr Howell opposed that move, together with yet another attempt by Mr Dillwyn and his brother-in-law, Matthew Moggridge, to increase the numbers of honorary staff to four physicians and four surgeons. This, declared the medical staff, was 'but little short of insanity', as each of them only had access to six or seven beds already. The real issue, according to Dr Bird, was that there were no proper medical wards because the physicians' patients were being crowded out by people being admitted after accidents.

The medical staff mustered enough support to win by sixty-nine votes, but not before Mr Moggridge had managed to quote the chairman, W. R. Grove, as having said:

> I wish something could be done with the doctors, but they are a quarrelsome set, and perhaps it would be better to leave them alone.[5]

Dr Howell retaliated by reminding him that they gave their services free, to which he was told that there always occurred 'plenty of canvassing' when vacancies arose.

Both Dillwyn and Moggridge had played an important part in the Infirmary's affairs but, having become increasingly disillusioned with the way in which its work was being organized, Dillwyn vowed that he would never again move the adoption of any new rules. This, together with his election as Member of Parliament for Swansea in the following year, proved to be the beginning of his estrangement of many years' duration from the Infirmary's affairs, although he continued to act as a Trustee. Both he and Moggridge accused the doctors of having issued false statements to obtain the proxies of absent subscribers. In spite of that, Moggridge soon started to attend the meetings again and to play a part, though less active, in the administration.

The disagreements between those who governed the Infirmary and the Poor House were largely concerned with financial matters. Already, in 1844, the Swansea Poor Law Guardians were paying a total of £140 a year in salaries to their four part-time medical officers (who provided a minimal level of service to the sick poor), £206 in poor relief, and £66 as housekeeping allowances to the poor, so that they were not well disposed to the idea of providing more money for the treatment of illness.[6] In spite of the allegedly more philanthropic style of the age, the collection of money from the Poor Law Guardians and others to continue with the hospital's work was made no easier. Long before the Hospital Sunday movement (started by Canon Miller in Birmingham in 1850) gained ground, the local clergy had been preaching sermons annually for the benefit of the Infirmary. From 1847, the churches were given a guarantee that clergymen whose congregations donated more than the requisite sum would be entitled to become Vice-Presidents with the privilege of recommending patients for treatment being extended to those congregations. (With their unfailing flair for splitting hairs, the committee soon found some difficulty in deciding on whom the privilege should be conferred if the service at which the collection was made was to be taken by a visiting minister.)

Possibly as a result of the difficulties which the voluntary infirmaries were having to face, attempts were made to put pressure on the government to take a positive interest in their work. In 1847, an application to Parliament to abolish legacy duty on bequests, had been supported and in 1855, the House of Lords was asked to support a bill to regulate charitable trusts. But these were isolated efforts and provided no immediate help in caring for those who were 'so heavy a Tax upon this Institution'. There was not enough money to meet the increasing need for expansion of the clinical services. An excess of expenditure over income was not unusual and it was suggested that there had to occur a change of policy so that those able to pay for themselves could be admitted. There were, however, other less likely sources which provided a little money. If the 'Opulent ... who are not already subscribers' were less responsive than had been hoped for, the Swansea Association for the Prosecution of Felons donated £100 in 1858, and for many years the owners of local pleasure steamers arranged day trips in aid of the funds. In 1857, the Mayor and between eighty and ninety ladies and gentlemen, who paid 4s.6d. for a 'Best Cabin' and 3s. for a 'Fore Cabin' took such a trip to Lundy Island, where they were given an excellent dinner. Having lingered too long 'over the good things in life', they were stranded there for the night, but the event produced a profit of £14 and a Presidency for the year for Mr Pockett, the ship's owner.[7]

By 1857, after persistent attempts caused by 'great want of funds' to collect subscriptions that were overdue, among the names struck out of the list 'as not being at all likely to be recovered' were the Earl of Ashburnam, Lady Charlotte Guest, and the Welsh Brothers' Friendly Society of Rhymni. Subscribers who defaulted but who continued to refer patients were dealt with sharply and a local clergyman and the Swansea Gas Company were summoned in the County Court.

The most healthy aspect of the Infirmary's finances arose from the committee's wise policy of increasing regularly the amounts invested in the Permanent Fund, which rose in value from £2,500 in 1840 to £7,470 in 1856. This increase in assets was due to the advice offered by some committee members, who regularly reviewed the investments made. The most striking example of the way in which timely advice safeguarded hospital funds occurred in 1852. The Glamorganshire Banking Company informed its customers that because of continued imports of gold on a large scale, the rate of interest on securities in which they usually invested had fallen. It followed that they were no longer able to pay more than one per cent on money invested with them. As the value of gold diminished, money had to be reinvested elsewhere in order to maintain the amount of interest obtained. By acting on the advice given by those committee members to redistribute investments, the Infirmary committee avoided a major financial crisis.

Soon afterwards, as a result of the large sum of money (£200) received after sermons had been preached by local clergymen, it was decided (in 1857) that the building could be thoroughly repaired and that six additional beds could be provided. More extensive alterations were then contemplated which were to include a new kitchen and washing room with sleeping accommodation for the dispenser and servants, after the health of one of them had deteriorated 'in consequence of his sleeping with the patients'.

From the 1830s, smaller dispensaries such as that at Crickhowell had been subscribing in order to take advantage of the in-patient facilities in Swansea. When other hospitals in south Wales were opened, however, they did nothing to relieve the clinical load in the Swansea Infirmary and only lessened the willingness of other localities to subscribe. When the Carmarthenshire Infirmary was opened in 1858, lectures were arranged in places such as Aberdare and Merthyr in aid of the new hospital as people from Carmarthen who had moved there to work tended to return home when their health failed. No such scheme was possible in Swansea. The continuing expansion of industry locally and the floating of the harbour would inevitably lead, it was thought, to a massive increase in the proportion of those unable to pay for medical treatment and therefore dependent on the Infirmary.[8]

In 1844, the Select Committee on Poor Law Medical Relief was told that in Swansea the Guardians employed midwives who were excessively ignorant and had no certificates of competence. There was little evidence that standards of nursing care in the Infirmary were more sophisticated than in the town. The new wards 'replete with comfort and convenience' by July 1836, were largely staffed by a girl sent from the House of Correction to help for a few hours each day under Mrs Couch's direction. While that situation lasted, there was no hope of increasing the number of indoor patients from fifteen, although there was room for fifty in all.

The first mention made of Mrs Couch as the Matron was in January 1840 when she was being paid 12 guineas a year with 6 shillings a week board wages. By then, the Head Nurse (a term often used interchangeably with Upper Nurse), Mary Hollbrook, was paid 9 guineas a year with meals, and there was also a second nurse whose wages were 6 guineas. In March 1840, it was agreed that 'a more effective staff of nurses should be established'. Mr W. R. Grove was asked to take whatever steps were necessary to bring about this change without being given any specific instructions as to how to proceed. The Director General of the Ordnance Medical Department failed to find a suitable Surgery Man and Nurse, so Robert Southward, who had been a military hospital sergeant for 16 years and who was stationed at Brecon, was taken on along with his wife at a combined wage of £45 a year ('dieted by themselves with a Bedroom, Coals and Candles').

At a time when there was less friction between the doctors and the committee, there were some indications that all was not well with the nursing staff. In October 1840, the nurse, Catherine Quick, had made it known that she wished to leave and, nine months after being appointed, Charlotte Padley felt no longer able to stay 'in consequence of being made uncomfortable by the Matron'. 'There does exist', maintained the Secretary, 'a want of command of temper on the part of the Matron' who, after being admonished, 'promised under a vow to manage better for the future'. The Under Nurse then agreed to stay but immediately afterwards Robert Southward complained that Mrs Couch had made his own and his wife's situation uncomfortable. Unless she could mend her ways, the committee decided that they would 'feel themselves under the necessity of making a change'.

She was also reprimanded for allowing ten-year-old James Couch (probably her grandson, who later practised as a surgeon in Swansea) to live in the hospital with her. That warning proved to be ineffective and when Charlotte Padley finally insisted on leaving, Mrs Couch was given a month's notice with a gratuity of a quarter's pay 'in consequence of her long servitude'. (She was well provided for financially and was listed in the Tithe Map records as a landowner who owned several small pieces of property). Apart from being asked to account for some missing articles and groceries costing £1.2s.10½d., which she had to repay, Mrs Couch had no further connection with the Infirmary to the time of her death in 1852 at the age of 81.

Her successor was to be 'without the care of a family' and from among the five applicants, Mrs Margaret Smith was elected. Her first quarrel with her employers occurred two years later after she had ordered cupboards and shelves that cost £1.12s. for her room without their permission. The committee refused to pay, but by October 1847, she had introduced sufficient stability into the administration of nursing affairs for her application for an 'advance' of salary from 12 to 15 guineas to be approved.

In February 1850, a visitor issued a summons against the Matron for assault. Mrs Mary Fulford, the wife of a boot-and-shoemaker, had been visiting her sister who was an indoor patient. In her evidence in court, she claimed:

> having gone into the ward to see her (sic) sister, the Matron had come in and shoved me violently out of the Room. Mrs Smith raved with passion and I could not understand what she said. She continued shoving me ... She then called for a Candle ... for me to see the Clock but I was so agitated ... [She] caught hold of my shoulder and threw me

right out ... I am in delicate health and subject to fits ... I believe that Mrs Smith insinuated that I was after time.[9]

The two other patients in the room testified that Mrs Smith was very angry but that they had no reason to believe that she had ill-treated Mrs Fulford. The case was dismissed by the magistrates, the committee felt satisfied at Mrs Smith's behaviour and Mrs Fulford was not allowed to visit again without their permission 'for the due protection of the Matron and Officers'.

When Mrs Smith resigned in July 1851, she left with the committee's 'unqualified approbation' at the way in which she had worked during her ten years there. She was replaced by Mrs Howe, the former Matron of the Poor House. The staff then consisted of the Matron herself, the Upper Nurse, the Under Nurse, the Cook and the Surgery Man whose work was largely concerned with the treatment of the outdoor patients. Mrs Howe's period of office was not particularly illustrious. It was acknowledged in 1853 that the nursing staff had to spend so much time cleaning the wards that they were prevented from caring for their patients effectively. Many of the patients were interviewed by committee members and afterwards the Matron was urged to develop a 'more vigilant and active performance of her duties' and to spend more time visiting the wards. When she resigned a year later, her former lack of vigilance had been forgotten and she again left with 'unqualified approbation'. Little is known of her successor, Miss Margaret Jones of Swansea, except that she refused to pay two months' wages due to a nurse in October 1858 and was 'discharged for general neglect of duty'. After a further enquiry, it was recommended that all the nurses and servants should be dismissed. The next Matron, Miss Mary Cox, started in her new post in November 1858 and she acquired a more elevated status by being invariably consulted by the subcommittee responsible for appointing nursing staff.

Eight years after his appointment as Surgery Man, Abraham Nachman acquired the title of Dispenser. Although he had not had any formal training, he was expected to prepare and dispense the medicines ordered 'with the utmost care', to apply bandages, dress wounds (starting not later than 7.30 a.m. in the summer and 8.30 a.m. in winter time), together with any other work that might be found for him. It was after he started at his new work that it was realized that he could not read prescriptions or write instructions on labels. For that reason and because of his general misconduct, he was dismissed and was appointed as a porter (with wages of five pounds a year). His successor as Dispenser was preferably to have passed the examination of the Pharmaceutical Society and was to receive £30 a year with board and lodging. With his appointment, the Dispensary was to have its own water supply for the first time, at a cost not exceeding £6.10s.

The difficulties with the staff continued after Miss Cox's appointment. It had already been decided that no employee responsible to the House Surgeon was to be allowed out after 11 p.m. and they were to see that indoor patients:

> were not allowed to play at cards, dice or any other game not approved of ... or smoke in the wards. [They were not to] swear or use abusive language, become intoxicated or behave themselves indecently in any other way, on pain of expulsion.

It became only too apparent later that Miss Cox had little sympathy with that form of regime. She had been instructed to provide a liberal supply of tea or coffee for the night nurses but it was thought essential that she should be instructed not to leave them spirits or wine on any account. Following the unsavoury experiences with two of her predecessors, the committee instructed her to keep an inventory of household goods and furniture and to weigh and measure the provisions brought into the house. On her twice-daily visits to the wards, she was to ensure that they were kept as quiet and as clean as possible. She was also meant to enforce the reading of the rules concerning their conduct to patients, nurses and servants every Saturday, to see that the doors were closed at 9 p.m., and opened at 7 a.m., and to report all cases of misconduct to the committee. The last measure taken to tighten discipline was that when subscribers recommended the admission of patients, they were expected to deposit a guinea with the Secretary for funeral expenses in case the patient should die, and for travelling expenses for the journey home if they were discharged alive. All indoor patients from then on were required to bring with them two shirts, and a doctor's letter if they lived in a distant place.

It could not have been apparent to the authorities that this trivial bundle of changes was inadequate, and at the Annual Meeting of 1860, they had 'pleasure in stating that they now have an efficient Household staff'. Their satisfaction, however, was to be short-lived and three months later, a subcommittee was set up to investigate irregularities in management. It was found that there had been neglect but that patients were often reluctant to oppose 'those who have it in their power to make their residence ... agreeable or very much the reverse'.

The accusation that one of the nurses had been drunk at work was proved, and when the House Surgeon and Matron were reminded that they should never be absent at the same time, Miss Cox treated the matter 'with more levity than was consistent with the importance of the subject'. Meals had often been served irregularly because she rarely got up early enough to supervise them, and the excessive consumption of beer, wine and spirits called for a more strict system of control 'so as to leave as little temptation as possible in the way of the nurses'. The discrepancy between the quantity of alcohol consumed and that accounted for led to a system of 'compensation in money in the place of Beer' for the Dispenser and the two servants. Miss Cox, as intransigent as ever, had her authority to appoint staff withdrawn. By that time, the visiting medical staff were again found, with one exception, not to be fulfilling their commitments, and the committee finally became convinced that they were faced with a severe problem.

From the early 1860s, a sense of lack of discipline had also been apparent in the other departments, with two successive porters being removed from their posts because of neglect and helpless drunkenness. In June 1866, even George Turton Stroud of the Glamorganshire Banking Company, who had been the Infirmary's Secretary since May 1831, was severely censured even though his inability to cope with his work was caused by illness. The hope that Edwin Probett, the Dispenser, and the Matron would 'go on more comfortably for the future' was not fulfilled, and in addition, a solicitor had to be instructed to investigate the discharge of one of the nurses by the Matron. Although no fault was found with Miss Cox's handling of that situation, she was told two months later that she must either resign or be given notice. Being of a more militant temperament than some of her equally blameworthy predecessors, she refused to leave and was given her notice in October 1865. The medical staff intervened at that stage with the opinion that a trained and efficient nurse, although more expensive, was necessary.

After the Crimean War, Florence Nightingale was active in the movement to train nurses properly for their work, and although she herself did not actively participate in their tuition, she was responsible for many of the innovations that were brought about. She made available large sums of money from the Nightingale Fund, into which £45,000 was paid by the public to commemorate her work in the Crimea. The intention at the Nursing School, which she helped to set up at St Thomas's Hospital, London, was to train nurses who could work elsewhere and who could in turn teach other nurses properly; at that time, nurses' tuition was commonly left to chance. ('No man,' she maintained, 'not even a doctor, ever gives any other definition of what a nurse should be than this—"devoted and obedient". This definition would do just as well for a porter. It might even do for a horse.'[10])

Among the Swansea Infirmary staff, devotion and obedience were certainly not unknown (even among the Matrons) but there is not much evidence that the qualities set out in the *Regulations as to the Training of Probationer Nurses under the Nightingale Fund*, which was published in 1860, had been found in great abundance there. Trained nurses were to be:

> sober, honest, truthful, punctual, quiet and orderly, cleanly and neat [and] skilful: 1. in the dressings of blisters, burns, sores, wounds, and in applying fomentations, poultices and minor dressings. 2. in the application of Leeches, externally and internally ... 4. in the management of trusses and appliances in uterine complaints ... 10. to be competent to cook gruel, arrowroot, eggflip, puddings, drinks for the sick. 11. to understand Ventilation ... 12. to make strict observations of the Sick in the following parties: The state of secretion, expectoration, pulse, skin, appetite, intelligence, as delirium or stupor, breathing, sleep, state of wounds, eruptions, formation of matter, effect of diet, or of stimulants, and of medicines. 13. And to learn the management of convalescents.[11]

For the wages paid by them (£40 a year), it might have been unrealistic of the Governors of the Swansea Infirmary to expect that they could attract someone of that calibre for the post of Matron, but Mrs Wardroper, the Matron at St Thomas's Hospital, recommended Mrs Tate for the post and she was selected from among fifteen candidates. (No mention can be found of Mrs Tate in the St Thomas's Hospital Nursing School papers so that it is unlikely that she was trained there.) In June 1866, Mrs Wardroper wrote to the House Surgeon to say that a trained nurse could be made available, but as the state of the funds would not allow an additional appointment to be made, and as Mrs Tate's six-month period of probation had proved to be most satisfactory, she was offered the permanent post as Matron. A fortnight later, after representations had been made by the medical staff, 'a perfect understanding' was reached on the need to appoint a trained nurse. Having read the letters received from Mrs Wardroper (which have not been preserved), the committee decided to accept Miss Markham from St Thomas's Hospital as Matron. She was only at St Thomas's Hospital for eight months and had hoped that she might be accepted in Swansea before starting her training. On being told that the arrangement with Miss Markham had been agreed to before her own appointment was made, Mrs Tate asked to be given a testimonial and left apparently without complaint.

The new Matron soon complained that she was having difficulty in enforcing the 'new System of discipline'. At her request, the revised rules for patients were printed and hung in the hall, with that portion that referred to visiting days and the introduction of spirits being 'in large type in English and Welsh'. Shortly afterwards, she was asked to deduct a month's wages from the Women's Nurse, who had been found guilty of 'illconduct' (*sic*). Anyone who had hoped that the Nightingale nurses would bring with them a new teetotal style of living was to be disappointed. Having already been allowed a pint of beer daily, the Head Nurse was given an extra half pint 'when needful' at the Matron's discretion. Miss Markham herself applied for and got permission to take a glass of wine each day. By the 1867 Anniversary Meeting, although everyone was well pleased with the increased efficiency of the nursing staff, she had not been successful in her attempt to curb the excessive consumption of beer and was required to keep all alcoholic drinks under lock and key. The authority that she was allowed (and obviously deserved) was far greater than that given to any previous matron. She was even allowed to use her discretion (a trait not recognized in most of her predecessors) in deciding whether to charge for the washing done for indoor patients.

The only member of the medical staff who advertised by regularly releasing details of his clinical work to the lay press was Mr Bird. When he published information concerning the treatment of a patient with a dislocated shoulder in *The Cambrian* on 3 July 1835, he received a rebuke from the other surgeon, Mr Rowland, who maintained that behaviour of that kind was 'contrary to established custom and the etiquette of the profession'. That did nothing to deter Mr Bird, who continued to satisfy the morbid curiosity of the readers of that newspaper for many years to come with accounts of cures of cancer, amputations of limbs and eye surgery. He did not restrict his publications to the local press. His account of 'two rare and important operations' was published in *The Lancet* of 10 February 1838, and later copied by *The Cambrian*.[12] As this interesting report was the first detailed publication of its kind by any of the hospital's doctors and as it provides a rare glimpse of the clinical work done then, it deserves to be described in some detail. The patient was a 38-year-old quay porter who had been used to carrying 5 cwt. loads about for wagers and who had 'lived freely and drunk hard'. For two years, he had noticed a swelling behind his right knee and for some weeks a similar smaller swelling on the left side. When he was first examined at the Infirmary, the swelling on the right knee was the size of an orange, and a diagnosis of 'bilateral popliteal artery aneurysms' was made. (An aneurysm is a swelling in an artery which is caused by a weakening of the arterial wall. The popliteal artery helps supply the leg with blood and runs behind the knee joint.)

Three days after his admission to hospital in January 1837 (and several years before general anaesthetics were first introduced), the aneurysm on the right was found to be increasing in size and it was feared that the wall of the artery might burst, which could have resulted in the death of the patient. After a consulation with Mr Rowland

and one of the physicians, Dr Cohen, Mr Bird decided to attempt to close the artery above the level of the aneurysm by tying it so that no blood could enter that area. 'A careful stethoscopic examination of the patient's person' was made to exclude the possibility that there might be other aneurysms elsewhere in the body, but none were found. After the operation, the patient recovered sufficiently to be able to walk about the ward in a short time. The wound was allowed to heal by first intention (without the use of artificial aids such as stitches). Two months later, a similar operation was performed on the other leg in the presence of several Swansea doctors:

> I [Mr Bird] laid the artery bare, and passed the needle under it ... Before I put the ligature around the vessel, I pressed the artery on the blade of the needle, to see that the pulsation stopped the tumour, which was the case. I then drew the thread round the vessel, and tied it firmly, the pulsation stopped in the aneurysm ... two or three days after the operation, we perceived a pulsatile movement in the tumour, which had, however, considerably diminished ... [On] applying the stethoscope, it was quite evident that secondary aneurysm existed ...

The patient was kept in bed for several weeks and by January 1838, he was 'able to carry a sack of flour as well as ever except that he finds some weakness in going upstairs'. In May 1840, Mr Bird resigned as surgeon so that he could apply for the vacant physician's post and he was elected to that position a month later.

On their retirement, members of the visiting medical staff who were highly thought of and who had served for longer than ten years could be appointed as Consulting Physicians or Surgeons. In 1854, after fourteen years of reasonably efficient service as a physician, marred only by his autocratic nature and occasional periods of poor attendance, Dr Bird was waited on by the Vicar of Swansea, the Reverend E. B. Squire, and two other gentlemen acting for the committee. He was told by them that if he should resign, he would, in view of his past services, be elected to 'such Office'. This was no more than an indirect way of trying to persuade him to leave. Having thanked them for their kind consideration (and surely having realized that they were not being kind or considerate towards him), he told them that before deciding, he would like to consult his friends. As it was, he replied:

> I am able to perform the duties devolving upon me in my present situation as effectively or nearly as effectively as at my former period ... I am therefore at present inclined to devote my humble experience and such energies as I still possess to the duties of active life.[13]

By April, the argument concerning his fitness to continue to practise had extended to another field. He was also the (paid) Medical Officer to the Swansea Prison and at the following quarter sessions, the visiting

Dr G. Gwynne Bird in 1853.

justices spoke highly of his work saying that more than 6,000 prisoners had been admitted there during his period of office at times when there had occurred epidemics of cholera, smallpox and several other highly infectious disorders. Only 20 people had died there during that time. Their expression of 'approbation of his work' was not universally accepted. One magistrate gave it as his opinion:

> that from Dr Bird being blind, it is impossible . . . under such an infliction for him to continue working effectively.[14]

But George Gwynne Bird was a seasoned campaigner and was not likely to yield easily. Although he did resign from his appointment at the prison, he continued on the Infirmary's staff for a further year when both Dr Howell and he resigned and were appointed Consulting Physicians.

Dr Bird was replaced by Dr William Rowland, who had started working there as an apprentice in 1818 and who became House Surgeon and then Visiting Surgeon until 1843 when he resigned through illness and was appointed a Consulting Surgeon. Dr Howell was replaced by Dr Thomas Williams who had withdrawn his application for the House Surgeon's post in 1840 to proceed to a most distinguished career as a physician in London. Mr Hall also resigned after fourteen years as House Surgeon, and the committee attributed its failure to find 'a fit successor [to the] present demand for Surgeons in consequence of the [Crimean] War'.

Virtually no information concerning clinical matters was recorded in the Infirmary's detailed records; even the introduction of anaesthetics, one of the most revolutionary advances ever made in medicine, was not mentioned. On 16 October 1846, in Massachusetts, the value of the inhalation of ether vapour as an anaesthetic agent had been demonstrated. On the night of 21 December, Mr Robert Liston, a surgeon at University College Hospital, London, wrote:

> I tried the ether inhalation today in a case of amputation of the thigh ... It is a very great matter to be able to destroy sensibility to such an extent...[15]

Among those present on that day were the young Joseph Lister, who later revolutionized the whole practice of surgery, and James Couch, who was possibly the grandson of Mrs Couch, the former Matron, who eventually returned to his native Swansea to practise as a surgeon and whose son worked as an anaesthetist at Swansea Hospital.

Within weeks, ether was being used at Edinburgh (where it had actually been tried many years before), Liverpool, and in every important London hospital. Less than three weeks after Liston's demonstration, it was being used for the first time in Swansea (and possibly in south Wales) in private practice, in his home, by an ex-pupil of Liston's, Henry Wiglesworth, who was one of the surgeons at the Infirmary. While his more famous colleagues published their results in *The Lancet*, Wiglesworth was satisfied with recording his impression of the new drug in *The Cambrian*:

> I feel very great pleasure in being able to announce that the remarkable discovery of rendering patients insensible to the pain of a surgical operation by the inhalation of sulphuric ether has been rectified in this town by myself ... [The patient inhaled] ether vapour through an apparatus invented by Mr Robinson [which cost four guineas] ... The operation consisted in the extraction of a large molar tooth from the lower jaw of a young lady, and was performed at my residence in the presence of several medical gentlemen of the town of Swansea.[16]

Six weeks or so later, under the heading 'painless operation at the Swansea Infirmary', *The Cambrian* described:

> the first capital operation performed under the influence of ether in Swansea, *or we believe in South Wales*, [on a man with] incurable disease of the knee joint ... the tenderness was so great that he could not endure

the most gentle touch of the finger ... [On] Friday last, in the presence of all the medical gentlemen of Swansea, with one or two exceptions, and several non-professional gentlemen ... [He] commenced inhaling the ether, from Robinson's apparatus ... at the expiration of three minutes he was sufficiently affected, and Mr Wiglesworth, the operating surgeon, commenced the incisions ... He moaned slightly as the sawing of the bone was nearly completed ... [and] afterwards stated that he was unconscious of this ... we are glad to have it in our power to announce, in addition to the many benefits which the Swansea Infirmary through its medical officers confers upon this town and South Wales generally, that operations may be rendered painless.[17]

Since 1835, outsiders who were not doctors had only been allowed to witness surgical operations with the permission of the Infirmary's Medical Board. On this occasion, as the surgeon was about to start, a gentleman suggested that the knee should be pinched and Mr Wiglesworth grasped it, 'but the poor fellow was unconscious of it'. This, the surgeon thought, was 'the philosopher's stone for which we have long been searching.'

The Lancet commented soon after (on 10 April 1847) that the number of surgical operations in some hospitals had more than doubled within months but that there were still doctors who refused to accept this advance. In Swansea, as in many other places, financial considerations took precedence over the need to take advantage of new developments in medicine. In the first full year after ether was introduced, the number of indoor patients admitted to the Infirmary fell and there is no evidence that the surgical department immediately increased the extent and scope of its work.

On 8 November 1847, James Young Simpson of Edinburgh had started using chloroform as an anaesthetic agent during labour. Within a month, this was being used in Swansea and again it was in *The Cambrian* that Dr Edward Howell wrote:

> you have doubtless heard and read of the use of chloroform ... in the practice of Midwifery, and as every new case cannot fail to give increased confidence in its administration, I beg to state that I have recently exhibited it in two instances with the most gratifying results.[18]

Mr Wiglesworth was later to go on to defend the use of ether in a spirited attack on Professor Simpson who had tried to justify the use of chloroform in the case of a patient who had died after its use. Considering the revolutionary nature of this innovation, it is surprising that so little reference was made in the Infirmary's records to its introduction, but Mr Long is known to have used an anaesthetic in performing an amputation of a thigh in June 1848.[19] He used chloroform, having previously found ether to have been 'unsuccessful'. Afterwards, his patient was quoted as having said, 'God bless the man who first found it out'. No further mention was made of the technique until 1859 when 'A Choroform Inhalr' (*sic*) was bought.

The medical profession throughout Britain was gradually organizing its activities in a more systematic manner. Since 1832, the Provincial Medical and Surgical Association (later to become the BMA) had been slowly increasing its membership and influence among practising doctors. The first full meeting in south Wales was held at Swansea in 1852, and in his Presidential Address, Dr Bird exhorted his fellow members to follow St Paul in their professional relationships in letting 'brotherly love prevail'.[20] A year later, he became the first of the two Swansea doctors (both of whom were associated with the hospital) to be elected to the Association's Presidency.

In October 1858, a far-reaching change in legislation occurred when the General Medical Council was formed under the provisions of the Medical Reform Act. The purpose of the act was to enable those requiring medical advice to 'distinguish qualified from unqualified people'. Until then, it had not been essential for doctors to hold formal qualifications. In Swansea there did not appear to have been any unqualified doctors in practice for many years so that the introduction of the new act had no impact on the practice of medicine in the town. (Patients were frequently sent to the Infirmary from west Wales and there the number of unqualified doctors practising was still a great enough problem for a Medical Registration Association to be formed 'to serve the efficient operation of the new Act'.) Within the Infirmary, it had been essential for many years for the honorary medical staff to hold certain qualifications and from 1856 onwards, the House Surgeon and Apothecary was obliged to be a member of a Royal College of Surgeons and of the Society of Apothecaries. In practice though, no one had ever been appointed to that post without holding those qualifications. It was Dr Thomas Williams, with his wide experience of working in a teaching hospital, who first raised the possibility of exploiting the teaching opportunities available by suggesting that a medical school should be formed in connection with the Infirmary so that:

> young men may be educated in their profession and be allowed to witness the many scientific operations performed there.[21]

Nothing came of that suggestion but the wealth of experience available at the Infirmary for young doctors and students was great and much of this was to be found in the variety of work provided outside the hospital by the Outdoor Department.

There, the infectious diseases continued to cause havoc regularly and indoor provisions were called for in order to deal with those disorders effectively. In 1817, the attempt to provide a 'Pest House' had failed but in 1836, five years after the first cholera epidemic, the Swansea Poor Law Guardians set aside a building 'in the garden' (on land which may have been shared with the Infirmary) as a Fever Hospital.[22] By February 1839, they decided that 'the female paupers now in the Cholera Hospital be removed as soon as the Medical Officer certifies that it can be done with safety'. Presumably this was meant to be a precautionary measure in case the facilities there should be required in the event of another epidemic. Ten years later, with the onset of the second great outbreak of cholera (when more than 200 people in Swansea died), Mr O. G. Williams, a local surgeon who was also a member of the Infirmary committee and the Board of Guardians, had to take it upon himself to prepare 'a part of the building in the Garden . . . as a Cholera Hospital' to take in those suffering from that disorder. He was thanked for his 'prompt initiative' and a nurse was loaned to the Guardians to care for the patients.

During epidemics, increased demands were invariably made on the services provided for the poor and it had been well said that 'the heaviest municipal tax is the fever tax'.[23] The hospital committee did not regard such matters as being relevant to its work. Provided that the main Infirmary wards were kept free from infection, the fact that the House Surgeon had to cope with large numbers of infected patients in the course of his outdoor work was of little interest to them. They merely noted the occurrence of such disorders when he was called on for help in dealing with them. By 1839, vaccination was being practised free of charge on a fairly wide scale by the druggists in the town so that the Infirmary had been relieved of an important and time-consuming task. With the end of the cholera outbreak, the other epidemic disorders had also (temporarily) taken on a milder form and at least one local doctor, Mr J. W. Gutch, was prompted to ask why this should be so. He concluded that increasing wages and regular employment rather than any other factors accounted for this change.[24]

Such questions and conclusions helped to pave the way for important changes in health legislation. Although the 1848 Public Health Act has since been judged by many to be ineffective, it was nonetheless a turning point in the history of public health legislation. In Swansea, a series of somewhat stormy public meetings eventually led to a petition being sent from the local ratepayers to the recently constituted General Board of Health. A Public Inquiry conducted by G. T. Clark ensued and this resulted in the setting up of a Local Board of Health. (Swansea's death rate in 1849 was twenty-three per thousand compared with fifteen per thousand in Gower.) None of the reports on the state of health of the local population, however, were ever recorded as discussed or even mentioned at the Infirmary's committee meetings. Nor was there any evidence submitted to the Inquiry by them. Not surprisingly, those who regulated the Infirmary's affairs were bereft of any notion as to the extent of the future impact of the new public health measures which were slowly taking form. Apart from the contribution which their smallpox vaccination service had previously offered, the only indication for many years that they regarded themselves as having a broader role than merely attempting to treat illness, occurred in June 1844 when they asked their Medical Board for an opinion as to the causes of the increasing level of sickness 'among the poor . . . and especially whether it is attributable to the imperfect drainage and otherwise dirty state of the town'. No reply has survived and it may be that none was given. The comparatively low mortality rate— not more than three and a half per cent in the outdoor patients and four and a half per cent among the indoor patients—probably led to complacency. These low rates may possibly be accounted for by the fact that untreatable patients, even if they were admitted, were quickly discharged and heroic surgical procedures (which carried a high mortality rate) were not often attempted in the 1840s.

The burden of illness dealt with by the House Surgeon, however, continued to increase and about the only economy never considered was the use of his time. With six out of every seven of the town's houses having a water supply that was likely to be polluted, a total lack of public health measures, and pressure from local industrialists to extend the geographical limits within which he was allowed to visit patients, it seems inconceivable that Mr Hall could have had the energy to remain as the resident doctor for as long as fourteen years. He undertook all the home consultations, and in 1841, he paid 637 such visits. By 1851, that number had increased to 1,380 so that it became necessary to set up a subcommittee to examine the reasons for the increase. It was found that several subscribers had been recommending more outdoor patients than they were entitled to, and of those, two local pharmacists, Mr Dawe and Mr Wilson, had between them recommended 89 from June to October 1851, whereas they were only entitled to refer 3 patients each in any one year. Having been presented with that explanation for the increased volume of work, the committee sought no other. Since the 1830s, the greater variety of clinical conditions treated had testified to the increasing scope, particularly of surgical practice, in the locality. That very expansion had added to the number of patients being treated.

There were signs though that more accurate assessments of the extent and effectiveness of the Infirmary's work were being attempted. By the time of the 1840 Annual Report, although amputations of the limbs were still classified as 'cures', a 'cancerous affection' earned the comment 'went out well but with the ultimate result doubtful', whereas an operation for a disunited fracture of the thigh-bone was thought to be 'not perfect union but considerably improved'. The 'vagrant who fell asleep on some heated cinders when intoxicated' was beyond all help by the time of his admission. On the other hand, an indication of the improvement in the outlook for some patients treated surgically is found in the suggestion that the death of a man with a strangulated hernia might have been avoided with more prompt attention.

As the range of work being undertaken was extended, better and more extensive facilities were called for. Caring for those injured in industrial accidents continued to drain the scarce resources, and there was no shortage of entrepreneurs in the locality who were prepared to take advantage of the service offered without being too ready to contribute. With various railway companies starting work in 1847 and the construction of the docks in 1854, there occurred an increase in the number of admissions to the Infirmary of casualties who, it was considered, could have been treated at their places of work. It was resolved that in future they could only be accepted when little else could be done for them, the funds 'being in a low state'. In spite of these difficulties, the committee and medical staff were sufficiently aware of their obligations to open what was their first specialist unit, an Accident Ward, in 1854. Arguments about priorities between the various medical departments were far from unknown, particularly as there were still only 26 beds available as late as 1861. There were then 14,722 beds available in voluntary hospitals and 50,000 in Poor Law units throughout Britain. The population of Swansea was nearly 34,000 (which excluded the wider catchment area) and unlike many other towns, there was no properly established Poor Law Hospital so that the Infirmary had to deal with numbers of patients that might elsewhere have been considered excessive.

Since 1828, trusses had been supplied free to patients with hernias (at a cost of £10.8s.6d. in that year). A vogue for buying specialized equipment started with the purchase of two orthopaedic beds in 1830. Five years afterwards, the House Surgeon asked for a fumigating box for treating patients 'in cutaneous disease and Rheumatism'. In later years, there followed a handsaw for 'an important operation', a Jarvis Surgical Adjuster (at a cost of ten guineas) for the reduction of severe dislocations, an electrogalvanic apparatus for £3.15s. 'found to be eminently advantageous in the restoration of drowned persons', and in 1847 an 'Apparatus for the Fractured Clavicle' was donated.

There were also alterations of a less concrete nature occurring. Many years were to pass before a complete after-care service was provided but an extension of the home visiting system which would take into account the wide-ranging social effects of illness was considered. Although Lewis Llewelyn Dillwyn's attempt to form a Ladies' Committee had failed four years previously, in December 1858 several ladies offered to form themselves into a group whose purpose would be to visit patients, a move which eventually had most beneficial effects. Within two and a half years, the Ladies' Committee had assumed a more active role and were asking permission to be given lists of names of discharged patients to enable them to do their work more effectively.

With the exception of a regular supply of beer and wine and their usual Christmas treat, there were few comforts to which the indoor patients were entitled. In 1855, it was decided to form a library ('Not of a Sectarian character') for their use, but any books donated were to be viewed by the committee first lest their contents should be offensive. This scheme was soon augmented with invitations for donations of not more than a shilling so that a patients' libarary could properly be set up. The patients' occasional misdemeanours continued to cause concern. Where 'squabbles' occurred between them, the 'Party chiefly to blame' was refused readmission. W. G., of Merthyr, having absconded after being entrusted by the Matron with two pounds 'for the purpose of getting change', was thought 'highly deserving of punishment'. As a result, half a crown from the funds was donated to the Society for the Prosecution of Felons (an organization whose ultimate aim was the prevention of crime and which occasionally donated its surplus funds to the Infirmary).

Although patients from widely differing backgrounds were admitted from time to time (including sailors from as far away as South America), little mention was made of problems arising from religious differences or practices. The infirmary had been open for more than forty years before any reference was made to dietary problems based on religious beliefs. Then 'I.P., being of the Hebrew persuasion and therefore having scruples about partaking of the ordinary diet of the House', was allowed two shillings a week to provide himself with food that was acceptable to him. The first sign of true religious discrimination occurred in the same year when efforts were made to secure the services of a clergyman at least twice a week. The Vicar of Swansea, the Reverend E. B. Squire, had made it known that he would be prepared to undertake the duties for £20 a year and this was accepted. It was emphasized that it was not intended to exclude dissenting ministers if they were willing to offer their services free of charge. Two weeks later, with an amazing show of force, twenty of the twenty-one members of the committee attended the weekly meeting (the largest for years), and the resolution concerning the chaplain was rescinded. 'No such officer' was recognized by them, and justice and courtesy demanded that those from other persuasions who had given so generously of their time and money should also be consulted so that 'religious equality and harmony' could be preserved. The original decision was later reintroduced, whereupon twelve dissenting ministers volunteered to take religious services without payment, or, it seems, causing any embarrassment to the committee. The limits of tolerance in this field of religious equality and harmony were reached when religious tracts which 'argued for a return to Primitive Christianity' were distributed in the wards by visitors from an unorthodox sect. The committee insisted on inspecting all such material afterwards. It is of some interest that when the House Surgeon was empowered to give all the old Bibles for which they had no further use to patients as they left, a third of those given away were in French, German, Italian or Spanish.

Apart from the House Surgeon's tendency to provide more expensive diets than could be afforded and the failure of the honorary staff to attend punctually, the year 1860 opened quietly enough with no hint of the great changes that were almost in sight. Although an argument had been presented for providing wards for the treatment of consumptive patients, there was insufficient money so that what would have been the first organized attempt to treat tuberculosis in south-west Wales was delayed for many years. In spite of this, it had become apparent that an effort must be made to enlarge the Infirmary as it was not possible to provide the service expected, especially for male patients.

In 1855, an attempt was made to obtain permission to build a railway to run in parallel with the Mumbles Railway and which would connect the Swansea Docks with the Llanelli Railway; the new railway would have to pass through the Infirmary grounds. After much disagreement, £1,000 was accepted in return for the land needed by the railway company and for the possible damage that might ensue from the closeness of the new line to the building. An embankment was to be constructed to separate the railway from the Infirmary and an option on selling the whole property for £4,000 was also considered. It then became apparent that the new tracks would actually envelop the building. Its pine-end would be exposed with the demolition of the old workhouse and a signal post was to be built directly opposite the female wards. All of this would prove to be:

> very injurious and so great an annoyance to the patients that it will be necessary to remove elsewhere.[25]

A subcommittee had been formed to 'watch the progress' of the Dunvant Railway Bill but it had hardly started its work when a Notice of Ejectment was served on the Infirmary and the Poor House in 1862. It was thought that this could best be challenged by withdrawing £500 of their investments to help enlarge and improve the building so that another 20 beds could be added. An attempt was made to buy the Poor House garden, which lay between the Infirmary and the Oystermouth Railway, However, with 99 subscribers having failed to pay their dues, the new plans were badly timed and the railway company's scheme proved to be something of a nuisance. The only alternative was to ask for the permission of the Corporation, who were the freeholders, to dispose of the property and to use the money already received as the nucleus of a building fund once another site had been found. Two acres and twenty perches of land in the more rural setting of St Helen's were bought for £2,100 and plans were to be made for a new hospital of 100 beds to replace the old Infirmary with its 35 indoor patients.

Since the publication of her *Notes on Nursing* (already 'in the hands of the committee'), Florence Nightingale had often been asked for advice on the design of hospitals. In September 1864, Dr Thomas Williams, at that time Physician at the Infirmary, sought her views as she was known to be 'ardently interested in the good cause'. The correspondence which passed between them (preserved in the London Record Office[26]) showed the immense influence that her work was having. He, by far the best known of the Infirmary's staff and its only doctor ever to be elected a Fellow of the Royal Society, was unusually sycophantic in his style of writing to her:

> Without flattery or nonsensical circumlocution [I] crave a few words of advice and assistance from you ... [The new hospital was to be built using] the most improved sanitary principles, but in the most economical manner—we want a good structure at minimum cost. Will you generously aid us with a helping hand?

He went on to ask if she knew of an architect who specialized in the design of hospitals and for her opinion about the choice of building materials:

> with a view to economy ... If you can favour us without ... the least inconvenience to your-self, with a few words of advice or suggestion, it will act upon the Committee like an Electrical impulse.

Only four days after his first letter to her, he wrote to thank her for:

> your generous and instructive letter ... Now that you have united us to the fountain head of the best instruction, I assure you that it is the desire of the committee to consult you at every step ... Your name has set fire to our undertaking—those who were once indifferent are now energetic.

For once in his distinguished career, Dr Thomas Williams, extraordinary physician as he was, was greatly mistaken. In her reply, Miss Nightingale had written:

> A hospital is almost as difficult a place of construction as a watch and there is no building which requires more special knowledge.

She believed that they must be prepared to spend at least £140 a bed, exclusive of the cost of the land 'and any outlay for ornament', and that they should commission plans from an architect experienced in the field. There were only two or three such men in the land and she recommended Mr Graham of Leeds as having 'large experience'.[27] He took the trouble to visit Swansea to inspect the site and, in November 1864, submitted his plans to Miss Nightingale for her views. They both failed to share Dr Williams's enthusiasm for the location; she because the 'shape' of the land was not suitable, and he because the excessive fall of the ground from one end to the other (twelve feet in all) would make it impossible to erect a building in one length. He asked for her advice on his decision to omit day rooms for convalescent patients and believed that his plans would not allow extensions to be built easily. Her replies were, as expected, detailed, and with the reverence to which she had become accustomed, he 'unhesitatingly' accepted her modifications. It seemed by then that the only major obstacle left was to try to persuade the committee to abandon the Turkish Baths scheme (which they regarded as being a source of income).

Mr Graham later wrote to Miss Nightingale to say that he had met the Building Committee and that they were much pleased with his designs. In spite of that, they had not reached any conclusion, as there was a 'small local architect' (referred to more bluntly by Dr Williams as 'a local Mason, who misnomers himself an architect') who might be asked to submit his own design. Dr Williams continued:

> You may readily imagine that under such circumstances, in an assembly of unmixed Celts, a boisterous storm arose. The Barometer rose to a high point [but] Mr Graham charmed even the most violent opposition ... I am doing everything in my power ...[28]

But neither Mr Graham's undoubted charm nor Dr Williams's distinct persuasive powers were sufficiently potent to prevent the postponing of the next meeting. This was brought about in deference to the absent Mr Vivian ('an imperious Copper-Prince [who] extravagantly overrides his influence as he does his hospital intelligence'[29]). There were also others who wished to delay making a decision. From among them, Mr Eaton and Mr Moggridge later decided that they must call at the Nightingale house in Hampstead. She was said to be too ill to see them, although they had a lengthy interview with one of her close associates.

The early enthusiasm for Miss Nightingale's opinions was soon forgotten. Dr Williams remained as virtually the sole local influential champion of her views and of Mr Graham's designs. His isolation may have been because of the fear that commissioning a first-rate architect would greatly increase the costs involved but it was probably of some importance that Dr Williams's initial approach to her was made without anyone else's knowledge or permission.

Mr Graham confided to Miss Nightingale that it was all very well for Dr Williams to encourage him to enter the public competition for the design of the new building that was then organized:

> quite forgetting [that they can] purchase any one of the Designs at the price of one or other of the premiums offered ... there is not one of them competent to give an opinion upon any hospital arrangements ...[30]

Twelve sets of plans each bearing a pseudonym were submitted and they were exhibited in the Town Hall for three days before the General Meeting on 7 April 1865, at which the final choice would be made. The designs submitted by 'Omega' (who was actually Mr Graham) were thought to be immeasurably superior to the others, especially as the final cost would not exceed £12,000, which was the largest amount to be spent on the project.

On obtaining subscriptions of £6,000, the work was to be allowed to proceed and by November, more than that sum had been promised, with further donations of £1,000 each by the Lord Lieutenant and Nash Vaughan Edwards-Vaughan of Rheola. Miss Nightingale was well pleased with the final arrangements. She wrote to Mr Eaton of the 'very great pleasure' which his account of the meeting at which they were accepted, had given her:

> Your enlightened committee has rendered a real service to the cause of humanity in adopting Mr Graham's plans. When completed, you will have perhaps the finest and most perfect small hospital in the kingdom. I was deeply grieved to hear of the death of Dr Williams ... I shall ... add my name to your list of subscribers [for] £25 when you are ready for it. I think it is an extremely good idea to interest the men (in the great iron and other works) in your hospital—as it takes away from the idea of a Charity and gives them a personal care and anxiety for a measure which ought to concern their feelings ...[31]

Affording her that 'very great pleasure' of which she wrote was no easy task and much was made of her letter. In commenting on her generosity, *The Cambrian* of 30 September 1864 said:

> In Wales there be hidden in obscurity many hundreds of charitable ladies. Let this touching example call them forth ...

Some of Swansea's charitable ladies had already been called forth by Mrs Moggridge in 1860 when the Infirmary's Ladies' Committee (or Relief Fund) was formed. Although there were signs that their work was becoming increasingly more important, there were also those (gentlemen) who would have preferred that they should have been left in obscurity. Possibly of even greater significance was the fact that although local workmen were already following the example of those employed at the nearby Gas Works in subscribing, they, too, were to be excluded from having any say in the hospital's affairs for many years.

While the more conscientious members of the committee, complete with the lithographic sketches of the proposed new building sent to each of them by their architect, were soliciting contributions, the medical staff had taken to quarrelling among themselves. In 1863, the Medical Board had suggested that the House Surgeon would have more time to attend to patients in their own homes if two new posts of Physician and Surgeon for the Outdoor Patients were created. Every doctor in the town, who was not already connected with the hospital, was informed of this decision. On 9 October, Mr Andrew Davies was elected to the surgical post and Dr Thomas Druslwyn Griffiths to the post of Physician.

Twice during the following year, attention was drawn to Dr Griffiths's poor attendance, and as his explanation was not satisfactory, the possibility of asking for his resignation was considered. He was not a man to be trifled with (as was to become apparent over a period of many years). In attempting to explain his own absences, he accused the other members of the medical staff of making false entries in the journal in which their attendances were recorded. He was challenged to produce proof of his assertions or to apologize, whereupon he claimed that his remarks had been misinterpreted and that he had only meant to suggest that a more accurate means of recording their visits was necessary. He later maintained that he had only meant to accuse Dr Thomas Williams of failing to meet his obligations. When Dr Williams died tragically at the age of forty-seven, three months later, Dr Griffiths resigned from his post in order to offer himself as Honorary Physician.

Having badly overestimated the amount of support available to him, he only obtained seven votes and Dr John Paddon was elected by a majority of fifteen. Dr Griffiths's connection with the Infirmary was then broken until he obtained a post in another speciality there nearly twenty years later. To mark his disapproval, he then withdrew his subscription and claimed that the guinea which he had given in the previous year was a non-recurring donation, even though he had used his privilege as a subscriber to vote for himself at the recent election for a new physician.

There were grave problems awaiting Dr Paddon. Shortly after the plans for the new hospital had been accepted, the barque *Hecla* put in to the nearby Swansea Docks from Cuba. One man had already died on the day before the ship's arrival. Dr Paddon was so concerned at the ten deaths that occurred subsequently from yellow fever that he wrote to the Privy Council and they sent down an expert to investigate. The *British Medical Journal* commented:

> Fever of one kind or another is chronic at Swansea and has long been so. To the inhabitants, it has become a terror, and the cause of much family bereavement ... The North-East and North-West portions of the town are scarcely ever free from disease ... slow fever and malignant diseases of all shapes and kinds are seldom absent ... The town has always been, upon the whole, a foul spot ...[32]

Amongst the doctors, the brotherly love which Dr Bird had longed for but had failed to practise in an earlier age became more apparent with the appointment of Dr Jabez Thomas to succeed Dr Griffiths. He had previously worked at the Infirmary as a locum House Surgeon for his brother, Mr Griffith R. Thomas, who was by then the other Medical Officer for Outdoor Patients. Seven months after starting work there, Dr Jabez Thomas asked for permission to open a clinic for the treatment of eye diseases, a field in which he later specialized, but the Medical Board was opposed to this in principle. Five months after that, the two Outdoor Medical Officers and the House Surgeon divided the town into districts so that the outdoor patient work could be done more systematically and the patients' treatment supervised more effectively. That system cannot have lasted for any great length of time as by 1868 the geographical extent of the area in which the House Surgeon could visit patients in their own homes was found to be far too extensive for one person to deal with.

That problem soon got submerged in the greater difficulties being faced. In 1865 the disruptive effect of the new railway caused a great deal of concern. The erection of the new hospital had not been commenced a moment too soon and there were hopes that it would be ready shortly. A vast sum of money was still required before the building could be furnished and there was already a deficit of more than £460. There was concern that the delays had proved to be expensive and even the tithes on the land at St Helen's had to be paid from the time when it was bought. One of the most promising signs was that workmen from the Swansea Brewery, the Briton Ferry Iron Works, and the Middle and Upper Bank Copper Works had joined their colleagues from the Gas Works and had collected nearly £21 in an attempt to ease the difficulties.

At that same time, it was found that the part of the Infirmary nearest the railway showed signs of collapsing and the risk of accidents due to carelessness on the part of the railway officials was thought to be considerable, as the trains passed the entrance to the building. The need to transfer to the St Helen's site was therefore pressing. By January 1868, the House Surgeon reported that the staff's state of health was very unsatisfactory as a result of the presence of 'disagreeable effluvia in all parts'. The Matron, Dispenser, nurses and servants had all complained of 'debility and enervation'. The House Surgeon had been aware of an overpowering and unwholesome smell throughout the house by day, which became intolerable in any room with closed doors and windows. For some months, he had provided carbolic acid to be poured into each drain every night, but without noticeable improvement. In spite of all the concern that was registered, and a severe epidemic of choleraic disease when the new building was nearing completion, large quantities of rubbish were regularly left directly opposite the Infirmary by the town's scavengers.

To add to the problem, the medical staff had to complain that no plans had been made to extend the town's drainage system to the locality of the new hospital. The surrounding houses with their cesspools were thought to constitute a hazard to the health of the in-patients and a deputation was sent to the local Board of Health to press on them the need for an expansion of the drains to that locality by the time that the hospital accepted patients.

The preparations for the laying of the foundation stone for the new building on the 4 March 1867 (fifty years exactly after the first Infirmary had been opened) were extensive. The Members of Parliament and the Mayor were invited and the function was to be followed by a public breakfast (later referred to as a luncheon, see Appendix II), held at the Music Hall, which ladies were also allowed to attend, at a cost of 4s.6d. each. Eventually, the tickets were bought at 5s. each and 200 places were reserved, except that the House Surgeon, the Secretary, his predecessor, the Dispenser, the Matron, the Superintendent of Police, the Toastmaster and representatives of *The Cambrian* did not have to pay.[33] Fifty copies of that paper were bought 'for distribution profitably'. Lt.-Col. Vivian and Major Dillwyn had already consented to the use of the bands of their respective Volunteer Corps during the day. Major George Grant Francis (who, as managing director of the railway company, must have been greatly relieved at the move) was refused permission to bring along the Artillery Volunteer Corps.

While the 'Inmates' of the Infirmary had to be content with a 'general holiday' (subject to the approval of the House Surgeon), more than 300 people sat down to the celebratory meal, while the balconies were well filled with spectators. In his speech, C. R. M. Talbot, in referring to the 25 dishes available in the main course, said:

> It was never possible to get as much money for a charitable institution as they could after a good dinner.

The usual burdensome toasts (to 'The Press', 'The Architect', 'The Army, the Navy, the Militia and the Volunteers—those noble defenders of their country by land and sea') followed. While its significance for the later history of the hospital was probably not appreciated, the inclusion of 'the Friendly Societies' and the response by one of their representatives was not without importance considering the major role which organized working-class contributions were to play in the hospital's development in later years.

Large contributions, such as those of John Dillwyn Llewelyn, who offered to provide all the furniture, were greatly appreciated. It was also soon realized that offers such as those of Mr Morgan of Hafod to exhibit his model of Oystermouth Castle (which raised nearly £40), and of Major Francis to show his collection of medals, coins, and china for the benefit of the hospital, were not to be spurned. Such haphazard means of financing the work of the main local provider of health care were gradually being accepted, although they had previously been viewed with a certain amount of distaste. The drastic revision in the collection of funds, which was so badly needed, belonged to a somewhat later age. In July 1868, while recognizing the 'arduous labour' connected with the organization of the annual bazaar, there was a growing awareness in the committee that, although events of that kind were useful, more regular and predictable sources of income were necessary. A modest start in this direction was made with the printing of 'Collecting Cards' and the concurrent move to canvass the town for subscriptions.

It was hoped that the removal to St Helen's would occur by June 1868, and work on the second (administration) block was to proceed before then if additional subscriptions of at least £2,500 could be found. Over the previous year, £1,100 had been made available, but of the £9,500 which had been promised, £2,500 was still unpaid. Given these circumstances, delays were inevitable. Towards the end of 1868, prolonged discussions were still taking place on the disposal of the old building. Meanwhile, concern continued to be voiced about the increased risks of injury because of the closeness of the railway. The danger to children attending the nearby parochial schools was highlighted when a six-year-old boy leaving a school building had his leg amputated by falling under a train. The railway company's reply to criticisms levelled at them was that their guards had been instructed to sound their whistles and drive slowly through the locality. That did little to alleviate matters; neither did the dangers hasten the closure of the old Infirmary.

When the preparations for the change were at their height, Miss Markham, by far the most efficient Matron yet appointed, 'begged' the committee to give her a testimonial as she wished to apply for a similar post at the Hereford Infirmary.[34] Mrs Elizabeth MacVey was appointed to succeed her at a salary of £35, with the possibility of an increase to £40 after a year. On 26 February 1869, a committee meeting was held in the new hospital building when it was possible 'to minutely Examine and inspect the progress of work'. Even with arrears of subscriptions of nearly £140 and a deficit of £1,500 in connection with the building work, an offer by a Mr Roose Jones to canvass the county for subscribers was refused by them. They were no nearer to disposing of the old building and several new options were considered. These included leasing the ground for building purposes (with 240 feet of frontage facing the road and 270 feet facing the beach) or leasing the building for use as a hotel or lodging house, although it was recognized that its proximity to the railway terminus and the South Dock was likely to make it more profitable to sell it for use as a siding store or workshop. An offer to the Corporation to buy the lease for £2,000 was refused but a figure of £1,000 was agreed on later.

Without any increase in the numbers of in-patients, it had been estimated that there would inevitably occur increases in expenditure with the opening of the new building. These were enlarged by the 'many deficiencies', the need for a boundary wall for which no provision had been made, for a stable for the doctors' horses and carriages, and for a 'Dead House'. When all these were finished, the new Swansea Hospital was insured for £2,500, and the furniture for £500. The most significant move in the history of medical practice in Swansea for many decades was about to occur. But the move to new facilities in November 1869 did not herald a great advance in the nature of health care available to the people of Swansea. Five weeks after the move, the editor of *The Cambrian*, in his last editorial column for that year on 31 December, wrote:

> If the year now closing has not been crowded by sensational events, it may be noted as one of steady progress.

Not every sick person in the town would have accepted that those words were true. Shortly before, a woman described as being 'in articulo mortis' had been refused admission because no guinea subscriber who had not already used up all his privileges for admitting patients could be traced. Her husband asked the Relieving Officer (an official one of whose functions was to provide aid for the needy from public funds) for help and was chided for possessing a watch which, he was told, should have been sold to pay a doctor's fee.

It was to take more than the opening of a new building in another part of the town, important though that was, to alter the system of health care.

CHAPTER FIVE

The Swansea Hospital

For many years past, it has been felt that Swansea had outgrown its old infirmary.[1]

The Age of Superstition past,
O'er all such Scenes her veil hath cast,
Such ne'er shall eye behold again . . .[2]

THE Reverend Ireland Jones's *Poems . . . for the benefit of the Swansea Infirmary*, published in 1840, had long since been forgotten by 1869, but it seemed to many of those connected with the hospital that the 'New Age' for which he had hoped had at last arrived. Armed with 250 newly printed collecting cards, the almost certain knowledge that their proper use would do no more than contain the debt, and a seemingly infinite degree of patience which would serve him well in his dealings with committee members, medical staff and subscribers, Mr John W. Morris, the new Secretary since 1868, embarked on his duties. He was to remain as Secretary almost until the turn of the century. He had prepared well for the Opening Ceremonial of the new hospital on Wednesday, 27 October 1869. The £14,000 which the building was thought to have cost had all been subscribed by the day and the contractors, Messrs Thomas, Watkins and Jenkins of Swansea, were highly complimented on their work, even though the building was faced with local stone in spite of George Grant Francis's protestations that only Bath stone would do. It had originally been intended to provide a hundred beds but the completion of the new North Wing was delayed, so that only half that number were available—an increase of twenty on the number in the old Infirmary.[3]

Although the day's events were meant to have a religious character 'rather than any public demonstration'[4], the two Trustees, one of the Presidents, thirteen Vice-Presidents, the seven members of the medical staff and eighteen committee members gathered at the old building so that they could walk in formal style to the new hospital. They were met on the way by Lewis Llewelyn Dillwyn MP, 'who turned and joined in the procession'. The ceremony was held in the large ward on whose walls had been hung several illuminated biblical quotations such as 'Lord, he whom thou lovest is sick' and 'This mortal must put on immortality'. The Mayor presided and representatives of the town's more important families and 'a large number of the General Public' joined in a religious service after which a collection was made and produced more than £13. On the following two days, the building was open for the public to visit and on Tuesday 2 November, arrangements were made (at a cost of £2. 16s.) 'for the removal of the household' to the new site.

The transfer of facilities had not been without its problems, whose extent varied from the lack of Norwegian and Greek Bibles to the risk of annoyance to those who lived nearby because of the presence of the Dead House. Shortly afterwards, a complaint had to be made to the architect about the number of imperfectly fixed tiles which had been blown off the roof. When a committee member protested that, on visiting the hospital at 8.30 p.m., he found the gas light still burning 'after the hour for lowering the light', he was informed that this was the only means available for maintaining the temperature in the wards. There was no means by which contaminated clothing could be fumigated until the Justices promised that a machine similar to the one in use at the House of Correction could be built by the prisoners there so that each patient in the hospital could be provided with clean clothes on their admission.

A further bill from the builders showed that they had not been paid the whole of the money due to them. It was C. R. M. Talbot who offered to clear the debt of more than £800. Soon, it became apparent that extra accommodation was urgently required for female in-patients. It was hoped that a general redistribution of beds could be brought about by reducing the size of the hospital's Dispensary and Outdoor Department and using one of the corridors as a ward. Again, the issue of the provision of therapeutic baths was raised and was resolved by a decision made by John Dillwyn Llewelyn of Penllergaer to subscribe as much money that year as he would have spent on the erection of a cottage hospital. By July 1871, the number of beds available had reached fifty, and it was believed that no other hospital in the kingdom could claim such economy of administration in comparison with the benefits provided.

By the time of the 1874 Anniversary Meeting, however, it was being shown that the hospital's resources were already under strain as a result of further increases in the population, and moreover the number of patients admitted following accidents was rising disproportionately to a level where they filled almost all the available beds. A combination of cleanliness, good nursing and the great attention which the medical staff ('under Providence') paid to their work was believed to be sufficiently potent to cope with virtually all the evils encountered in medical practice, except, of course, their greatest difficulty of all, namely that of the debt. In discussing the vast improvements that had come about, the Secretary, in an eloquent mood, quoted twenty-eight lines of Milton's poetry at its most sombre, but for those who sought help there, he believed that the hospital was 'their chief and final hope'. The medical staff report for that year certainly tended to confirm that view, particularly as the nature of the work being undertaken by the surgeons was gradually expanding.

In July 1870, largely through the work of the Secretary in collecting subscriptions that were overdue, a debt of £460 had been changed into a balance of £23. 18s. For his achievements, the Secretary was given a gratuity of £20 and the Matron was paid £5 for introducing 'the strictest economy' by reducing the cost of the dietary from £729 to £638. About £7,000 would be needed if the plan to complete the North Wing was to be brought about, and the possibility of withdrawing money from the Permanent Capital Fund was considered. Mr Griffith Llewellyn of Baglan Hall offered to pay £3,000 if proof could be given to him by the end of that year that the additional sum required had been obtained from other sources. Within three weeks, more than £4,000 had been subscribed, and an additional appeal 'to those whom Providence has blessed with means' was launched.

In spite of all the difficulties, by 1876, tenders were finally being invited for the erection of the North Wing. A new infectious diseases ward was also to be built and some reconstruction of the older building to form an accident ward was planned. With the removal of the hot water pipes and the addition of a post-mortem room and mortuary, the final cost was set at £7,085. Of the generous donations received, £100 was given anonymously to help build a children's ward and a promise was made that this would soon be accomplished as the numbers of children being admitted to the adult wards had increased greatly.

In spite of this generosity, more cutbacks were obviously needed by 1877 to ensure that the building could be completed, and the clinical work could proceed and develop properly. An application by the Dispenser, Mr Blackmore, for an increase in wages had to be refused, the resident medical staff's supply of free beer was cancelled, and it was not long before the Assistant House Surgeon had to leave because it was unlikely that there would be sufficient money to pay his salary.

Yet further attempts had to be made to extend the facilities, particularly as it was thought to be 'a slur and a blot on the fair character of the Welsh people' that there was still no recognized School of Medicine and Surgery in the Principality. In addition an increasing number of applications for indoor treatment was having to be refused and strong steps to remedy the situation were called for. The favourite (and often successful) remedy for this situation, namely to call a public meeting at which the Lord Lieutenant or the Mayor would preside, had been tried and found to be reasonably effective but there were limits to the extent to which such measures could be invoked. Local industrial concerns were major users of the hospital's facilities and it was decided that the 'heads' of all the large works in the district should again be asked to consider contributing larger sums of money.

For some time past working men's organizations had been donating sporadically but no real attempt had been made to exploit this source in a systematic manner. 'The noble example' set by the workmen of the Amman Valley Iron Works, who had voluntarily subscribed a penny a month each (without asking for subscribers' privileges) was at one time thought to point the way to a new source of income. However, apart from a special appeal at which employees were told 'simply and in their own language' of the difficulties faced by the hospital, no sustained efforts had ever been made in that field. It was the workmen themselves who set in motion the machinery which, in the long term, came closest to solving the financial difficulties.

It was the resignation of Mr Mowatt from his post as House Surgeon in 1869 that proved to be the eventual turning point in the collection of funds. His work was so much appreciated that a 'Working Men's Testimonial' was set up as a means of showing their appreciation. At the presentation, it was proposed by the Superintendent of the Swansea Harbour Trust, Mr J. W. James, that a quarter of a day's pay once a year, which would amount to less than one-fifth of a penny from each pound earned, would yield a regular and large sum of money, and so the matter was given serious consideration by the committee for the first time.

It was strongly felt by some members of the committee that the Swansea artisan or labourer was not contributing enough towards the cost of his treatment at times of illness. At the same time, great efforts were made by the committee to ensure that when bodies of workmen did donate money to the hospital, they should be denied the privilege of being known as subscribers, irrespective of the amount of money received. In spite of the ever-increasing emancipation of the working classes which had occurred since the old Infirmary was first opened, the composition of the bodies that governed the hospital had not altered significantly. All the indications are that the rank and file of the town of Swansea were not thought to be capable of taking control of their hospital. It seems that the Governors cannot have realized (or, more likely, actively resisted the notion) that ordinary workers had already taken significant steps in asserting themselves and in protecting their rights. At times, though, this form of development seems to have been welcomed at annual meetings:

> Working men, too, have learned, by becoming better educated, to join Friendly Societies, and by this means they are free from needing the advantages of this Institution. Friendly Societies have increased both in strength and numbers, and their funds have been much augmented of late years, thus showing that men are being taught by education to provide for a day of sickness and distress. (Cheers) Happily we are living in an age where the virtue of charity is more widely exercised than of old.[5]

In spite of this apparent acceptance of the Friendly Societies, the hospital authorities occasionally saw them as a threat to the more established forms of medical aid. The so-called 'club system', whereby workmen employed doctors on a part-time basis to provide them and their families with medical services, was well established. With their increased membership and bargaining power, the Friendly Societies were no longer prepared to tolerate the somewhat patronizing attitude previously displayed towards them. While the Cambrian Lodge of Odd Fellows had been able to pay out to their members £126 more in 1882 than in the previous year, their Patriotic Lodge meeting at Alltwen found it 'very disagreeable' that the doctor paid by them should oppose hospital treatment for those already under his care. In an attempt to force him to change his views, they seriously considered withdrawing their subscriptions to the hospital altogether.[6] (The general level of unrest reached its peak in the Maesteg area in 1882, when all the workmen of the Llynvi and Tondu Iron Works and Collieries went on strike for a day in order to assert their right to choose their own doctor rather than the management's.) A deputation from the Swansea Trades Council visited the hospital committee to discuss their views on the operation of the club system.[7] As no children over the age of fourteen were catered for by their scheme, the deputation asked for an extension of the hospital's facilities to include them. They felt justified in asking for that concession particularly as the Hospital Saturday movement (which arranged weekly collections for the hospital and had raised £393 in that year) had proved to be so successful among those represented by them. Because the hospital debt had risen to nearly £800, the only way in which the committee could see the Trades Council request being put into practice while retaining the conditions of admission unaltered was by cutting the out-patient facilities in other ways. The request was therefore refused.

It would have been no consolation to the Trades Council's delegates to realize that Swansea's tradesmen did not fare any better in their dealings with the hospital. They were often deprived of the advantages offered by membership of the Friendly Societies and were usually only eligible for hospital treatment on becoming subscribers themselves. Their dilemma and the committee's attitude to them was well summarized by one correspondent in discussing the hospital's Annual Ball, which provided a recurring source of income, when he said:

> [it] would all the better attain its object ... if the empty space on the [ballroom] floor were filled up by such of the respectable commercial people as can afford to pay for the tickets, and who know how to behave themselves accordingly.[8]

For several generations yet, the management of the hospital was to remain in the hands of those who were sufficiently well off not to have to rely on its services. Indeed, the general attitude of the committee became even more apparent when Dr Jabez Thomas attempted to arrange a meeting in the hospital board room between the doctors and the Friendly Societies in May 1873. As the building had recently been painted and new carpets had been laid, the request was refused, and when the committee was asked to reconsider, it allowed the meeting to take place in the surgery. The price which the artisans paid for being prudent was high. If they joined clubs which had their own doctors, they were refused outdoor treatment at the hospital. It was only after a deputation from the Loyal Hafod Lodge of Odd Fellows had put their case most forcibly, in 1874, that it was agreed that there would be no objection in future to working-class people having access to two sources of medical advice.

In view of the great problems being faced, the level of optimism among some of the committee members bordered on being totally unrealistic. But, in the end it was that obstinate approach that ensured that the hospital survived. At the Anniversary Meeting for 1878, William Thomas of Lan House, who was the Mayor for that year, voiced the general satisfaction that when the North Wing was completed, it would be possible to accept 120 indoor patients. He went on to express his concern that £277. 17s. was owed to the Treasurers and blamed this on an abysmal lack of public support. His speech ended with what had become a fairly regular warning that, in spite of the enlarged facilities, the committee, as 'provident housekeepers', might well be forced to limit the benefits conferred in proportion to public generosity.

By 1879, the furnishing of the new North Wing was completed. Even though it was claimed that 'all is paid for', nearly £500 of the ordinary debt remained. In spite of that, the Anniversary Report for that year took on a near-ecstatic tone. The hospital was said to be:

> second to none in the kingdom for architectural beauty and arrangement, and so situated that the sea breezes are wafted straight across the broad

Atlantic into its very wards. It is also within easy walk (*sic*) for the convalescent, of our charming sands. Every modern appliance that skill and money could procure has been brought into requisition so as to make it a perfect Hospital, and your committee may be acquitted of conceit when they say, without fear of contradiction, that *it is* such.[9]

Three weeks after the writing of that report, the patients from the South Wing had to be removed to the new building because the drains were blocked. Dr Morgan, the Public Analyst, was asked to examine the water in the hospital well in case it should have been polluted. He found it to be excellent drinking water but it was too hard for use in washing and cooking and it did not compare with that provided by the Urban Sanitary Authority. Yet, illness (of an unspecified kind) among the indoor patients led the medical staff to believe that there must be defects in the drainage and sanitary system.

There were indications that from the time of the opening of the new hospital, patient care was becoming more highly organized and efficient and more attention was being paid to patients' social circumstances. This was by no means an innovation. Since 1860, the Ladies' Visiting Committee had spent more than £170 'for the relief of patients'. Money for that purpose was also being made available from other sources. (One such example was that of Lewis Llewelyn Dillwyn who had temporarily forgotten the disharmony of former years and had made available £100 left by his father to aid patients who were being discharged from the hospital.) Although the need for the services of the Ladies' Visiting Committee had become increasingly apparent, the hospital committee failed to agree to any of the requests made by Mrs Webber on their behalf. Possibly as a result of her despair, when the appointment of a chaplain was being considered in 1874, she suggested that the interest on the Dillwyn Bequest should be handed to him to be used for the relief of impoverished patients rather than be used by the Ladies' Fund.

The administration of the hospital was gradually becoming more complex. A revision of the rules was called for in 1869 and two committee members were asked to review these and to correct any grammatical errors in time for a Special General Meeting called to repeal the old regulations. Of the revised rules, the most important was that henceforth the Matron was to be considered the head of the household so that her administrative powers were enhanced. Like her predecessors, she was expected to visit the wards at least twice daily, to inspect the bed-linen regularly, and to ensure that every new patient was given clean bed-sheets on their admission. The nursing and household departments were to be kept separate and the servants were not to enter the wards on any pretext. The nurses were to behave with kindness to the patients and with civility and respect to the hospital's officers. They were to refuse money or other rewards from those under their care and were to ensure that those patients who were well enough to sit up should not lie on their beds with their shoes on, take their meals there, or play cards or dice.

When Mr Mowatt resigned (within months of the opening of the new hospital) after nearly six years as House Surgeon, he was presented, in a flood of generosity not witnessed since the time of the very first doctor to hold that post, with a binocular microscope, a magneto-electric machine, a caustic holder in a case and a self-reading thermometer, each of which was engraved with a silver plate, together with a resolution illuminated on vellum. His successor was Dr Henry Thomas Sylvester of Bath, who had been shrewd enough to introduce himself well beforehand by attending the opening ceremony of the new building. He was the grandson of the Dr Sylvester who had helped found the original Dispensary and his father had also worked in Swansea as a physician. He had entered the army as an Assistant Surgeon in 1854 and had worked with Florence Nightingale in the hospitals at Sebastopol and Scutari during the Crimean War. There, for his extraordinary courage in caring for wounded soldiers, he became the only doctor associated with the hospital ever to be awarded the Victoria Cross. His appointment as House Surgeon began a new era in the medical history of the hospital.

Lister had begun his pioneering work with the introduction of antiseptic surgery in 1867 (first with the use of carbolic dressings and later, with the carbolic spray), but his work was strongly opposed by many doctors. In 1874, even *The Lancet* was of the opinion that 'with every public appearance, Professor Lister's carbolic solutions grow weaker and weaker while his faith grows more and more'. Within a year, the same journal's viewpoint was that 'in matters of hygiene, no precaution is now too trivial'[10]—a statement that might well have been echoed by the hospital's medical staff.

The Report of the Medical and Surgical Staff in reference to 'Traumatic Infection' in the hospital was written after they had investigated the possible causes of the fouling of the wards by erysipelas and other unspecified conditions in 1876. The Medical Board met on several occasions and carefully considered what had developed into a major crisis. At that time, they had no true appreciation of the origin of infections; the importance and significance of Pasteur's work on the causes of such conditions had not been generally appreciated. For more than three years, especially in the men's wards, infections had occurred for which no cause other than 'an unhealthy condition of Ward atmosphere' could be discovered. Such infections had been most common where there were injuries with a breach of the skin surface and in those undergoing 'what are called major operations'. The result was:

> traumatic infections [which] poison a building very persistently; they will render persons and things occupying a ward such for example, as the hands and clothes of dressers and nurses, beds and bed clothes and even surgical Instruments the carriers of contagion to healthy wounds, just as certainly as the poison of scarlatina or smallpox can be carried from the infected to the healthy.[11]

While it was acknowledged that such infections could have been brought in from outside the hospital, the possibility was considered that they were 'generated within' and that this was, in some way, related to overcrowding of patients whose wounds were already severely infected or which showed extensive destruction of tissue. It had been apparent from the start of the inquiry that isolation facilities were needed and that 'any limitation of the mischief' would be made more difficult by the insufficient supply of nurses. In one instance, a day nurse, helped by a 'scrubber', had to care for thirty-two patients. The nurse was thought to be 'active and kind' but, having started work herself as a scrubber and having received no training except while working in the hospital, she had no adequate conception of the risks incurred for patients by her being, almost of necessity, 'a carrier of contagion as she ministers by turns to infected and non infected persons.' Only one night nurse was employed and the most highly infected of the patients were those who had the most regular contact with her:

> [The patients] want change of position, they want nourishment, stimulants and perhaps medicine in the night as in the day.

The Matron was greatly praised, particularly as she had volunteered to care at night for a patient who had since died of a generalized infection. It was believed that her duties were sufficiently onerous to make a repetition of this situation undesirable. A plea was made for the provision of cotton dresses which could be washed each week for the nurses, and a reduction in the number of beds in the large ward was called for. The women's ward at the foot of the stairs should also be emptied as soon as possible so that it could be used as a combined accident and surgical ward.

Lister's antiseptic techniques were not used in the hospital until 1876, when the medical staff made a special plea for their use.

> The success of [the] Antiseptic system of treatment of wounds, with which Mr Lister's name is inseparably associated, has been in his hands (and in those of others when carefully and thoroughly adapted) so remarkable not to say brilliant, that we recommend that every facility should be given for its use here. It ... involves much care and trouble, but we feel assured that under the supervision of the Surgical Staff and the present Resident Medical Officer it will not disappoint the hopes and expectations which we indulge ... It is certainly expensive, but in as much as when well applied, it does not require, like other dressings, frequent renewals, and as foul wounds and profuse discharges and poisoned blood, are not often seen accompanying it, the probability of a good financial, is almost as great as of a good sanitary, result.[12]

A 'spray producer' (used to dissipate the carbolic acid) at a cost not exceeding £7.10s. was ordered and before the end of that year, an operation involving the removal of a cyst from the ovary of a 12-year-old girl was performed 'under the Carbolic Spray'.

The medical staff were displeased at the fact that the disinfection of beds and bedding could not be carried out effectively at the hospital. As merely soaking clothing and bedding in a disinfecting solution for a few hours was unsatisfactory, they recommended that the disinfecting chamber owned by the Urban Sanitary Authority, which was kept at the old Infirmary, should be used. They went on to offer an opinion that the traumatic infection was carried by 'ward dust' which was to be found in abundance on the hot air pipes in the long ward. They recommended that these should be more frequently cleaned and that the ward walls must be brushed down with disinfecting solution. No clothes or bandages were to be washed in any of the offices attached to the wards and no clothes should be dried on the roof of the ward corridor. Again, a special plea was made for the erection of Isolation Buildings with accommodation for two women and two men, but they believed that if their other recommendations were effectively implemented, the need for separate isolation facilities would be reduced.

Their last recommendation was that careful records should be kept on all those admitted as this would provide an 'early warning system when infection occurred'. All this advice was accepted with the exception of that concerning the isolation block; this was rejected on the grounds that concentrating their resources on the construction of the new wing would provide a more effective solution. If there were an emergency, a house in the neighbourhood could be rented for the nursing of grossly infected patients. Implicit in the acceptance of the medical staff's report was a new awareness that the spread of infection in hospital might be preventable. This signalled a change of attitude that was of far greater significance than could have been realized at the time.

There had become apparent a greater tendency for patients themselves to complain about their treatment. At a time when it could least be afforded, disparaging remarks were widely circulated about the hospital's work. A police inspector had suffered a severe shortening of his leg after being treated for a fracture of the thigh in 1879 and the surgeon concerned, Dr Jabez Thomas, who had not attended to the patient himself, was sent 'an expression of great regret and strong disapproval' by the committee. Later, Dr Thomas, who claimed that he attended to his work at the hospital every day, had to face an accusation that two patients had died but that no inquests were held even though the cause of death was not known. An investigation by the medical staff showed that, in one case, a dislocation of the hip had occurred sixteen weeks before the admission and that a doctor elsewhere had attempted (unsuccessfully) to correct this. After a consultation in the hospital, the patient:

> was placed under Chloroform, and every legitimate means was employed for that purpose. [Eventually, the patient was] sent back to bed in a state only usual after such manipulation.[13]

The patient died that evening. The second problem occurred when a lady with an abdominal tumour had asked to have it removed despite Dr Thomas's warnings that there were many dangers. At operation, he found 'many untoward circumstances' and the patient 'sank from shock'. It was not considered necessary to hold inquests on patients who had died after surgical operations and this view, it seems, was shared by the coroner.

Even if Dr Thomas was thus spared any further embarrassment (particularly as he had been able to quote the former President of the Royal College of Surgeons, Sir James Paget, in his defence in the case of the first patient), the activities of some of his colleagues were also questioned. Dr Padley, who had held the post of Physician for almost fourteen years, was bluntly asked if he would resign after a prolonged absence due to ill health, but he refused to do so. At the same time, Dr Griffiths, who was no longer a member of the honorary staff, claimed that the number of deaths during the previous year (1876) was far greater than had been recorded in the Annual Report. This was not true but his episodic outbursts invariably drew attention. They were never well received as it was feared that they might affect the level of contributions on which the hospital was so dependent and as they were made, on this occasion, at a time of economic depression in 1877, this caused an additional degree of concern.

Attention was eventually diverted from this issue with a major argument about the use of alcohol in treatment. Whenever its value as a medicinal agent was challenged (often by the abstainers among the honorary staff), that view was countered with such statements as that made by Dr Paddon when he insisted that he had the right to prescribe what he believed was best for the patient:

> [For] people coming in to hospital in a poor and bloodless condition, something more than milk was required (HEAR, HEAR), namely a mild form of claret... The hospital [is] not only supported by teetotallers and if they want to have one of their own, let them get on with it.[14]

The 1870s had seen a great deal of activity occurring locally in medical fields outside the hospital. The passing of Disraeli's Public Health Act of 1871 made it compulsory for each district to appoint a Medical Officer of Health. The Borough of Swansea had made its first appointment of that kind in 1853 and the Urban and Rural Sanitary Authorities, which served the surrounding localities, were eventually compelled to follow. The sporadic recurrence of smallpox, which had such a devastating effect on a population that was by then largely unvaccinated, served to emphasize the importance of the new public health measures and the hopelessness of attempting to treat the major infectious disorders once they were established. The committee, with uncharacteristic boldness, went so far as to present a strongly worded 'memorial' to the Swansea Board of Health. In it, they drew attention to the possible relationship between the state of the streets and the unhealthy condition of the town's population. It was thought that:

> the Exhalations arising from the admixture of mud, the Excrement of horses, dogs &c combined with animal and vegetable matter in all stages of decomposition cannot be otherwise than prejudicial to health. We think the plan of removing this liquid filth from one street and pouring it over the newly laid stones in another is most objectionable and ought to be discontinued unless some disinfectants (such as carbolic acid) is (*sic*) first mixed with it, our best authorities on the subject advising the use of that.[15]

The 'memorial' ended with the stern reminder that one of Swansea's most important by-laws insisted that every occupier of premises was obliged to keep clean and free from filth the pavements outside his premises and that due to the absence of 'crossways', the pavements were often covered with 'the filth before alluded to'.

No explanation exists for the committee's sudden (if rather belated) interest in the topic of preventive medicine. It is certain that the doctors had long since been emphasizing its importance, particularly with regard to the isolation of patients suffering from infectious disorders. Not that they were totally in agreement on such matters themselves. When the incidence of typhoid (by then clearly distinguishable from typhus) in the town reached epidemic levels in 1881, Dr Griffiths alienated himself from most of the members of the Swansea Medical Society; to the annoyance of the Mayor, Dr James Rogers, himself an expert on public health matters, and Dr Ebenezer Davies, the Medical Officer of Health, Dr Griffiths claimed at a meeting of that society that the town's drains had been choked for several weeks and that it was neglect and failure to correct this that had brought the typhoid to Swansea. On a show of hands, the vast majority of those present failed to accept that 'a backward escape of sewer gas', as Dr Griffiths claimed, had precipitated the epidemic. (Although Miss Nightingale would have supported him in his views, there were probably few other doctors in Swansea who believed in that theory by that time as it was almost universally accepted that the infectious disorders were caused by the transmission of bacteria.) Further disagreements recurred at the next outbreak of the same disease in 1885. 'When doctors differ', it was said then, 'patients die . . . [and] Swansea doctors are not altogether in agreement.'[16] Then, the arguments centred on the means by which patients suffering from the disorder should be isolated. 'The collection of sheds and tents on our foreshore', as the old Infirmary was called, became quickly filled, and Dr Ebenezer Davies made a strong plea for the loan of a ward at the hospital. He promised that any additional expense incurred would be borne by the Corporation, which was, by then, much more aware of its duties in the public health field. The death rate had risen considerably during July but he was certain that no danger existed, provided that great care was taken by the nurses. The matter was eventually deferred for a week in spite of Dr Rawlings's protests that there existed a grave emergency and that a decision should be made at once. The medical staff were divided in their views. After much arguing among themselves, they decided that it was undesirable that typhoid patients should be allowed to enter the hospital; later, however, when the suggestion was made that a part of the new workhouse buildings should be used, the workmen employed on the site threatened to go on strike. Once again, therefore, no decision on an isolation building was taken at this time.

When Miss Grenfell wrote to the hospital in 1875 to ask if 'a Lady' could be allowed to attend the hospital to be trained as a nurse 'with a view to her taking a post as matron of a County Hospital', the main objection was that the accommodation available 'would not admit of receiving a lady'. But if the status of the hospital nurse was low, that of the district nurse was even more inferior. The first attempt in Britain to organize a scheme for training district nurses had occurred in Liverpool in 1859. Since 1870, the Swansea Nursing Institute had operated on a comparatively generous scale by employing three nurses at first. It had been set up by a few ladies and its purpose was to provide the sick poor with nursing care in their own homes. The nurses were meant to see to their patients' spiritual and temporal needs and were encouraged to read and pray with them, 'acting the part of the scripture reader and town missionary as well as nurse'. There was never any attempt to co-ordinate the work of the Nursing Institute with the hospital, although occasional appeals were made to hospital subscribers to make available to these nurses letters of recommendation so that the needy could be referred to the Outdoor Department. The creation of the nursing organization did not have an adverse effect on the hospital's financial situation. (It was also fortunate for the hospital that a proposal made in Neath in 1871 to build a cottage hospital, which would have cost £150 a year to maintain, failed, as that would certainly have diverted money away from the larger institution.)

In 1879, Mrs Griffith Llewellyn of Baglan Hall attempted to interest several people in forming another institution which would supply nurses who would visit both the sick poor and private patients in their own homes, and she hoped that the hospital would participate in the new training scheme. The matter was never formally discussed by the hospital committee at that time. In 1882, however, in a meeting held at Dr Ebenezer Davies's house, Mrs Llewellyn, her sister Miss Grenfell, and nine other ladies (including Mrs Ebenezer Davies and Mrs T. D. Griffiths) set about forming a new Nursing Institute. Dr Ebenezer Davies was anxious that they should not put an end to the existing institute, and it was decided to name the new body the 'Nursing Institution for Swansea and South Wales' on the suggestion of Dr Farrant Fry who was intent on 'taking a rise out of Cardiff', where there was no similar organization.

The first district nurse employed (with 87 Bryn-y-môr Road as her headquarters) started work in 1883. She made 2,362 calls on patients in the course of her first year and it was said of her work that:

> there are cases in which [she] cannot entrust to a member of the family the duty of fetching an egg or milk; she must herself provide, prepare and administer it while she is in the house, to be sure that the patient gets it ... [17]

In that same year, the Institution sent a probationer nurse to the hospital to be trained under the Matron's supervision, for a period of a month in the first instance. If she were to remain for a year, the hospital would provide her with free board in return for her services. Trained district nurses were to be paid from £14 to £30 a year, together with their board and lodge, medical attendance and uniform. In a later review of the Institution's work in September 1893, it was shown that its six nurses had travelled as far as Merthyr and Tenby and had been quite unable to provide help in every case where an application had been made.

In January 1888, it was announced in *The Times* that Queen Victoria had requested that the surplus money from the Women's Jubilee Offering should be used to encourage the development of nursing services.[18] It was suggested that an institute concerned with the education of nurses who worked with the sick poor should be formed. Centres were to be established in London, Edinburgh and Dublin, to which organizations already doing similar work could be affiliated. The Swansea and South Wales Nursing Institution was already employing eleven nurses by then and when Dr Ebenezer Davies discovered that a petition from Cardiff had already been sent to the Queen asking for a centre to be established there, he objected strongly. In the end, neither town was able to attract such a centre.

A curious by-product of the move to the St Helen's district had been that those who lived immediately around the new hospital could not be visited by the medical staff as they lived outside the geographical limits previously set for consultations in patients' homes. By the month of May 1872, the hospital committee (by this time called the House Committee) were so concerned about the escalating costs of the Indoor Department that they wished to disband the service to outdoor patients altogether. In addition, the absence of the House Surgeon for several hours each day while he was visiting patients in their homes concerned them. It was estimated that the catchment area had a population of 100,000 and although the cost of maintaining one indoor patient (twelve to fourteen shillings a week in 1877) compared favourably with most other hospitals in Britain, additional expenditure of any kind was difficult to justify.

A decision to appoint an assistant resident doctor had to be rescinded at one stage and it was the overwhelming demands made on the House Surgeon's time that gave an impetus to the move to create a separate Providential Dispensary in the town in 1876. This, it was thought, was the only means by which the free provision of medical advice and medicines for those able to pay could be checked. (There had been strong opposition to an attempt to introduce a charge of threepence for each supply of medicine provided at the hospital as this would have involved a change in the 'fundamental rules'.)

The intention in forming the dispensary had at first been to ask for subscriptions of a penny a week from single people and fourpence a week from families. Schemes of that kind had been found to be effective elsewhere and the Medical Committee of the Charity Organization Society had concluded that 'providence and self-reliance' would be encouraged under such circumstances. Such arguments appealed to the hospital's committee and it was of no great interest to them and of no great importance at the time that the new organization would cause a further fragmentation of the available services.

For reasons that are not clear, the first attempt to form a dispensary failed. In March 1876, a group of twelve Swansea doctors, who included among their number the honorary staff, were of the opinion that the opening of a Providential Dispensary should be given the most serious consideration. They were partly motivated by a genuine concern because of the increasing numbers of people, not strictly 'impoverished', who were using the free clinical facilities at the hospital. In addition, though, there must have been some disquiet among them at the increasing power of the Friendly Societies. These were sometimes able to impose on the doctors who worked for them conditions which were not acceptable to most members of the medical profession. This seems to have given rise to an ambivalent attitude on the part of the more well-to-do doctors (and many members of the committee) to the excellent work of the Friendly Societies.

It was the hospital's strained financial situation that finally brought about the move to open a dispensary. Once formed, the new (separate) organization was eminently successful. In the previous year, the largest number of outdoor patients ever (4,288) had attended the hospital's clinics, but in the first year after the opening of the Dispensary in 1878, that number fell to 2,757.[19] The visiting medical staff then recommended that the number of out-patient clinics at the hospital could be reduced to three a week and that was accepted by the Governors. No subscriber of one guinea a year was to be allowed to refer more than six patients (instead of twelve). No people entitled to the services of a doctor by any other means were to be accepted for assessment unless they brought with them a letter from their doctor requesting advice and specialized help which could not be made available elsewhere.[20] From December 1878, it was possible to discontinue the Resident Medical Officer's home visits except where those recently discharged from the hospital needed to be examined. The committee which had dealt with the proposed 'disbanding' of the Outdoor Department had agreed with the Providential Dispensary that if they were to pay half the hospital Dispenser's salary for the first year, they would be allowed to share the services of the hospital's Dispensing Department and obtain their drugs at cost price.

Lesser problems were temporarily forgotten some months later when a deputation from the Providential Dispensary laid a claim to a tenth of the money collected by the hospital on the grounds that it had taken over more of the clinical work than had been expected. The request was refused, but two and a half years after that, in February

1882, it became known that the amount of money received by the Providential Dispensary in the previous year had been considerably less than had been anticipated. On the other hand, the number of out-patients attending at the hospital had not decreased as had been hoped. (This might have been foreseen considering that the hospital was continuing to offer a free service which was also of a specialized nature.) The hospital was then asked if its out-patient services could be curtailed in the hope that more patients would be forced to subscribe to the Dispensary. That was agreed to in the hope that it might help deter that most awful of sins, improvidence. It was thus hoped that eventually the hospital need only provide a specialized service in its clinics, including the provision of advice to patients referred by the Dispensary's doctors and the Poor Law Medical Officers. Patients catered for by the Friendly Societies were not mentioned but those who lived in more distant parts, where facilities were more sparse, were to be allowed to continue using the clinics. As it happened, the number of patients being referred for specialist assessment continued to rise so that those discussions proved to be fruitless.

The arrangement with the Dispensary concerning the provision of drugs was allowed to continue far beyond the agreed period. When it was discovered in 1884 that the hospital had been subsidizing the other organization to the extent of more than £112 a year, the Secretary was instructed to act immediately to terminate the agreement. This situation had arisen in spite of the fact that it was widely known that the Dispensary's income (and the amount of work that their doctors were called on to do, of course) had increased substantially during that period. A deputation hastily sent to plead the Dispensary's cause showed that their doctors had carried out more than 6,500 consultations in the previous year, of which nearly a third occurred in patients' homes. They (erroneously) concluded that had it not been for their work, the Outdoor Department at the hospital would have had to cope with that burden. They had not realized that a substantial part of their work dealt with less serious, previously untreated, illnesses which would never have reached the hospital's clinics.

One important event that occurred in 1878 had a far more divisive influence than the formation of the Providential Dispensary. Dr Jabez Thomas had already shown an interest in the treatment of eye disorders for a considerable time. When he was first appointed Medical Officer to the Outdoor Department, he had asked for permission to start a clinic in ophthalmology but this request was refused on the advice of the other members of the medical staff. Eye surgery had been practised at the hospital virtually from the time of its opening and there is no evidence that the extent of that work had increased for some time after Dr Thomas was appointed Visiting General Surgeon. As he was a man of some considerable energy, it is not surprising that he should have looked elsewhere for an opportunity to practise what later became his specialty. Having been dissatisfied with the lack of opportunity to proceed with his plans at the hospital, he was very much concerned with the formation of the Swansea Providential Dispensary for Diseases of the Eye, which was set up in July 1878. A public meeting was held at the YMCA building in May, with Mr Coke Fowler, the Stipendiary Magistrate, presiding. A move to amalgamate with the recently formed Providential Dispensary failed and the two dispensaries continued to function separately. Dr Thomas was described as having 'considerable ophthalmic experience' and he proved to be more than capable of taking charge of the new venture. Temporary premises in a schoolroom were placed at his disposal at the back of the Pell Street Chapel. It was hoped that the organization would be self-supporting and about £40 was obtained from the subscribers in the first year. Two beds for indoor patients were provided and, in the first three months, 58 people sought advice, 214 consultations were held with them, and 20 eye operations were performed.[21]

As the nearest similar institution was at Bristol, the aim was to provide the best possible advice locally for those who were unable to travel elsewhere for their treatment. It was maintained that it was not intended that it should be 'antagonistic' to the hospital, although it is now clear that Dr Thomas had no objection to his differences with the hospital on this matter being made public. In addition to his work as the Visiting General Surgeon to the hospital and his other clinical commitments, Dr Thomas held 1,133 consultations with 203 patients during the Eye Dispensary's first year. When new premises were found in Mansel Street, indoor patients were received on a larger scale and many 'delicate operations' were performed there. These included (among others) 7 for the creation of 'artificial pupils and iridectomy', 1 for cataract, 5 for the removal of chips of steel, 7 for squint, 3 for tumours of the eyelids and 1 for ulceration of the cornea.[22]

In 1880, a further move occurred (to Herbert Place), and until 1884, Dr Thomas continued as the only doctor. In that year, in the course of a conversation which he had with Mr Nettleship, an ophthalmologist at St Thomas's Hospital, London, it was arranged that Dr Alex Davidson, an assistant at that hospital, should join Dr Thomas as a member of the Swansea Eye Dispensary's staff.

Although most of the hospital's medical staff had been at its inaugural meeting, 'this useful institution'[23] was not mentioned in the hospital records at that time. It was later claimed by Dr Thomas that he only set about forming the new Eye Dispensary because the general hospital had refused to provide specialist facilities for treating eye diseases there. Consequently, while the Providential Dispensary was started with the agreement, and at the request of, the hospital authorities, the Eye Dispensary was regarded by them as an unnecessary rival and later became the cause of considerable dissension and unpleasantness.

In 1879 (the year after the Eye Dispensary was formed), Mr Clouston Scott, the hospital's Surgeon-Dentist and a prominent member of the committee, and Mr Latimer, one of the medical officers in the Outdoor Department, proposed that a department for eye diseases should be created in the hospital, and that one or more ophthalmic surgeons should be appointed to work exclusively in that discipline. No attempt was made to amalgamate with the Eye Dispensary at that stage. During that year, only thirteen indoor patients had been treated for eye conditions at the hospital, far fewer than were being dealt with by Dr Jabez Thomas at his other place of work, under far less suitable conditions. An anonymous letter to the *Western Mail*, written in 1880,[24] alleged that no patients with eye diseases could be treated at the general hospital. This led to the presentation of a requisition for a special meeting of governors to alter the rules so that an Ophthalmic Surgeon could be appointed. Dr Jabez Thomas did not take part in the discussions; nor did he apply for the new post. There were two applicants, Dr T. D. Griffiths, who had resigned as Medical Officer for the Outdoor Department in 1865, and Mr Latimer, who had seconded the proposal which led to the formation of the new department. All the hospital's medical staff (with the exception of Dr Jabez Thomas, who was not at the meeting) voted for Mr Latimer, but Dr Griffiths, who had always been able to muster a large measure of support from among the non-medical governors, was elected. (Almost immediately afterwards, Mr Latimer was elected Visiting General Surgeon to replace Mr J. Griffith Hall, who had retired after nearly twenty-five years as a member of the honorary staff.) Dr Jabez Thomas continued to work as a Visiting General Surgeon but it is not clear if he practised eye surgery at the general hospital at all.

In the meantime, his work at the Eye Dispensary continued to attract attention and admiration. It is impossible to avoid the conclusion that he, with his vast specialist experience, must have been far superior to Dr Griffiths as an ophthalmologist. His lecture on *Remedies introduced in Ophthalmic Practice*, which he delivered to the South Wales Branch of the British Medical Association at the hospital in July 1880, included a discussion on the use of the ophthalmoscope and the drugs available to dilate the pupil of the eye.[25] In the same year, his enthusiasm as ever seasoned with great energy, he was able to address the same Association on such different subjects as a new and immediate method for curing hernia, and removal of a foreign body from the knee joint.

Nothing is known of the relationship between Dr Griffiths and Dr Thomas. The former is known to have been an able and experienced general surgeon, yet, at the hospital, he was restricted to practising eye surgery. As has been mentioned, Dr Thomas did not apply for the post as ophthalmologist and, in spite of his versatility, there can be no doubt that he was far more interested in eye surgery than in any other branch of medicine. Dr Griffiths was the older of the two men. In 1885, when he was 48 years of age, having failed in his attempt to abolish the rule which did not allow the honorary staff to retain their posts after reaching the age of 50, he resigned as Ophthalmic Surgeon. The official thanks bestowed on retiring doctors was usually generous and often exaggerated the extent of their contributions; in his case, the comments were so curt as surely to have reflected the sense of relief almost universally felt at his departure.

His retirement was to raise difficult problems. Dr Rawlings at once suggested that negotiations should be opened with the Swansea Eye Dispensary in the hope that an amalgamation of the two bodies could be brought about, although he feared that their chances of success would not be very great. The reply received confirmed his fears. It was said that no move aimed at creating a single combined hospital could be considered. The best that could be hoped for was that they should work 'harmoniously together' (which presumably meant that they should continue to ignore each other). When the medical staff discussed the matter, there were three votes in favour of asking one of the existing general surgeons to assume responsibility for the work of the Eye Department, but there were five abstentions. It was then agreed that the appointment of an ophthalmic surgeon should be made. (This gave Dr Rawlings the opportunity to give notice that he would again propose that departments for skin diseases and diseases peculiar to women should be formed, and that they too should be in charge of members of the existing staff who were to be recommended by their colleagues. His proposals, which reflected his own interest in obstetrics, were 'negatived by a large majority'.)

The only applicant for the eye surgeon's post was Dr W. T. F. Davies, who was the son of Dr Ebenezer Davies, the town's Medical Officer of Health. He was to care for all patients admitted suffering from eye diseases and an unsuccessful attempt was made to ensure that he was not automatically entitled to a seat on the committee.

Several other important matters were overshadowed by these discussions about the Eye Dispensary. At the 1886 Anniversary Meeting, it was shown that 105 more indoor patients had been admitted to the general hospital during that year and that it had been possible to diminish the expenditure. The level of attendance at the meeting prompted the Mayor to say that:

> political gatherings possessed a greater charm for the multitude than did the proceedings of the hospital.

An offer was made in June 1886 by the Western Counties and South Wales Telephone Company to connect the hospital free of charge with their new exchange in Wind Street by means of an overground wire system. Even the blowing down of the turreting of the south wing caused only a minor stir compared with the agony of realizing that, in the public's view, all the important local developments in ophthalmic surgery took place at the Eye Dispensary rather than in the General Hospital. The supporters of the smaller unit rarely lost an opportunity of reminding the public of Dr Jabez Thomas's far greater experience and phenomenal efforts (in spite of his commitments as a general surgeon). In 1885, he had drawn more attention to his work by operating on a patient with a disfiguring 'staring white patch', which covered most of the visible part of one of his eyes. He ingeniously:

> introduced into the white patch some pigment which would darken it, and so lessen the disfigurment (sic) [by] smearing ... Indian ink over the white patch and then puncturing the surface with a sharp instrument, [so that] the pigment was introduced and the disfigurment 'blotted out'.[26]

Such acts of publicity, together with an account in the local press which gave the impression that the 'Swansea Eye Hospital' was the only place in Wales which dealt with the treatment of eye conditions, only served to exaggerate the situation. A statement was sent to a variety of newspapers saying that the general hospital also had a fully qualified ophthalmic surgeon who regularly treated patients from as far away as Monmouthshire.[27] In this, they were helped by Dr Ebenezer Davies, who wrote to the *British Medical Journal* in 1886 drawing attention to the fact that Dr Thomas was also an honorary general surgeon at the hospital and inferring that his loyalties were divided. He went on:

> Cardiff has an efficient ophthalmic department in its new infirmary, and it is said that following the evil example of Swansea, a special Cardiff Eye Hospital is to be built ... Much of the poverty of the general hospital seems to be caused by the diversion of funds into the coffers of special hospitals which do no service to medical education and deprive the general hospitals of cases specially suited for treatment there, and for the clinical instruction which is so important a feature of a public hospital.[28]

This was countered by a letter to *The Cambrian* written by Lewis Llewelyn Dillwyn MP, revealing that, as the extent of the Eye Hospital's work had increased to a point where its accommodation was insufficient to cope with the demands made on it, it was intended that the Eye Hospital should 'erect a suitable building without delay'.[29]

Since his differences of opinion with the governors of the old Infirmary many years previously, Dillwyn had, from time to time, helped with the general hospital's affairs, but he was not averse to behaving in a way which undermined its work. In this, he may have been encouraged by the attitude of Dr Griffiths.

The previous failure to negotiate constructively towards an amalgamation at the time of Dr Griffiths's resignation was far from forgotten, and neither side, a year later, had any illusions that they could come to an agreement with ease. Both bodies claimed that they were interested in pooling their resources, but neither was prepared to yield to any significant extent on the contested issues. While each was prepared to blame the other for their failure to agree, it seemed that the only course open was for each to continue with its own separate existence.

The records of the Swansea Eye Hospital again show the extraordinary extent of Dr Jabez Thomas's commitment to his work in ophthalmology. His contributions had already been recognized by his election to the Fellowship of the Royal College of Surgeons of England in 1878. Even as late as that, the qualification (FRCS) was not commonly held by doctors working in south-west Wales. At a more practical level, he himself volunteered to obtain subscriptions and promises of support for the new Eye Hospital building and the matter was left entirely in his hands. He was prepared to go to the greatest lengths in order to proceed with the plan even to the extent of personally arranging a concert with the singer Mary Davies, to help to raise funds (and from which a profit of £50 was made). He was sufficiently optimistic that a new building was within reach to give notice to the landlady that the Eye Hospital was likely to move sometime after the autumn of 1887. A house became available, for which they were prepared to pay £1,500 (for the freehold, the fixtures and the fittings), but this was not acceptable to the owner.

Meanwhile the meeting between the two committees was not at first a great success. Dr Ebenezer Davies, who was probably only partially motivated by the fact that his son was the ophthalmologist at the general hospital, insisted that the town was already flooded with charitable organizations. A dilution of funds must, of necessity, occur when claims were made on behalf of both hospitals. He believed that the previous negotiations had failed because of the reluctance on the part of the general hospital to accept that one doctor should have a monopoly of the ophthalmic work.

It is evident that the determination shown by Dr Thomas and his collaborators was a major factor in deciding the outcome of the joint discussions, and at last in 1887 it was unanimously agreed in principle that amalgamation should occur. The combined institution was to be named The Swansea General and Eye Hospital, and a separate part of the building was to be devoted solely to ophthalmic work. Special efforts were to be made to extend the work of the new department and a guarantee would be given that it would not suffer by any future extension of the general departments. The new committee would include some of those who had previously been connected with the Eye Hospital and the funds raised by Dr Jabez Thomas would be transferred to a common bank account. It was at first agreed that Dr W. T. F. Davies was to be allowed to continue with his work, so that there would be three Visiting Surgeons in the new department. The Eye Hospital committee insisted that the ground floor of the South Wing should be available for the ophthalmologists, who should have their own operating room. This was refused and after a great deal of further discussion, they had to be content with the North (and newer) Wing. For some reason, they also insisted that their department must have an entrance from St Helen's Road. As there were already six entrances to the building, and the Matron had difficulty in exercising a proper degree of supervision over nurses, servants and patients, the creation of yet another entrance was unacceptable to the general hospital committee.

Having had to yield on that (seemingly unimportant) matter, the Eye Hospital committee refused to proceed unless Dr W. T. F. Davies resigned from his post to enable Dr Jabez Thomas and Dr Alex Davidson to be the sole surgeons in charge. Dr Davies agreed to this on condition that he should be appointed a Medical Officer in the Outdoor Department, but not before he had protested about the lack of courtesy shown towards him. The hospital committee, however, refused his request. He did not resign and the negotiations, so near successful completion, were again discontinued.

By April 1888, the Eye Hospital authorities were preparing a Special Appeal in order to proceed with the work on their new building. It was this defiance on their part that led to a request from the general hospital that talks between them should be resumed. The preparations for the new discussions started with the threat that unless they were conducted speedily, the Appeal would continue. The other conditions were virtually identical to those which had been found unacceptable previously, with the additional proviso that a suitable plot of ground was to be apportioned for the erection of a new Ophthalmic Department with an entrance from St Helen's Road. Three members of the Eye Hospital committee were to be added to the new committee and the reorganized department was to be under the sole charge of Dr Jabez Thomas and Dr Davidson, who were also to be allowed to continue with their work in the general departments. (Since 1883, Dr Davidson had also worked on the staff of the general hospital's Outdoor

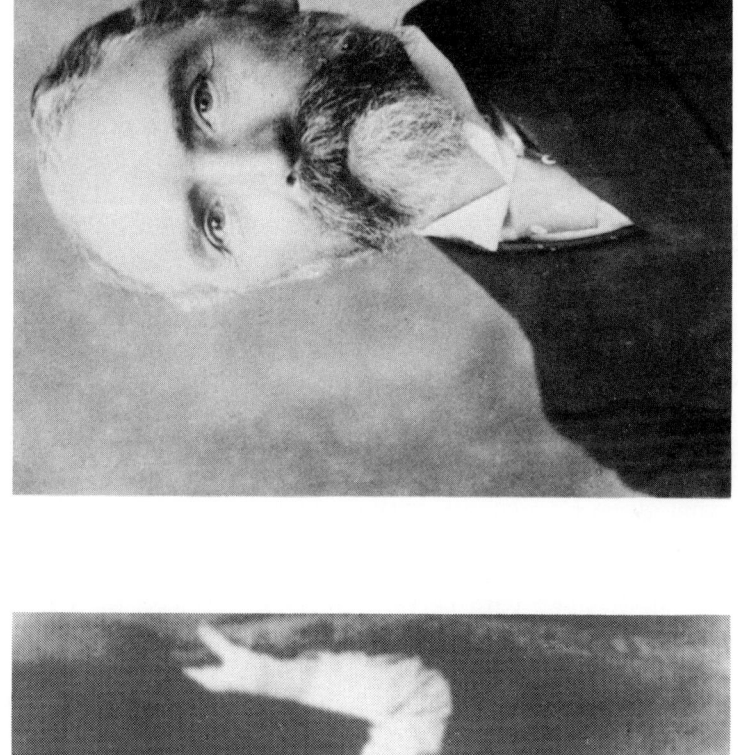

Head Nurse in the 1880s. (*By kind permission of Mrs A. Arthur.*)

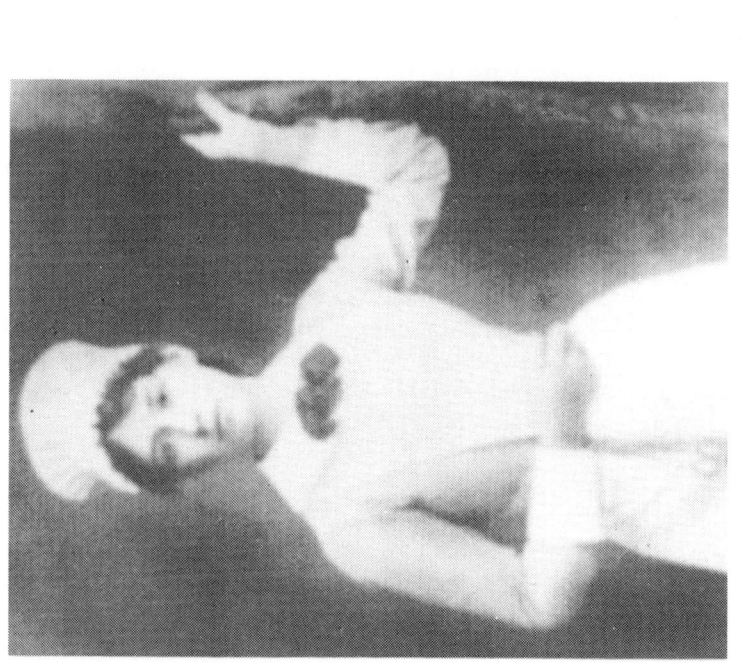

Dr Jabez Thomas, c. 1880s. (*By kind permission of West Glamorgan Health Authority.*)

Department.) Dr Thomas was able to give an undertaking that not less than £750 would be made available for the erection of the new building and no objection would be raised if part of it were used to accommodate nursing staff. Dr W. T. F. Davies, having been abysmally treated, was left with no alternative but to resign in July 1888, and he left Swansea for Johannesburg.

In February 1889, Mrs Griffith Llewellyn of Baglan Hall presented the hospital with £5,000 to be used for whatever purpose the committee decided was appropriate. Dr Thomas's wish that he should have an entirely new department was, therefore, made possible within a short space of time. Of the eleven tenders received for the erection of the building (which varied from £1,920 to £2,587), the lowest was submitted by G. W. Palmer of Neath and this was accepted. The Agreement was signed on 25 March 1889, and if the building was not completed by 11 January 1890, the contractor would forfeit £5 a week thereafter until his work was finished.

Since Mrs Llewellyn was still in mourning after the death of her husband, her sister, Miss Grenfell, laid the Foundation Stone (on 7 June 1889), using a silver trowel (not to exceed £10 in price). After a brief religious service, Dr Jabez Thomas proclaimed that the names of Grenfell and Llewellyn would become known as the greatest benefactors that the hospital had known, and the proceedings were drawn to a somewhat gloomy conclusion with the singing of the hymn 'Brief life is here our portion'. Built of native stone, the new department was similar in appearance to the general hospital. The entrance porch was made of Bath stone with carved panels surrounded by a bold cornice and baluster. In the entrance hall-cum-waiting room there was a large leaded and glazed window, and on the ground floor were the Head Nurse's room, the consulting room and operating room with a dark room, the large ward (which measured 30 by 20 feet), and the kitchen and scullery; from here there were lifts to the first floor, where there was a smaller ward and three nurses' rooms. The architect's suggestion that a large tank for the storage of rain water should be placed on the roof was not accepted and the connection with the general hospital was by a 'wooden structure similar to a Green House, six feet wide...' The unity symbolized by that structure had been bought at a considerable cost.

In the fifteen years when he had not been connected with the hospital, that most pernicious of medical dissidents, Dr T. D. Griffiths, had lost none of his capacity for quarrelling. One of his first activities after being appointed in 1880 as Ophthalmic Surgeon had been to object to the manner in which Mr Latimer and Dr Rawlings had been appointed Honorary Surgeon and Physician. He disturbed the tranquillity of the Anniversary Meeting in 1881 by objecting to the reappointment of the committee and his suggestions for reforming the administrative structure 'stirred up an amount of feeling that was quite painful to see', according to *The Cambrian* of 8 July 1881. His view that the committee of management should be changed every three years might well have been accepted, according to the description of the day's events that have survived, had it not been that his abrasive manner antagonized many of those present. The debt had risen by nearly £200 that year and the number of beds empty for lack of funds to pay for their use was higher than ever. In spite of that, his suggestion that the empty wards ought to be used for paying patients to relieve the financial situation was not accepted.

Within weeks, Dr Griffiths had taken issue with his employers on another matter. He wrote to the Clerk of the Cirencester Union (which subscribed two guineas a year to the hospital) complaining that a young girl from that town, who had been admitted to the Eye Department suffering from scrofulous [tuberculous] ophthalmia, had not been able to get hot and cold sea-water baths in the hospital. As those were among the benefits advertised as being available, he accused the governors of 'gulling the public'. Usually, the committee commented, Dr Griffiths confined himself to 'vague generalities' to which they paid little attention, but that was not so in this case. In their reply, they were able to show that he had never ordered sea-water baths for the child and that there had never been an instance of a patient failing to have such treatment after it had been prescribed, either in the hospital, or if the patient could walk, on the 'Machine' on the beach, which was paid for by the hospital.[30] Typically, he refused to withdraw his 'untrue and offensive language' and was asked to resign. This he refused to do because the request had not come from a Special General Meeting, which was then called for that purpose. In readiness for it, he wrote to *The Cambrian* describing the technique used in preparing for bathing:

> The outdoor porter is supplied with one or two tin cans to fetch some water from the sea, which is about a quarter of a mile distant when the tide is in and half a mile when the tide is out ... [The] water on the beach is extremely shallow ... and surcharged with filth from our drains and refuse of our town which is more or less washed ashore ... How is the porter to fill his tin cans from the shallow ripples which lick our sandy beach?[31]

As usual, he was well prepared for the inevitable confrontation. The committee had issued a statement proclaiming that they were unable to work with one who, instead of helping to make the place as efficient as possible, had persistently done all that he could to injure the hospital publicly and detract from its popularity. Again, in spite of the vitriolic nature of his remarks, the backing that he got from the governors was so strong that it was impossible to proceed with the move to force him to resign. It must have been his work in specialties other than ophthalmology that was responsible for his prestige. Because of his status as a doctor the oldest subscriber present, Mr George B. Brook, had no doubt that, had he been ejected, there would have occurred a 'continual agitation' until he had been reinstated. His supporters included the High Sheriff and so many eminent men spoke in his favour by praising his skill and work with the poor that he was actually cheered, and 150 guineas were collected towards providing sea-water baths. Eventually, both sides withdrew their allegations, but support for Dr Griffiths continued when *The Lancet* and *Medical Times and Gazette* of September 1881 congratulated the hospital on having available the services of:

> a gentleman clear-sighted enough to see his duty, and bold and resolute enough to incur the risk of personal unpopularity and professional and pecuniary injury in doing it.[32]

Still the debate went on. Several decades previously, doubts had been raised as to the effectiveness of cold-water baths. A letter written to *The Lancet* in 1847 had claimed:

> It is the misfortune of medical men residing in the neighbourhood of cold-water establishments to be eternally bored about the miraculous virtues of cold water and wet bandages...[33]

Thirty-five years later, Swansea's medical men remained divided on the issue. Several doctors spoke out strongly against entering into expensive schemes for recovering sea-water, when dissolving salt in water would be just as useful at a time when so many beds in the hospital were still empty for lack of money to provide a better service. On the other hand, the recently formed Swansea Baths Company (which intended to raise £4,000 in capital in £5 shares, and to which the hospital later had to subscribe for the hire of its Turkish baths for the use of patients), had five doctors, including Dr Griffiths himself and the town's Medical Officer of Health, among its directors.

Dr Griffiths had not yet finally settled with the committee. His opportunity was to come some weeks later when the Swansea East Dock was opened by the Prince and Princess of Wales. It had been hoped that they could have been persuaded to call at the hospital during the day but permission was refused by the Duke of Beaufort who had made the arrangements for the visit. Dr Joseph Parry had asked if his choir of 2,000 voices could sing within the hospital enclosure as the procession passed by, but this was not thought to be wise because it might impede the admission of patients in an emergency. On the day of the opening, Dr Griffiths sought and obtained an introduction to the Prince, who agreed to visit the hospital after the official proceedings. As no one else had been informed of the sudden change of plans, the Prince and Princess were met only by Dr Griffiths himself and the House Surgeon, Mr Humphreys. As his adversaries were, by and large, people who would have given much to have been there for the occasion, his actions on that day represented the ultimate triumph of craftiness over snobbery.

Gradually, both the nature of the work undertaken at the hospital and its organization changed. For many years, children had been admitted to the adult wards, and the promise made several decades earlier that a ward to deal only with sick children would be opened, had never been kept. It was in September 1882 that the world-famous soprano, Adelina Patti, who lived at Craig-y-nos in the Swansea Valley, consented to give the first of her many morning concerts at the Albert Hall, for the benefit of the hospital, and it was described as an 'unparalleled success'.[34] The prices of admission were a guinea, half a guinea and five shillings, and after 100 guineas had been deducted, at Patti's request, for the distressed poor who lived in the locality of her home, £731. 10s. was given to the funds. A deputation, consisting of Dr Padley, Mr Thomas Hall, and the Secretary, delivered an illuminated scroll (which had cost fourteen guineas) to her. She, in turn, promised to visit the hospital on her return from America and expressed a wish that the ward in the North Wing that was to be named after her should be the Children's Ward.

A disagreement followed over the offer made by Mr Ll. W. Howell to publish a full-length portrait of Madame Patti. The original was to be given to 'La Diva' herself. Copies were to be produced and sold at a guinea each, with no expense being incurred by the hospital. Mr Deffet Francis then offered to paint the portrait on condition that he should first be allowed to exhibit it at the Royal Academy. This offer was not accepted, and the artist who was eventually commissioned was James Sant, whose painting was shown at the Academy. After ten sittings (eight at Craig-y-nos and two in London), the finished work was presented to her by Sir Hussey Vivian MP, at a private reception in 1887, after which it occupied 'a prominent position in her boudoir'.[35]

The year 1883 had passed quietly enough. The number of surgical operations performed, although few by more recent standards, was 119, which was higher than ever before. A new mortuary had been built, and for the first time, the hospital paid for a day's outing to Crawley Wood for the nurses. A fire escape and a reel of hose ('for use at the hospital and Surrounding District') was provided by the Head Constable, Captain Colquhoun, and a small portable fire-engine, valued at two pounds, was acquired. The Matron suggested that a donkey should be bought to draw the invalid carriage which had been donated, and one was presented by a local clergyman.

By March 1884, the excess of expenditure (£3,000) over income was more than £1,200. This called for one of the committee's periodic threats to close a ward (which in the past had seemed to have surprisingly little effect on most of the readers of the newspapers in which this was made known). It is not known why the response should have been so different this time; Mr Arthur Gilbertson, the Pontardawe industrialist, appealed to those of his workers who earned more than five pounds a month to subscribe a shilling in every pound, and those earning less than that to give sixpence in the pound. This triggered off the organization of a series of events. One was an auction, at which livestock, furniture, china, ironmongery, carriages, horses and harness, which had been given for the purpose, were sold in aid of the funds. A challenge by a Mr Cumberland that he could read the number on a five-pound note in a seance at the Albert Hall was not a great success financially but a great deal of attention was drawn to the hospital's monetary problems. Consequently, between the Bazaar, which produced £490, and Patti's second concert, for which £644 was received, the situation again improved. More than 800 ships' masters, whose vessels had docked at Swansea over the previous year, and who had provided the accident ward with a great deal of work, agreed to contribute as part of a more organized system of collecting funds.

Disagreements of varying degrees of importance continued to occur frequently. A keen supporter of the hospital's work, the Reverend Eli Clarke of Christ Church, proposed (with the support of Dr Jabez Thomas) to begin each meeting with a prayer, but this motion failed as it was 'feared many difficulties might arise'. Nor did he succeed in getting the text *Non Nobis Domine* ('Not unto us, O Lord') hung on the wall of the Board Room.

Administratively, the most important decision taken was to refuse the request of the Provisional Committee of the Hospitals Association for help with their work. The Association's aims were simply summarized in a statement to *The Times* by their Secretary as 'mainly to diffuse a sound knowledge of hospital economy and to strengthen and widen the public interest in ... hospitals'.[36]

This they did admirably, largely through the efforts of Mr (later Sir) Henry Burdett, but the amount of support which they got at first varied. This serves to emphasize the fact that the sharing of common problems between hospitals was of no great interest to many people working in this field.

That year did not pass entirely without complaints about the quality of the service provided. Two women who were indoor patients complained to a visiting clergyman that the nurses frequently neglected their duties. Poultices and dressings were sometimes not changed for two or three days, and, it was alleged, when the attention of a nurse was drawn to this, the patient was told to 'shut up'. When the chairman of the committee, Mr Thomas Hall, interviewed the main complainant, she denied ever having had any cause to complain. The members of the committee tended grossly to underestimate the intimidating effect which an interview of the kind held by their chairman would be likely to have on most of the underprivileged people who made up the bulk of the hospital's patients.

It had become apparent after her appointment in 1869 that Mrs MacVey and the nursing staff were unable to work well together and her inefficiency had caused the Resident Medical Officer a great deal of trouble. She was later told that she could only remain in her post if no trained Matron could be found to replace her. One of the Head Nurses from St Mary's Hospital, Paddington, Anne John, was appointed 'subject to her being a Protestant and under fifty years of age'. As she was an Anglican communicant and of the requisite age, she was considered to be suitable and, as two of the nurses had resigned, she was asked to bring two of her colleagues with her from London.[37]

Not long after their arrival, in November 1871, the possibility of training probationer nurses 'for our own and public use' was considered. These were expected to be between twenty-four and thirty years of age, of good character, to be able to read and write well and be willing to accept nursing as their calling in life (which was certainly more than had ever been asked of any of the previous members of the nursing staff, but which would have been expected of the Nightingale nurses). In 1872, the hospital's first probationer nurse, Elizabeth June Heard, was appointed and when the Head Nurse left, it was the Matron's opinion that, with her five months' training, Miss Heard and the other recently appointed probationers were 'sufficient to work the Hospital'.

After eleven years as Matron, Mrs John retired in 1882. Some of the medical staff proposed that her duties should be shared between a Matron and a Lady Superintendent of Nurses. That was not accepted and although the committee (in common with most of the other hospitals in Britain) was later to ignore an appeal from the British Nurses' Association to form a board to organize nurse education, it was decided that a Matron must be sought who could undertake the training of nurses. Thirty-four applications were received and three were invited to attend for interview. One of those withdrew and one missed the train at Paddington, so that the remaining candidate, Miss Bann, of the Manchester Royal Infirmary, was appointed.

Even if his previous suggestions had not been accepted with enthusiasm, Dr Rawlings was intent on bringing about changes in the nursing administration. On his suggestion, it was agreed that probationer nurses should be kept on the staff after completing their two-year training period and that the Head Nurse on each ward should henceforth (from January 1890) be known as a Sister. Within weeks, the title was withdrawn, possibly because that would have entitled them to demand a higher salary. Before that, there had occurred another upset in relationships between members of the staff. It had been many years since attention had been drawn to quarrels between the Matron and House Surgeon, but by November 1888 their differences had become only too apparent. Apart from occasional meagre compliments that were paid to her, little is known of the work of Mrs Foulkes as Matron until that year, four years after her appointment. Objections were raised when she appointed her own daughter as a probationer nurse, and a complaint was made that patients who failed to get out of bed promptly at 5 a.m. in winter time frequently had their bedclothes stripped from them by the nurses. 'Half recovered patients' were expected to sweep the ward floors twice daily and to carry their breakfast to those unable to get up.[38] It was suggested that the dissensions between Mrs Foulkes and the House Surgeon, Dr Kerr, had brought about insubordination among the nurses and that this in turn reflected on their treatment of patients. It was concluded that Dr Kerr's tendency to interfere and to upset the peace and quiet arose from his inexperience but both were told that they must leave, and the Matron's request for a testimonial was refused. At the same time, it was acknowledged that some of the complaints about the nursing staff were attributable to the fact that there were insufficient of them. In May 1889, their numbers were increased so that there were four qualified and trained nurses, nine probationers and four ward maids. With that move, it was thought that there was no need to accept Mr Latimer's plan for the 'co-optation' of a committee of twelve ladies who would visit the wards to survey the behaviour of the nurses and the comfort of the patients.

There were thirty-seven applications for the Matron's post (to which Miss Edith Bellars of Bristol was appointed) and thirty for that of the Resident Medical Officer. Four days before Mrs Foulkes and Dr Kerr were meant to leave, it was made known that one of the nurses who had been given ten days' sick leave to care for a relative who was ill had in fact gone to Gateshead to act as a locum tenens for the matron of a Children's Hospital. She returned four days later and was dismissed. On the following day, the committee were hastily brought together to discuss a letter from the outgoing Matron who complained that:

> the House Surgeon [Dr Kerr] is taking a high hand and has forbidden me to discharge Nurse Jenkins ... If he prevents her going, what am I to do?

Nurse Jenkins was allowed to stay the night but was forbidden to enter the wards and the honorary solicitor advised them to 'get rid of the Doctor at the earliest possible moment'. He was sent written notice and was asked to confine himself to the duties of his office until he left. He threatened to stay until January 1890 unless he was given specific instructions to leave. Eventually, he was paid a quarter's salary so that he might depart at once.

Another report on the organization of the medical services had been commissioned in 1882 and, as a result, for the first time, the duties of the outdoor medical staff were fully defined. In addition to holding at least one clinic a week each at which there was to be no strict division into 'medical' and 'surgical' patients, they were to care for any patients delegated to them by the indoor staff, to assist at operations and to act in the absence of their seniors. They were also to have access to two in-patient beds each which could only be used for treating patients already examined by them in one of the hospital's clinics. Of far greater significance was the recommendation to create a 'Department for the treatment of Diseases of Women' or an 'Obstetric Department' (*sic*) with a physician, and a 'Department of Diseases of the Skin' in the charge of a member of the medical staff who was to be nominated by them on an annual basis. Although these changes were not implemented for many years, they did signify a great alteration in the attitude of the honorary staff in that they were more willing to accept that the time-honoured divisions of medical practice warranted revision.

A Medical Subcommittee was formed with Dr Jabez Thomas as its convener, and he was also elected their representative on the House (Hospital) Committee. This was the first move to provide the committee with a regular source of advice on medical matters (although the Medical Board had previously met and for some decades, the visiting medical staff had attended House Committee meetings somewhat inconsistently). The first investigation instigated by the new medical committee was into the continuing infectious illnesses among patients and staff in the upper ward of the South Wing in the autumn of 1882. It was of great concern to them that the hospital was still not able to get its water supply from the town's system. The wards were provided (irregularly) with water from cisterns which also supplied the lavatories and were filled from the well in the grounds. (The municipal system only made water available for a few hours each day, and whenever there were any extra demands to be met, supplies were usually drastically reduced.) The mortuary was found to be unfit for use and it was suggested that it should be kept for the reception of dirty clothes or for use as a disinfecting chamber. No lessons, it seems, had been learned from the results of investigations of previous contagious disorders. Again, 'dirt, the accumulation of unused food and a lack of ventilation', all familiar words in that context, were thought to be the causative agents.

The periodic revival of the somewhat grandiose idea that a medical school could be formed to work in conjunction with the hospital seemed to be a constant feature of the committee's history. (One of the more surprising arguments provided for such a move was that the parents of local young men might thus be saved a 'considerable outlay'.) Already, the hospital had a long tradition of postgraduate medical education which was maintained throughout its history. The newly resurrected branch of the BMA held its meetings at the hospital and in September 1885, the Swansea Medical Society, which had not met for three years, was re-established with a slightly increased membership. Their monthly meetings at the hospital again represented a superb attempt to meet the need for postgraduate medical education in the locality. The subjects discussed over the following year included enteric fever, the treatment of syphilis, the best intra-uterine applications, the surgical treatment of tuberculous glands of the neck, the notification of infectious diseases—on which views were severely divided—and the new splint for use in the treatment of fractured thigh-bones that had been devised by the new House Surgeon, Mr Nelson Jones. He had been trained under Lister's supervision and was greatly praised by his more senior colleagues for his new invention.

The hospital's role of teaching in other spheres also continued to expand. Apart from accepting medical students occasionally and probationer nurses from the Nursing Institute more regularly, there were irregular visitors such as the male missionary who wanted to acquire 'a little knowledge' of surgery before starting on his work in distant lands. In 1883, Dr Farrant Fry was responsible for establishing a St John's Ambulance Association Centre in Swansea and, with the introduction of their courses of lectures, some interest was roused locally in learning about first aid. In 1886, a group of ladies asked for permission to meet at the hospital for that purpose and rightly pointed out that their aim was totally in sympathy with the object of the hospital. Although their lecturer was one of the hospital's surgeons, Mr Latimer, they had to look elsewhere for facilities.

In 1882, an attempt, not originally connected with the hospital, was made to attract the new university college planned for south Wales, to Swansea. 'A warm and continued agitation', it was thought, would surely be effective in showing that all the arguments put forward in favour of Cardiff applied equally to Swansea.[39] The Memorial which the Corporation of Swansea addressed to the Lords of the Committee on Education[40] included comments on the 'healthfulness' of the town with its low death rate of only 21.5 per thousand. At one of the several public meetings held to discuss the issue, the Reverend A. G. Edwards, 'assuming that the medical department in the new college would be an important one', hoped that the immense advantages offered at the Swansea Hospital would be taken into account when a decision was made about the siting of the college.[41] While the facilities at the hospital would have been good and the range of clinical experience available for teaching purposes considerable, little else had changed since the previous discussions about the possibility of establishing an independent medical school. By the time the final decision had been reached in favour of Cardiff, it seemed likely that the number of beds at the hospital would have to be reduced because of the extent of the debt.

If Dr Rawlings's 'Suggestions for the Increased Efficiency of the Swansea Hospital',[42] which represented one of his several attempts to reorganize the clinical work, had been accepted in its entirety at an earlier date, it might have added some weight to the case for establishing a medical school at Swansea. An attempt was being made in Cardiff at that time to meet the requirements of the various medical examination boards in the hope that a medical school could be affiliated to the new University of Wales, which it was hoped would be formed. As the University College at Cardiff was already in existence and the number of general hospital beds available there was greater, the likelihood of obtaining a medical school at Swansea had diminished greatly but that did not deter Dr Rawlings. He wished to reintroduce the monthly consultations among the medical staff, which were meant to have been a feature of the clinical work from the beginning but which had frequently been allowed to lapse. Taking-in days should be established so that it would be known which specialist would be responsible for patients admitted on any particular day, and a timetable of attendances of visiting medical staff should be published. The outpatient work would have to be separated into 'medical' and 'surgical' according to the nature of the clinical problem, and the Outdoor Medical Officers should be replaced by Assistant Physicians and Surgeons. One certain way of ensuring that most of the medical staff would undermine the proposals was to suggest that a third post for a Visiting

Surgeon was needed. He again suggested that separate departments of skin diseases and obstetrics or gynaecology must be created, and that an entirely new position of Pathologist and Chloroformist (who would perform autopsies and administer anaesthetics) was necessary, but that these functions might be undertaken separately by existing staff members. With these changes, he believed that the hospital would be the best equipped in Wales. Apart from an agreement that there was a need for a pathologist and anaesthetist, there was little support for Dr Rawlings's views.

The necessity for an anaesthetist can be seen from the fact that by 1888, the number of operations performed in the year had risen to 245. It is not known why it was thought necessary to appoint a pathologist at that time and very few references were ever made to his later work. Autopsies had first been performed in prehistoric times. Later civilizations prohibited the dissection and examination of dead bodies, and even after being reintroduced in the eighteenth century, autopsies again became less fashionable for a period. The first account of an autopsy performed in Swansea that it has been possible to trace occurred in 1838, at a time when each doctor was expected to carry out such examinations himself.[43] Such investigations must have been undertaken rather earlier at the hospital, as a rule was made in 1835 that no post-mortems were to take place there unless the physician or surgeon concerned was present, or had given his consent and had arranged for the House Surgeon to attend in his absence.

In 1889, Dr James Kynaston Couch (probably the great-grandson of Mrs Couch, one of the hospital's first Matrons, and whose father had been present at the first operation in Britain when an anaesthetic was used), was appointed as Pathologist and Chloroformist.

The creation of that post was as sensitive an indicator as any of the developments that were slowly occurring. It might seem that not a great deal had changed in medical practice in Swansea since the new hospital had opened twenty-one years previously. Certainly, the extent of the quarrelling which seemed to be a necessary concomitant of the institution's administration had not diminished. Yet, the number of indoor patients being admitted there (and the amount owed to the bank) had more than quadrupled in that time. Medical concepts which were unknown when the oldest member of the honorary staff had started his career were by then accepted as commonplace. Vast improvements of a kind that were as yet unheard of were to occur during the lifetime of many of those starting as medical students then. During the last decade of the nineteenth century, it was to become increasingly more apparent that hospital treatment for the many should no longer be regarded as a privilege that could only be made available by the courtesy of the wealthy few.

CHAPTER SIX

The Swansea General and Eye Hospital

> With all the material and mental progress of the nineteenth century, we have found no means of lifting into comfort the lower strata of life ...[1]

THE day of the opening of the Eye Hospital, 24 July 1890, was a public holiday but the wet weather, and particularly the drenching which many people got on the St Helen's Field earlier that day, reduced the attendance to a far lower level than had been hoped for. The visitors assembled in the empty ward and walked in procession to the Ophthalmic Department. What was described as 'an end to an unhappy schism' was only slightly marred by the hasty departure of the Mayor and Sir John Talbot Dillwyn Llewelyn, who had to attend a meeting of 'Y Gorsedd' (sic), in connection with the Eisteddfod, at the Assembly Rooms.[2] It was fitting that the first celebration to be held afterwards took the form of a tribute to the doctor to whom Dr Jabez Thomas had been apprenticed for seven years. Mr James Griffith Hall had been House Surgeon at the Infirmary for 14 years and, since his retirement as Visiting Surgeon in 1881, a Consulting Surgeon to the hospital. At the gathering to mark the fiftieth anniversary of his association with the hospital, it was Dr Padley who reminded those who had gathered to pay their respects to him that there had never been 'one dissentient word' between Mr Hall and his colleagues.[3]

The festive season did not last for long. Henry Burdett had met with little success in Swansea with his early attempts to investigate the work of the voluntary hospitals. When the Hospitals Association, of which he was Secretary, wrote in 1887 to ask for information on 'practical points of hospital administration', the matter was abruptly referred to the Matron and was not discussed again. The attitude to Burdett became noticeably warmer following an account which he published in 1890 in *The Hospital* of the visit which he had made to the Swansea Hospital. He wrote:

> We happened to be at the Swansea Infirmary (sic) ... each patient was brought the most temptingly served food we have ever seen offered to

patients. It appears that the plan is to send up the food from the general kitchen to the ward kitchen, where the plates are kept hot until the patients are ready ... [We] congratulate the committee upon the efficiency of the House Surgeon, Mr Hopkins, an old University College man, and the Matron ...[4]

No detailed account of his visit has survived but almost immediately afterwards, it was agreed that there should occur an increase in the amount of accommodation available for nurses. Henry Burdett was obviously not altogether pleased that, in spite of his complimentary remarks, none of the suggestions made by him had been accepted, although he was promised that they would be reconsidered later. The only permanent memorial to his visit was the porcelain bath that he had sent there for the use of the nurses, but it may be that it was he who encouraged the Matron to request that a Night Superintendent who would be a 'responsible person in charge to whom the subordinates might be able to refer in an emergency', should be appointed.

As the hospital got larger, so did its management become more complex. Since the 1870s, a Committee of Management had met once a month (or more often if necessary), and a House Committee of twelve (three of whom were females and one a member of the honorary staff) were elected once a year to meet weekly.[5] Later, two of its members were appointed monthly as House Visitors and they were expected to record an account of their visits.

The new system of management did nothing to discourage the committee's seemingly infinite capacity for discussing relatively trivial matters in the face of the most severe crises. There were many among them who believed that the greatest crisis that had occurred was the increase in the number of people demanding a say in the hospital's affairs. The Swansea Guardians, who had not had any serious disagreements with the hospital for many years, complained that they had not been allowed a representative on the committee in spite of the fact that they subscribed £50 a year. Their plea was heard with more sympathy than would have been credible some decades previously, and it was agreed that they should nominate one from among themselves to serve. But there were also new arguments being put forward concerning the governance of the hospital. The rules simply and clearly inferred that those wealthy and interested enough to donate certain stipulated sums of money could secure for themselves that sole right to be a Governor. There were occasional signs, though, that the rudiments of a more liberal system of administration were about to appear.

On her admission to hospital in 1892, a lady who had suffered from a gynaecological complaint brought with her a letter from one of the Indoor Medical Staff (who was not named but who may well have been Dr Rawlings) which said that she had already been physically examined by him and that a further examination would be unnecessary. She took exception to the fact that the House Surgeon insisted on re-examining her and the matter was subsequently discussed at a meeting of more than a hundred Sunday School teachers of both sexes. There, it was decided that, having committed themselves for some time past to collecting money on the afternoon of Hospital Sunday for the treatment of children, they now wished to increase the amount so as to be eligible to have a representative on the hospital's committee. They considered that women patients at the hospital were:

> improperly treated, especially considering their sex, when they are used for schooling purposes by medical men—generally juniors.

Colonel Morgan, soon to be Chairman of the Board of Management, promised to present a resolution that would somehow eliminate the practice of examination of women patients by the house staff, and Dr Rawlings, himself a keen supporter of Sunday Schools and already disgruntled at his failure to be appointed Obstetric Physician, gave his support. (On the other hand, he had been the most keen supporter among that generation of Swansea doctors for creating a medical school. Had that move succeeded, the amount of bedside teaching would have been greatly increased.) As it was, it was alleged that the rules did not allow for teaching of this nature and that it had been carried out without the permission of patients and against their wishes. There were no such rules in being and eventually the letter of complaint was allowed to lie on the table.

That was far from the end of the matter. In December 1891, Colonel Morgan, who was not known as one of the most radical of Swansea's upper middle-class population, drew attention to the continuing abuse among subscribers of sponsoring the admission of patients who were not entitled to indoor treatment. He proposed that anyone who was suffering from severe injuries could be admitted at any time on the authority of the Resident Medical Officer but that well-to-do patients should not be allowed to stay unless they were 'immovable'. Those bearing subscribers' letters should also be allowed entry if they were considered suitable by the doctor who examined them; those who recommended them for treatment should be obliged to enquire into patients' financial circumstances before signing the necessary papers. If they were receiving parish relief, they were to be referred to the Board of Guardians, and if they could pay for their own treatment or had friends who were willing to do so, they ought to be admitted as paying patients. His proposal, however, was not even discussed at any length.

Elsewhere, the view that health care was too important to be left to charitable organizations was gaining ground. On 24 February 1892, the *Western Mail* went as far as to suggest that the time had come for the municipalization of the Cardiff Royal Infirmary. Similar opinions were never actually voiced at hospital meetings in Swansea but requests to state-controlled bodies for help for the hospital were regularly refused. As a result, there occurred a definite hardening of attitude towards these bodies which was reminiscent of the disagreements with the Guardians in Henry Sockett's day. From April 1892, children from the Truant School were refused admission when they were ill and all such bodies were expected to make their own arrangements for the treatment of those for whom they were responsible.

It was known that in other places, collections of money from workmen were taking place in a regular and systematic way. The continuing success of the Hospital Saturday and Sunday movements, when weekly collections were made in the streets and special sermons were preached in an attempt to raise money, had at last made it apparent that there was much that could be done to exploit the willingness of the less well-endowed members of the community. Even so, apart from employing half a dozen men with collecting boxes on the day of the Horse Parade procession, the committee continued to rely on other sources although their income had fallen drastically. With debts of more than £700, legal advice had to be taken to determine whether the Board members were individually responsible or whether money could be taken from the endowment funds if the bank should demand immediate payment.

For decades past, the peace between the working classes and the wealthy who were interested in the work of the hospital had been uneasy. Since 1851, attempts had been made to exclude from the hospital workers from industries where medical aid was provided or where clubs had been formed to provide such aid. That had done nothing to improve relationships and in 1893, there occurred a further complication. The Welsh Church Suspensory Bill, which was the first step taken towards the disestablishment of the Anglican Church in Wales, had its first reading in the House of Commons in that year. The House Surgeon heard that it was proposed to bring in to the hospital a petition to Parliament against the Bill. He asked for instructions as to whether this was to be allowed. It had always been held that no patients should ever be presented with such documents, as this might suggest that advantage was being taken of their position at times of illness. Complaints were made in the press and Colonel Morgan maintained that he had been wrongly blamed for organizing the petition. The employees of the Clayton Tinplate Works at Pontarddulais sent a donation of twelve guineas accompanied by a letter of protest in which it was said:

> The workmen are very indignant at the attempt made by Rev Mr Pollock

and Col Morgan to convert the unsectarian Institution for Tory and Church purposes...[6]

Typically, Colonel Morgan retaliated by refusing to visit any local works on behalf of the hospital as his character was said to be under a cloud. His resignation from the committee—one of several—was accepted in 1897 after he had used language that was inappropriately strong to several members of the House Committee. He obviously found it difficult to accept any challenge to his authority and was not well prepared for the general air of rebelliousness which was gradually permeating into the hospital's affairs. Generous to a fault, he was regularly prepared to devote endless hours of his time to the hospital's business providing that he was allowed to play a dominant role in those affairs. Perhaps it was fortunate for the hospital that he rarely stayed away long after resigning and soon returned with his usual vigorous and authoritarian ways.

Such incidents bore witness to the immense difficulties faced by those whose task it was to organize the services provided. Viewed a century later, their ineptness at solving such problems is only too apparent, and it is surprising that in the last decade of the nineteenth century, no more satisfactory means of continuing with the hospital's work had been devised. With the worsening state of the funds, it occurred even to the hospital committee in the fullness of time that trifling schemes of the kind that had taken their fancy for so long, were not likely to solve their problems. By far the most revolutionary move made in that sphere was the appointment in 1894 of an Assistant Secretary (at a salary of sixty pounds a year) who was to be responsible for collecting subscriptions and enrolling new subscribers. In the same year, a request was made by the Swansea Trades and Labour Council for a discussion on the possibility of electing workmen's representatives to the committee.

Presidents, Vice-Presidents and Governors held office by virtue of their individual subscriptions, and ministers of religion through the generosity of their congregations. The principle that regular collective gifts entitled other bodies to a say in the hospital's affairs had always been resisted until that time. After much discussion, it was conceded that 'the time has arrived [when] representation should be given to them', although it might have been more accurate to have admitted that it could no longer be avoided. The terms were more generous than the workmen could have hoped for. Any body of workmen giving twenty-five guineas annually were to be entitled to nominate one from among their number as a Governor with all its privileges (which were not many and only carried an entitlement to vote at the Anniversary Meeting). For fifty guineas a year, they might nominate a Vice-President (which carried no additional privileges apart from the status and the possibility of being named in the local newspaper at least once a year).

After that decision had been taken, a deputation was received from the Trades and Labour Council to enlarge on their proposals. They promised that if they were to be allowed to elect representatives on to the committee, a more systematic effort would be made to collect money and they asked for the right to put forward four such names at once. This move was viewed with the greatest suspicion and they were eventually told that the extent of their representation was to be in direct proportion to the amount of money subscribed by them. In the following year, their contributions were raised from £698 to £1,028. The long-awaited era was about to dawn when the working-class people of the locality were to be allowed to exercise their democratic right to play an active part in the hospital's management—and to prove in the fullness of time that they were no more skilled at that task than their better-off predecessors had been.

The previous objection to accepting private patients in order to boost the funds was waning, and at a time when more working-class people were agitating for an increased say in the hospital's affairs, it was decided that private patients could be accepted at a cost of a guinea a week. This arrangement did not last for long as it was found to give offence to many and led to even greater problems. When a temporary Clinical Assistant was appointed to help the House Surgeon (before the first House Physician had arrived), he was expected to 'assort' the outdoor patients not only according to the urgency of their clinical problems but by their 'social need' as well. The intention was to avoid giving free treatment to people who could afford to pay. Whenever doubts concerning the financial status of patients were raised, the matter was no longer to be left in the doctors' hands. The Assistant Secretary was expected to assume a new role and was instructed to investigate the circumstances quite irrespective of the severity of the clinical problem.

The medical staff had recently insisted that no more than fifteen outdoor patients should attend each clinic and they were convinced that this could be achieved by reducing the abuse of charity which they believed was rife. They thought that the workmen's contributions were being viewed as payments by which hospital attendance could be bought 'just as commodities are purchased in all the other affairs of the world'. They were anxious to make it known that the fundamental difference in financial organization between clubs and hospitals was that the latter operated as charities whereas all workmen's aid societies were really commercial undertakings. The tension was not eased when members of clubs who contributed at least ten guineas a year asked for the right to nominate a Vice-President from among their members. The argument was effectively ended by Colonel Morgan, whose feud with the working classes was over, when he protested that he knew of no examples where they had misused the hospital's facilities.

Irrespective of the extent to which he had hidden his true feelings in making that statement, it cannot have escaped his notice that working people's contributions were being made increasingly available. There were three sources. The Friendly Societies continued with their work, and in 1898 it was decided that any individual Lodge of a Benefit Society subscribing ten guineas a year was entitled to a representative on the Board. While they and their Sick Visitors (who were given certificates of identification and allowed to visit indoor patients in their official capacity) had been accepted, the trade unions were viewed with more suspicion. When a deputation from the Swansea Trades and Labour Council asked for the six seats on the Board to which they believed they were entitled together with the rights accorded to Vice-Presidents, no decision was made. It was Colonel Morgan who subsequently moved that those proposals should be accepted but it was his intention that they should not be allowed to vote in the election of any other members of the Board. One workmen's representative was also allowed on the House Committee. Even before Mr T. W. Hughes of the Cwmfelin Tin Works had been elected to that position, a protest was made that two managers had attended the Annual Meeting on behalf of their workmen and the Board was left in no doubt that 'only workmen can ... represent workmen'. Mr Hughes's only contribution for quite some time was to propose that the committee minutes should be printed, but the principle had now been accepted that ordinary working men had earned the right to concern themselves with the decision-making processes of the hospital. It was a suggestion by the Mayor, Mr Richard Martin, that brought into being the third source of funds. He proposed a scheme for collecting small weekly contributions from every house in the borough. In March 1899, six full-time collectors were engaged. While their straw hats were paid for by the hospital, it was the irascible Colonel Morgan who provided them with uniforms. They carried with them locked boxes 'with an aperture to admit of contributions' and were instructed to record gifts of more than three pence a week. Their wages were £1. 3s. 4d. a week and, in their first month at work, they collected £73. 14s. 5d., but shortly afterwards two of them were given a month's notice as their collections were not satisfactory.

The Works Governors, as the workmen's representatives were called, gradually assumed an increased degree of importance. At their third Annual Meeting in 1903, it was shown that the combined annual subscriptions of those represented by them during the previous year had made up forty-seven per cent of all the money subscribed and this sum was increasing annually. They believed that they should have an additional say in the management of the hospital and 'respectfully called' on those in the hospital's annual meeting to nominate a committee to meet them. It was their wish that they should have one Governor for every ten guineas subscribed annually.

The medical staff, always suspicious of threats to their own position in the control of the institution's affairs, regarded those demands as being unjust and a violation of the conditions laid down by the original donors. Had the proposals been accepted, the Works Governors would have had an absolute majority on all the hospital's committees. The doctors pointed out (quite justifiably) that while the workmen subscribed for their own benefit, there were others who gave purely from charitable motives. A meeting between the medical staff, the working men's representatives, the ordinary subscribers and the Chairmen of the Board of Management and the House Committee was held to consider any changes that might be called for in the rules. No account of that day's events has been preserved. All that is known of it is that the workmen, whose militant attitude was to cause so much unpleasantness in the years that followed, expressed their regret at the 'uncalled for and personal remarks' made by Mr Goldberg, the Board's Chairman, to their spokesman, Mr H. S. Thomas.

The workmen's persistence served them well in the end. By May 1904, the most remarkable concessions were being considered. At a specially-called meeting to discuss the possibility of a revision in the rules, the minority report presented by Colonel Morgan and Mr Brook, the senior surgeon, was accepted; they believed that the large size of the Board made it 'unwieldy and unworkable'. Far from wanting to add further committees, it was their wish to reduce its size. There were 28 Presidents and 38 Vice-Presidents and it was suggested that they should retain their right to vote during their lifetime (especially as 33 of them had never exercised that right and many of the others had only done so 'very sparingly'.) They asked, and their views were accepted, that any group of employees who subscribed twenty guineas after giving a basic donation of five guineas, should be allowed to elect one member as a Governor. The General Body of Governors were then to continue to elect 16 representatives to the Board of Management, with an additional 8 being taken from among the Works Governors and another 8 from the honorary medical staff.

In spite of those exciting new changes, the rather unambitious style of working that had played far too prominent a part in the hospital's housekeeping affairs still survived. So, the hospital still had to rely heavily on the enterprise of a few forward-looking individuals who usually sought their medical advice elsewhere. A plan was put forward in April 1905 by Mr Roger Beck and Mr Eccles which concerned the appointment of correspondents for soliciting subscriptions from more local industries. They themselves were prepared to seek out 'gentlemen who would be prepared to accept the office'. A Workmen's Contribution Committee was appointed and an attempt was made to correct the anomaly whereby the collection of money was centred on Swansea whereas patients were accepted from a far wider district. Later, that work came to be shared with the Works Governors.

After the Board of Governors had found conclusive evidence of an abuse of the charity, it was recommended in March 1905 that all out-patients who were to be treated free of charge would have to sign a declaration of inability to pay for private treatment. They would be required to reveal information about their occupation, the size of their families, their earnings, and the duration of their illnesses. Where any doubt arose, the matter would be referred to the Charity Organization Society for arbitration.

That clear declaration of intent concerning the creation of a new policy did not provide a guarantee that major changes in administration would follow. More than a year later, the BMA asked that their proposals for hospital reform, which were concerned with the same problems, should be discussed by the hospital Board.[7] Those were based on the principle that the inability to pay for treatment should be the only criterion considered in arranging the admission of in-patients. 'Poor-law cases' were thought to be in a separate category. This presumably meant that the recommendations made were not meant to offer the Poor Law Guardians a means of abdicating their responsibilities in localities where their medical services were more inadequate than the average. The most radical change called for was embodied in an attempt to dispose, wherever possible, of subscribers' letters, so that patients need no longer concern themselves with having to find someone who would sponsor them before they could be guaranteed treatment. No attempt had been made by the BMA to avoid the contentious issue of investigating patients' financial circumstances and they had no objection to the opening of 'pay wards' for those who could afford private treatment in voluntary hospitals. A 'system of co-ordination' between the public medical services, the Provident Dispensaries and the voluntary hospitals was thought to be quite essential, although it was not envisaged that the extent of the association would extend beyond the redirecting of patients who had been inappropriately sent to any of those three agencies. (This was something that had been done after a fashion at the hospital from the very beginning. One of the first matters ever discussed by the committee concerned a patient who had been wrongly admitted as he was able to pay for his treatment.) It was claimed by the Board that with the exception of the abolition of subscribers' letters, the whole of the BMA's plan had been accepted by them. Although Mr Brook more or less confirmed that view at a meeting of the BMA's Swansea Division in January 1907, he had sufficient doubts to want to suggest that 'an expression by the Division [voicing their concern] would be opportune'. That expression urged:

> the appointment of a special officer to investigate the circumstances of all applicants for relief, before they are seen by the Medical Staff.[8]

The members of the Board were divided in their attitude to that request, with one Works Governor appearing to accept that the people he represented were sometimes guilty of misusing the hospital's services. The majority view, though, was that appointing an enquiry officer would do nothing more than cause 'expense and ... irritation' as the proportion of patients who were able to pay would be too small for that to add greatly to the hospital's income. A minority report of uncertain origin stressed that without some form of systematic investigation of the circumstances of those who applied for help, the unfairness and the criticisms would continue. They wanted the questioning of patients to be undertaken by the Secretary (recently deprived of the opportunity to be elevated to the position of Secretary-Superintendent) and his staff so that the doctors would not be involved and need not discuss such matters with their patients. Eventually, the majority view prevailed and so the matter was not taken any further at that time. That did not prevent one of the honorary staff from questioning some patients about their income. No attempt was made to censure him as several instances of abuse had been brought to light by various means. The Board was asked by the Works Governors to arrange a meeting between eight of its members and an equal number from among themselves to discuss the alleged misuse of the clinical facilities. By then though, it had become apparent that there was a strong body of opinion among the Governors generally that such questioning of patients was fully justified and that being a subscriber quite definitely did not confer an automatic right to the benefits provided.

The House Committee reserved the right to decide if any one letter of recommendation from a subscriber carried an entitlement to treatment. During the first decade of the twentieth century, their attitude towards other agencies who referred patients stiffened again. Poor Law authorities who did not subscribe were at first charged when their patients were accepted and then the hospital soon reverted to the nineteenth-century practice of refusing to accept those patients. The Admiralty had already been informed that their Fleet Surgeon at the

Naval Establishment at Pembroke Dock was no longer to ask for appointments for patients with eye injuries. Indeed, the financial situation had become so difficult that even when companies whose workmen had covenanted to pay subscriptions went into liquidation, the honorary solicitor was asked to demand the money owing from those employees.

In spite of the increased militancy of the workmen and the hospital's doctors, there was no severe deterioration in relations between them at this stage, but the peace was short-lived. Already, the Friendly Societies in Gower were falling out with their Medical Officers (none of whom were connected with the hospital) and there was more widespread dissent in years to come. (The hospital's senior doctors were still unpaid, of course, and were in a powerful position when the subject of abuse of the facilities was discussed.)

Later, in 1907, the dissatisfaction over procedures for the admission of patients was as evident as ever and a rule was made which allowed the clergy or a responsible householder to testify about any individual's eligibility for treatment. As that failed to resolve the matter, the medical staff themselves decided to mount their own preliminary investigation of 'doubtful cases' before they accepted patients. There is no evidence from the hospital records or from local newspapers (which usually contained detailed accounts of any quarrels of this kind) that this in any way alienated the workmen's delegates at that time. It is impossible to escape the conclusion that the Board largely agreed with the stance taken by the doctors on this issue, and they may even have secretly welcomed such acts of defiance. In spite of that, the decision taken at the Annual General Meeting had been that patients' circumstances were not to be investigated, so there the matter was left.

The Works Governors themselves had been making greater efforts to raise money and at the hospital's Annual Meeting in 1905, some prominence was given to the visits paid by them to the various Trades Councils and Associations to plead the hospital's cause. This work was of the greatest importance, not least because it led to their being allowed to assume a more active part in the process of management. In July 1906, the first of their representatives to have been elected to the Board was unanimously appointed its Chairman for that year. Mr T. W. Hughes's dedication to that work was great and his task was a large one, particularly with the persistent claims that more people were able to pay for their treatment than actually did. His assumption of this position signalled a change of the greatest importance. He performed his task with great skill and tact and without attempting to over-assert himself or to displace or devalue those whom he had replaced. Indeed, the only obvious immediate change that occurred was that committee meetings, which had always previously been held in the daytime (at great inconvenience to Mr Hughes and his colleagues) took place from that time on at 4 p.m.

A new source of abuse came to light after the passing of the Education Act in 1907. A new generation of school medical officers had been appointed who referred large numbers of schoolchildren to the Eye Clinic for further assessment. This led to strong objections concerning what was considered to be a gross misuse of the hospital's facilities. Between the Admiralty and the Schools Medical Service, both of which had flooded that department with patients who could have been treated elsewhere, the additional expense to the hospital was considerable. Mr Frank Thomas, the Ophthalmologist, was allowed to take whatever steps he considered necessary to prevent the ordinary out-patients from being crowded out. Unfortunately Mr Thomas exacerbated the situation when he refused to examine the eyes of a child whose father earned only thirty-five shillings a week. He was supported in this by the House Committee although they preferred that such matters were left to the Reception Committee formed specifically at that time to deal with problems of that kind. The workmen's representatives had never objected to the decisions made by that committee and their attitude at the time tends to confirm the existence of the widespread abuse which it was alleged existed. Indeed, it was one of their number who seconded Mr Brook's motion in September 1910 which said that it was unjustified to call on subscribers to take on the burden of treating children with defective eyesight, as this was really the work of the education authority.

The main concern of the workmen's representatives at the time was to increase their number even further (from the twelve seats which they were given on the Board in 1910). But there were other greater problems which faced them and the other Governors. For reasons that are not known, the Providential Dispensary had been closed in the early years of this century and that continued to add to the hospital's problems. Disputes between the Friendly Societies and their medical officers added to the general uneasiness which faced everyone concerned with health care at that time. The Secretary of the local Division of the BMA wrote to the hospital again to remind them of the extent of the problem of abuse but by then it had been decided to formulate a new rule which made it obligatory for all out-patients continuing to have treatment for more than two months to have an enquiry made into their financial circumstances. In addition, no medicines were to be dispensed to patients who were members of Benefit Clubs or Friendly Societies.

Financial crisis were commonplace in the hospital's history. The clinical facilities available were generally regarded as being quite first-rate but they were not sufficiently extensive. The average number of in-patient beds in 1890 was 76 but this increase in hospital beds had not kept up with the average increase for England and Wales over the previous thirty years.[9] The pace of the clinical work in Swansea continued to expand at a faster rate, with a hundred more admissions and an increase of 46 per cent in the number of operations performed in 1894 compared with 1890. Equally disturbing was the fact that the numbers of patients attending the hospital Outdoor Department clinics had increased to the levels reached before the Provident Dispensary had opened. It was shown from Burdett's Hospital Annual[10] that of fifty-seven general hospitals, in only seven was the cost per head lower than the Swansea Hospital, and only five towns in England and Wales showed a lower collection per thousand of the population on Hospital Sunday. All these facts testified to the increasing medical needs of the community and to the admirable manner in which the hospital had attempted to meet those requirements.

The increasing status of the hospital contrasted severely with the state of the building. The Catholic priest felt bound to complain in 1895 that conditions in the mortuary were a violation of the sanctity of the dead. The attempts that were made to disinfect the already inadequate operating theatre, to lessen the serious risks to which patients were being exposed, failed. The servants' upper bedroom had to be boarded up to the ceiling with the coming of the cold weather because of the draught and the North Wing had to be emptied of female patients to house the nursing staff. At least two major additions to the building were thought to be necessary.

Sadly, the number of patrons available who were sufficiently wealthy to alleviate these problems, was small. The committee was anxious not to displease their major benefactors, but still seemed to have an infinite capacity for giving offence. Adelina Patti, less uncharitable but more sensitive than most, was deeply hurt by the decision to reduce the prices of admission for her annual charitable appearance in Swansea in 1896. It was later realized that it might have been wiser to have consulted her first but it would have been an unenviable task to have attempted to explain to her that the demand for tickets was lower than ever before. A request to receive a deputation who would present an apology was met with a curt reply by telegram:

> Impossible to give concert this year—much regret cannot receive deputation. Patti-Nicolini.[11]

Occasionally, a large subscriber would offer advice. Mr Studt (whose annual fête that year raised £907) was a man whose opinion was never sought and, when it was offered, it was usually ignored, possibly because of his humble origins. After the cancellation of Patti's concert, a plan to build a Nurses' Home in the grounds was set aside. Already, the ward and laundry maids might have to sleep in their own homes because of the overcrowding. Mr Studt suggested that one or two houses in Brunswick Street, whose back gardens adjoined the hospital, should be bought. The committee had always been attracted to short-term solutions to their financial problems. This explains the total lack of cohesion and sense of perspective that plagued the hospital's planning for most of the century. Mr Studt's proposal prompted Mr J. M. Leeder to donate £20 towards the cost of a new building if twenty-five other gentlemen were prepared to donate a similar sum, and a subscription list for £500 was opened for a new Nurses' Home.

Of the many other problems being faced, the one that caused most concern arose from the inadequate facilities available for performing surgical operations. The immediate solution to this, namely asking the ophthalmic surgeons for the use of their operating theatre, met with a blunt refusal from Dr Jabez Thomas. He was still something of a force to be reckoned with, particularly when he issued his periodic reminders of the conditions under which he had agreed to the amalgamation of the Eye Hospital with the General Hospital.

More disagreements with the ophthalmic surgeons occurred in August 1898; while the heating apparatus in the Out-patient Department was being renewed, it had been decided, more or less by common consent, that all the out-patient clinics should be held in the Eye Hospital. It was not unusual for the medical staff to concur on such matters and, considering the extent by which the number of patients dealt with had increased, they were able to agree on their working priorities to a surprising degree. In September, Dr Jabez Thomas, forever on the look-out for anyone who was liable to invade his domain, ordered that the furniture from the clinic, which had been taken there on the committee's instructions, should be removed.[12] After this had happened twice, Dr Alexander Davidson, the other eye surgeon, wrote to the committee to say that:

> if any motion is passed infringing the terms of amalgamation with the old Eye Hospital, you may consider my resignation in your hands ... Although always opposed to amalgamation, when it did take place, I made up my mind to do my best to make it a success ... I am perfectly aware that this action will be called selfish, but the clauses of amalgamation were specifically drawn up to safeguard against any such contingency as the present ...[13]

Such a threat from the Eye Department was guaranteed to make the Board of Management succumb. Dr Davidson was at once told that he had misunderstood the extent of the powers held by the Board and was asked to withdraw his resignation. This he refused to do until the Honorary Solicitor had been sent the documents concerning the merger of the two hospitals and had given his opinion as to whether there had occurred an infringement of the conditions laid down. Eventually, so powerful was the ophthalmologists' position that the minute criticizing Dr Thomas's actions had to be expunged from the records and an uneasy peace was restored. Although clinics had to be held in the Anaesthetizing Room and it was considered 'indecent and immoral to consult and treat male and female patients indiscriminately in the presence of their fellow patients', and although the ceiling of the old theatre had to be whitewashed with disinfectant and the floor cemented and washed with 'perchloride' (*sic*) before each operation, the extent of the inconvenience caused to patients and staff left the two ophthalmologists quite unaffected and unrepentant. When it seemed that this state of affairs might have to continue permanently, a local draper, Mr Ben Evans, offered to build a new theatre at his own expense. The only condition he made was that the mortuary must be removed to another part of the premises and a site ('just outside the North corridor') was found. The architect was asked to visit several other recently designed surgical departments and Mrs Evans was invited to lay the foundation stone in March 1897. At its rear, it was planned to build a single-storey Nurses' Home (for which a subscription would confer the same privileges as a subscription to the hospital), to house at least thirteen nurses, with foundations sufficiently strong to take a further unspecified number of floors. Mr Buckley Wilson, a local architect, resigned from the Board of Management on accepting the commission to design both buildings. He and his junior partner, Mr Glendinning Moxham, should have claimed five per cent of the total cost but they contributed the fees to the Building Fund in spite of the decision that the donation would not carry any privileges with it.[14] The opening of the new operating theatre on 28 October 1898 was sufficiently important an event for Sir William McCormac, the President of the Royal College of Surgeons of England, to be invited to perform the opening ceremony.[15] Built at a cost of £1,500, the operating theatre was to be used only for patients from wards where adequate pre-operative preparation was possible so that the risk of infection was reduced.

The days of relatively inexpensive medicine of the past were over. More advanced medical services posed increased problems for the organizers. The hospital laundry was inadequate, the hot-water supply old-fashioned and, less than two years after the Nurses' Home had been opened, there was insufficient accommodation—the Sisters had to sleep in the rooms adjoining the wards, which effectively prevented the nursing of patients singly. The pantry for the use of the Matron and resident doctor was 'most objectionable, being in the lavatory' and the out-patients' waiting room was so uncomfortable that many patients had to wait in the hall. The impure air and smell of anaesthetics from the operating theatre permeated through the whole of the Nurses' Home 'and if the door be closed, the ventilation ceases'.

There were few new sources of money to deal with these increasing difficulties. Adelina Patti had continued to give charity concerts but Mr Studt's attitude had changed by 1900. His new terms were that he should be allowed to keep a third of the profits from the fête, but the committee refused him more than £200 and he was not allowed to charge expenses for the use of his fairground 'machines'. Rumours were rife in the town that the committee had made some form of financial arrangement with him, which did not meet with general approval. As a donor of more than £2,000, he was entitled to have a ward named after him and the protests seem to have arisen not from any doubts about his generosity but because of his assumption of what had hitherto been an undisputed upper or upper middle-class role.

While his previous benevolence had done little to elevate his status, he was soon removed from all criticism by a relatively trivial act on his part. The original motto of the hospital, *Deeds not words*, devised in 1881, was replaced by the more cumbersome *Pity and Need make all flesh kin* in 1895, and a banner bearing those words was presented by Mr Studt for use on public occasions. The banner consisted of a view of the hospital surmounted by the borough coat of arms, with a patient being treated by a doctor—Mr James Griffith Hall—and a nurse, with the Geneva cross and the motto on its other side.

Moonlight cruises, the Annual Ball, 'eisteddfodau' and occasional theatre performances at which the nurses were expected to sell programmes, all continued to provide useful sources of income, especially as the sale of stocks and shares had to be considered in 1899 to pay off the overdraft on the building. A timely donation of £500 from Mrs Griffith Llewellyn was sent with the request that it should be used to provide adequate hot water. Colonel Morgan's *Suggestions for Remedying the Structural Defects* which he had printed in 1901[16] contained so many Utopian measures (where he was able to suggest any at all) that they only served to emphasize the increasing financial difficulties. For £4,000 (£2,000 of which was to be provided by an anonymous donor, who was Mrs Llewellyn), he believed that a new wing could be added to the Nurses' Home which had been opened in May 1899, a new out-patient department could be built and the Dispensary could be converted into a minor operating theatre so that the older of the two theatres could be 'swept away'. By 1903, Colonel Morgan's seemingly unrealistic plans had been largely brought about with the building of a second Nurses' Home, a new out-patient department so that the former building could be used for casualty work, and a new minor theatre for which the late Mr James Griffith Hall had left £500.

In 1901, it had been agreed with the Borough Streets Committee that the boundary wall of the hospital and footpath should be set back without expense to the hospital. This would allow for more space between the kerb and the rail of the tramway and so lessen the danger to pedestrians and vehicles. In the same year, Mr and Mrs Dyer gave £800 to maintain a ward which was to be called the 'Devon and Dyer Ward' for children.[17] They stipulated that it should have twenty new beds and a teak floor and that 'an efficient nurse should be found, a Kind, Motherly Lady, who understands Children'. The hospital's only stipulation was that the hair of any child admitted might be cut if necessary. By 1904, the ward would have been closed had it not been for the further £500 donated by the same benefactors as a result of which the name was altered to that of Dyer Ward.

When epidemics of infectious disease occurred, the Children's Ward frequently had to be closed as a temporary measure. This was unavoidable as the original intention of having a small but properly-built isolation ward to deal with such events had never been carried out. In 1905, the Building Committee were again persuaded by Dr Ebenezer Davies to prepare plans for such a unit. These might easily have been forgotten as they had so frequently been in the past but it happened that the Borough Council had been concerned with providing an adequate supply of water for the town. They had built a reservoir at Cray in Breconshire and during the construction work there it had been necessary to build a Smallpox Hospital (complete with mortuary) at the site as part of the general public health measures which were necessary in case an epidemic should occur and affect their workers. In April 1906, an approach was made to the Council's Cray Water Works Committee suggesting that they might present the building to the general hospital as an isolation unit. This was agreed to and Henry Billings, who could always be relied on to provide less expensive estimates for building work than any of his competitors, removed and re-erected the building in the Swansea hospital grounds, at the 'northern end of the shrubbery, near the Laundry'.

In June 1908, a comprehensive building scheme which would both increase the accommodation and bring about greatly needed improvements in the hospital building were called for. It was thought that these plans were sufficiently ambitious to need the advice of an architect before they could be properly proceeded with. No maintenance work had been done on the existing building and there were fifty patients waiting for admission. When the Talbot and Penllergaer Wards were closed for the reconstruction to start in July, patients had to be transferred to the hospital's Convalescent Home (opened in 1903). This raised difficulties and the Head Constable had to be asked for the loan of the town's motor ambulance.

Raising the North and South Wings by one storey would give an immediate increase of 8 beds with living space for 8 nurses and 10 servants. The kitchens were to be remodelled and the Electro-Therapeutic Room, the Casualty Department and the Dispensary would be enlarged. The Llewelyn and Patti Wards, Casualty, the Eye Hospital and the offices were to be lit by electricity. Since 1879, more than £20,000 had been spent on new buildings and improvements and this new scheme was likely to cost £25,000 with the eventual provision of 80 extra beds. By 1913, as a result of an Appeal organized by the Chairman and several large donations, four new wards had been built with a new operating theatre for the Eye Hospital.

A quite extraordinary triumph for the ladies connected with the hospital had been brought about in 1899 when two from among them (Mrs Travers Wood and Miss Lindsay) had been elected to the Board in the place of two men who had resigned. None of the women who had previously worked on behalf of the hospital had been particularly forceful and their influence was hardly felt in committee, in spite of their hard work on behalf of patients. With the arrival of Lewis Llewelyn Dillwyn's daughter, Elizabeth Amy Dillwyn, that situation changed drastically. She had already accomplished a great deal as Secretary of the Nursing Institution from which she resigned in 1886. Not for her the genteel tactics of the Ladies' Samaritan Fund with their fine ways and inferior status. In 1899 she was merely asked to take the initiative in organizing the Hospital Ball, but by 1901 she had become Chairman both of the Board of Management and of the newly constituted committee of workmen's representatives, the Works Governors; a year later she was a member of four of the hospital's subcommittees.

Her interest in the possibility of providing a Convalescent Home for the hospital brought her to prominence. Such a possibility had first been raised in 1871 at a public meeting which was not connected with the hospital, but which considered means of establishing 'a Rest or Convalescent Home for the working classes of this and adjoining counties'. In 1878, Miss Dillwyn's uncle, John Dillwyn Llewelyn, had made it known that 'the Convalescent Home at Gorseinon' was ready and that two patients might be sent there from the hospital.[18] Shortly afterwards, Colonel Turberville of Ewenny Priory was prepared to arrange for patients to be sent to 'The Rest' at Porthcawl at his expense. He had been willing to sponsor as many as six patients at any one time but little enthusiasm was shown for his ideas by the hospital authorities and virtually no one was able to take advantage of his offer, even though he wished to subscribe to 'The Rest' in the hospital's name. Eventually, a subscription (for six guineas a year) was taken out by the hospital and this sum was paid back to them by Colonel Turberville. This connection was kept up at least until 1896 when some of the available admission tickets were given to the House Surgeon for distribution and the remainder to the ladies of the Samaritan Fund. In 1893, in a lecture unrelated to health care, on 'Gowerland's Beauty' at the Swansea Scientific Society, the issue had been raised again. There, it was suggested that another committee to consider building a home might be set up. By 1899, no patients were being sent to Porthcawl but a year later, 'the great majority' of those admitted to hospital were thought to be capable of benefiting from a period of convalescence, especially as it was those very people who 'occupy our beds for several months'.

An anonymous donor, who was to be known as 'X', then promised Miss Dillwyn a donation of £500 if that were used for the building of a Convalescent Home. It was clear that this sum would not be sufficient for that purpose and that at least £10,000 would be needed. It was believed in some quarters that Miss Dillwyn herself was 'X' but some doubts were raised when the original donation was increased to £10,000 after Miss Dillwyn had promised £100 if nine other people would contribute identical sums. Several sites within easy reach of the hospital were considered and eventually the one behind Cwmdonkin Park was thought to be the best. The plans drawn up were submitted to 'X' for approval and when they had been accepted with some modifications, the Foundation Stone was laid by Lord Windsor on 30 August 1902.

It was inevitable with the opening of the Convalescent Home that the turnover of patients managed at the hospital would increase and that the clinical work would be greatly facilitated. The opening ceremony for the Home took place on 17 July 1903, but advertisements for staff did not appear for a further month. The 'Working Matron' was expected to be between thirty-five and fifty years of age and was to have undergone training as a nurse for three years. There were thirty-one applicants and Mrs Gainwell was appointed, with a salary of £50 together with a uniform. The cook was to be paid £20 a year and the porter ('abstainer preferred') the same money as the Matron, although he was soon given two months' notice as there was insufficient work for him there. The building was thought to suit their needs:

> the cubic space is satisfactory for the number of beds but the wall space is not quite sufficient.

Only patients of good character were to be taken there and one of the resident doctors would visit whenever necessary. The Matron was given the right to engage and dismiss female members of staff but decisions about the admission of patients were made by the House Committee on the advice of the honorary staff. (Disagreements sometimes occurred and in 1906, Colonel Morgan was quoted in a local newspaper as having said that 'If one went to the Convalescent Home, one would see the slums of the town . . .') In July 1904, Miss Dillwyn was asked to approach 'X' to enquire if she would be prepared to pay for the additional work which needed to be done there. The identity of 'X' had still not been generally revealed but a reply was received saying that Miss Clara Thomas of Llwynmadoc, Breconshire (who was actually 'X') would denote £300 for this work. The whole of the subsequent history of the hospital shows that the service provided after that time would not have been nearly as successful without the facilities of the Convalescent Home.

Miss Dillwyn's interest in the hospital's affairs came to an end in much the same way that her father's had many years previously. In 1901, she judged herself to have been harshly treated and wrote to Mr Hyam Goldberg, the Board's Chairman:

> If I were to bring an action against the Hospital for the privileges refused me this morning to which I claim to be entitled, I have a strong opinion that I should win my case. I do not choose to bring such an action but have decided to make no further personal efforts to complete the Convalescent Home Building Fund.[19]

Some months later, she allowed her name to be put forward at an election for new trustees, but she got very few votes and immediately announced that she would be 'withdrawing from the hospital'.

In March 1897, Dr Jabez Thomas suggested that it might be appropriate to celebrate Queen Victoria's 'Record Reign' Jubilee (which had already earned a picnic and an extra week's holiday for the nursing staff) by creating yet another Nursing Institution with its own improved system of training. There were fears that this might interfere with the work of the existing institution which had already asked the hospital to be responsible for training all its nurses on payment of ten pounds a year together with their wages and keep. The medical staff decided that two nurses a year could be trained (for the 'old' organization) for a period of two years during which time they would have the same status as the hospital's own probationers and be under 'the absolute control of the Matron'.

Already a 'Nurses Cooperation' (with whose organization Dr Griffiths and Mr Brook had been concerned) had been formed in London. Its aim was to provide a full level of remuneration for nurses and an attempt had been made to form a branch in Swansea.[20] That plan failed but a move to establish a private nursing system in connection with the hospital came into effect under the control of the Nursing Subcommittee of the hospital in February 1893 but there was to be no amalgamation with the Nursing Institution. Four years later, the medical staff were grieved that applications for nursing appointments continued to be advertised externally, and they were convinced that by far the best policy would be to appoint locally trained nurses to vacant posts. This was agreed to, and they were asked to formulate a scheme for the proper training of probationer nurses leading to an examination, in addition to the issue of certificates on successful completion. Much had happened in a short space of time. Only eight years before, when the most ambitious plans were being considered for the reorganization of district nursing in the town, the hospital committee, in keeping with the policy of most other voluntary hospitals, had not even considered the suggestion made by the Hospitals Association that a Board should be set up to organize nurses' education. Under the new scheme, probationer nurses would be bound to work at the hospital for three years and in their final year they might be sent to do private work. The Nursing Subcommittee, which at that time consisted of two of the honorary staff and three ladies, acknowledged that the medical staff's *Scheme for the Instruction and Training of Nurses* was well-planned and ambitious. Although they were not pioneers in the field, their scheme was as forward-looking as those in existence elsewhere and was certainly the most important move brought about in the Nursing Department up to that time. It was of some considerable significance that when Miss Bellars resigned from her post as Matron, her successor Miss Sykes, who already worked in the hospital, was expected to be able to undertake the training of nurses.

In the first three months of their probationary period, nurses would attend lectures in anatomy and physiology followed by tuition in medicine and surgery for a further three months each. The lecturers were to be those members of the honorary staff who were prepared to participate, and each course would be followed by an examination where the examiners would be those visiting doctors who had not acted as lecturers. Those who passed would be given a certificate of qualification signed by the examiners and lecturers, and there would be another form of certificate for nurses who failed after completing their probationary period. Finally, it was felt to be important that no nurse should remain on night duty for longer than six months and, soon afterwards, three months at a time.

By 1893, the term 'Sister' was in common use to describe the senior nurse in charge of each ward, with each of them being known not by their surnames but by the names of the wards on which they worked. There were no standard salary scales for hospital staff, and nurses were entirely at the mercy of their employers unless the Matron interceded on their behalf, which she occasionally did. Sister 'Penllergare's' (*sic*) earnings were increased from twenty-five to thirty pounds a year at a time when Miss Nightingale was finding some difficulty in providing the Cardiff Infirmary with 'a really good Superintendent Nurse' at thirty-five to forty pounds a year. The other requests for salary increases from ward sisters at Swansea were 'declined' without any reasons being given. In September 1894, a Staff Nurse was also appointed to each ward (at the same time that locked cupboards were provided 'for the custody of the poisons' for the first time in the Talbot, Penllergaer and Llewelyn wards). The duties of the new staff nurse were not vastly different from those of her modern counterpart and, although she was expected 'to do the duties of Senior Probationers', she was in all respects a deputy ward sister.

The Matron's opinion was being sought on nursing matters to a greater extent than had been allowed for a considerable time, and she was even allowed to object to the appointment of one staff nurse. A move to make ward sisters liable to be called out at night to assist in the operating theatre failed and this inevitably increased the responsibility placed on the Matron and the Night Superintendent. At the same time, it was agreed that sisters should have the right to enter their own wards at any time, but rather than risk a further disagreement, this was later rescinded. Probationer nurses were, in future, to be presented to the House Committee when they were first appointed, there, doubtless, to be lectured on the virtues of the Spartan existence that was to be their lot and about which most of the committee members knew little. They were expected to produce a certificate of physical fitness from the Senior Physician, and the Matron was obliged to provide a periodic report on their progress. There was talk of 'an unpleasant state of things between the Matron and some of the officials', and Miss Sykes was ultimately invited to put into writing any complaints concerning insubordination or inefficiency. Sister Talbot was at once accused of being insubordinate and of being inclined to disregard any rules concerning the behaviour of nursing staff. After a two-hour discussion, even though it was thought that Miss Sykes had exaggerated the difficulties, Colonel Morgan and his colleagues acknowledged that allowances should be made for the Sister's show of temper as she had been under great pressure recently, but they were determined to uphold the Matron's authority and Sister Talbot resigned a week later.

Although the staff worked long hours (reduced to twelve hours a day for the laundry maids in 1896), life for their more junior contemporaries had become slightly less strait-laced. A Christmas tree ('as usual') was provided for the Talbot Ward in 1893 and each nurse was allowed to invite a friend to a 'Christmas Supper in the Sitting Room from 8 to 11 p.m.', with 'the usual entertainment' being allowed in their own room without any restriction on time, although the House Surgeon was requested to see that none of the patients was disturbed. By the following year, it was stipulated that no dancing should occur within the hospital and most of the committee members would have preferred the event to have been held elsewhere. A private subscription list was opened among them to pay for the event but Colonel Morgan's attitude epitomized that of most of his colleagues; while he gave five pounds, he wished to make it known that he could never approve of dancing as a pastime. (He was slightly less rigid in his attitude to the light entertainment provided in January 1896 by Mr Harper of Brunswick Street; that was allowed to go ahead on condition that the concert should finish by 9 p.m.).

Miss Sykes had managed to escape the committee's wrath for a considerable time, but she found herself in difficulties by April 1896 when she tried to prevent 'the boy' from working for part of each day in the Dispensary. This, together with press statements she had made about the character and professional capacity of some of the nursing staff, led to a request that she should meet Colonel Morgan and Dr Rawlings to discuss her relationship with her employers. The quality of nursing at night under her superintendence was thought to be poor, but there was insufficient money to appoint a staff nurse to each ward and the best compromise available was that no nurse should take charge of a ward at night without first having had a year's experience of daytime nursing. Soon, for reasons that are not known, Sister Llewelyn, who looked after the Female and Children's Ward, was asked to resign. Once she had agreed to this, a special meeting was called to decide whether she deserved a testimonial. It was eventually agreed that a testimonial should state that she had come from Guy's Hospital three years previously with the highest recommendations, and:

> Her wards were always in perfect order and the interest of her patients most carefully studied. [Her qualifications] are of the highest class and she carried out her duties with great ability.

Having thus been told to leave, and then praised to the utmost in quick succession, she was asked if she would consider remaining in a locum tenens capacity before she left the country. This was followed by the publication of a statement recording the committee's 'unabated confidence' in their nurses. It was not long before Miss Sykes resigned because 'I feel it necessary that I should take a little rest'. Of her it was said that:

> The position occupied by this Hospital in the Statistical Tables by Sir Henry Burdett ... amply demonstrates without further testimony Miss Sykes (*sic*) capacities ...

In comparison with her predecessors, she had been found to have few faults, although her main virtue was said to be her ability to manage economically what had become a large household. As many as 101 applications were received for her vacant post and Miss Rigney of Burnley was appointed Matron.

The whole profession of nursing was gradually assuming a more sophisticated air. In future, probationers would be expected to sign contracts which would require them to complete their full three years' training after which they would receive the hospital's parchment certificate. For any of them who left before that time, the penalties were severe. A fine equivalent to six months' salary would be imposed and, if necessary, legal proceedings would be taken to ensure its payment. At a more senior level, in November 1898, two of the ward sisters resigned following 'friction with the Matron'. Some further uneasiness concerning the new Matron's behaviour came to light with the resignation of the Night Superintendent. When another Ward Sister claimed that she had been called 'a good for nothing blackguard' (*sic*), the medical staff were asked to set up their own investigation into standards of care and efficiency in that department.

They found that 'the Nursing affairs of the Hospital are in a most unsatisfactory state' but that there was insufficient corroborative evidence to warrant taking drastic measures. It was certain, they said, that:

> the Matron has not always been happy in her choice of language [and] the whole evidence shows pettiness of administration ... that she is in the habit of allowing Sisters and nurses to dispute her authority and herself to be drawn into wrangling not consistent with the dignity of Matron—in short, she shows want of tact and firmness ... the graver charges are not proved.

They did not wish to remove her from office but feared that the insubordination was in danger of spreading to the junior staff. Sister

Llewelyn's ideas concerning hospital discipline had been sufficiently unusual to make any Matron's life intolerable and Sister Margaret, the senior Sister, was also difficult but no action against her was contemplated because of the state of her health and her length of service.

Dr Jabez Thomas's views were heard separately by the Board. He believed that the Matron lacked the capacity to discharge her duties effectively. Not only was she tactless and uncontrolled, but her suspiciousness, callousness and tendency to be 'bothering about nothing' interfered with the well-being of a hard-working staff. She was even incapable of arranging special diets for patients without 'making vexations', and her cruelty in allowing Sister Margaret to go without her dinner for many months even though she was a diabetic provides sufficient cause, he thought, for regarding her as unworthy.

In her reply, the Matron complained that 'something is pulling against me' and that the committee's lack of support had made it difficult for her to maintain discipline. She had heard that the sisters 'did not love each other very much', and the House Surgeon had once spent an hour in a sister's bedroom having his hand dressed.

It seemed that it was the fate of many of the women appointed to the position of Matron at the Swansea Hospital that they should be found to be unequal to the task and were doomed to face an inglorious departure. Ultimately, Miss Rigney (and Sister Llewelyn) resigned and, of the thirty-eight candidates for the Matron's post, Miss Bridges, who was already the Acting Matron, was appointed in December 1899. In August 1900, she asked that consideration should be given to 'allowing her an assistant', and the first Assistant Matron was appointed at a salary of £40. Her duties were to include those delegated to her by the Matron and she was to be responsible for the operating theatres on the two main operating days.

An incident which was later a source of great embarrassment to the hospital occurred at this time, though it could scarcely be called mismanagement. In March 1901, and again in November 1902, two separate applications were made by Edith Cavell to join the nursing staff, but were refused.[21] She later became famous after her execution by the Germans for her role in helping Allied soldiers to escape from Belgium. There is no known reason for Miss Cavell's obvious wish to work in Swansea. There would, of course, have been no cause for her request to be treated differently from the many others which were regularly received.

The only insurance provisions made until almost the end of the nineteenth century concerned the buildings (which were valued at £30,000 in 1900). With the passing of the Workmen's Compensation Act of 1897, it became apparent that it would be necessary to insure the staff against injury or disease at work. In 1899, the Secretary of the Royal Pension Fund for Nurses sent their prospectus to the hospital and Colonel Morgan and Principal David Salmon of the Training College were asked to provide a report on its contents but they felt that they could not recommend the acceptance of its proposals. Further information was then sought from insurance companies with the intention of insuring only nurses who were exposed to infectious disease. The first members of the staff to be insured (against accidents and infectious disorders only) were those involved in private nursing and the general porter.

The uneasiness concerning the nursing staff continued. In August 1901, the two resident doctors, having 'exercised all possible forbearance', found that they could no longer work with Sister Penllergaer because of her attitude to the patients and to them. They found her manner in dealing with patients to be overbearing and at times cruel, especially when they were 'poor'. She had refused the relatives of a dying patient permission to visit him. She sometimes directed the nurses to disobey the medical staff's instructions. Having been reported to the Matron three times, she had refused to resign when asked to do so.

'The nursing world', said a witness to the Select Committee on the Registration of Nurses in 1905, 'is in a state of chaos just now'.[22] This view was clearly shared by the honorary medical staff at the Swansea Hospital. Their attempt to increase the period of nurses' training from three to four years was never given serious consideration in 1902, and one of the honorary surgeons, Mr Elsworth, made it known that he would refuse to sign certificates of training for nurses who had spent time working in the private department while they were employed as probationers. It was this pronouncement that led to the formation of another Nursing Subcommittee. Their first decision was that, if nurses were to choose to remain for a fourth year, the extra year had to be spent in the private department, which from then on had to be conducted 'so as to pay its own expenses only'. The Subcommittee also drew attention to the need to develop facilities for private nursing in the town. The Swansea Nursing Association dealt largely with the less wealthy population, and private nurses were being brought in from as far away as London at far greater expense than was necessary, and usually the nurse was not known to the doctor concerned. The work of the private nursing department in the hospital was liable to fluctuations in demand; whereas in 1901 a profit of nearly £200 was handed over to the hospital, in 1903 there occurred a loss of more than £40. After six months of an unusually low death rate in the town (extraordinary in view of the unprecedented high rate of illness at the same time), Miss Dillwyn proposed in 1904 that the private nursing service in the hospital should be discontinued as it was no longer necessary. This was not accepted and within a further six months, more patients were again being nursed privately.

When Miss Bridges resigned in 1902 in order to accept a post at Gibraltar, there must have been relief that at last a Matron could actually be greatly praised on leaving the hospital, for a Testimonial Fund was formed for her. She was presented with a set of silver-backed brushes and it was said of her:

> She has raised the tone of the hospital ... by a combination of strength and tact in doing so much without friction ...

Her successor was Miss Prudence Crispin of the Paddington Infirmary.

In 1906, Dr Ebenezer Davies attended a Hospital Committee meeting on behalf of the Town Council to enquire whether facilities could be provided for giving lectures for the Midwives' Centre which was to be established; this was agreed to.

Miss Musson, the next Matron, remained only two years in her post, leaving in December 1908 on her appointment as Matron of Birmingham General Hospital; but she was to have a distinguished career. She was the first nurse to become Chairman of the General Nursing Council (1926–44). She also became the Honorary Treasurer of the International Council of Nurses, President of the National Council of Nurses (which was later amalgamated with the Royal College of Nursing) and Vice-President of the Royal College of Nursing (in 1950).[23]

Miss Scovell of Newcastle, who was to remain in that post for almost a quarter of a century, replaced her. Soon after starting work, she asked that four new nurses should be appointed. From 1909, probationer nurses were allowed a half-day free in every fortnight 'subject to the work of the hospital permitting such extensions'. Eleven months after being appointed, Miss Scovell handed in her resignation but this was allowed to lie on the table for a month and no more was heard of it. She, like her predecessor, had made a good impression, and it is not known why she should have wished to leave so very soon after being appointed. A possible explanation might be that Colonel Morgan had recently handed in his resignation from all the hospital's committees, and the two events may have been in some way connected. He, according to his usual habit, returned (quickly on that occasion), and that may have solved her difficulties. Soon after she had arrived, the first pension (of £30 a year) ever awarded to a member of the staff was given to Sister Margaret 'on account of failing health and in recognition of long service'. As a direct result of Miss Scovell's work, the first masseuse–nurse was appointed in 1910.

For all the tumult that had accompanied the workings of the nursing department, there were other matters which regularly distracted the committee. Apart from his interest in the Nurses' Cooperation, Dr Griffiths had drawn more attention to himself by announcing, in 1893, that it was necessary to form a separate Throat and Ear Hospital, as such facilities were lacking in the general hospital. Sir John Talbot Dillwyn Llewelyn suggested to him that it might be more appropriate to consider forming a 'lying-in hospital' for maternity cases, while Colonel Morgan regretted that a meeting to discuss the proposal should have been called without consulting the General Hospital's Board. Dr Rawlings hoped that they 'should all gather together under [the general hospital's] motherly wing', but he was doubtless saddened by his own experience and, like the more inflammatory Dr Griffiths, held out no great hopes that fruitful discussions could occur. Mr Brook, who later became one of the most outstanding general surgeons that the hospital had known, and was at that time one of the very few Fellows of the Royal College of Surgeons in south Wales, and Dr Lancaster, one of the hospital's Outdoor Medical Officers, had volunteered to act as visiting doctors. It was believed that for £50 the new Throat and Ear Hospital could be furnished but that at least £150 a year would be necessary to maintain it properly. At the hospital committee, a letter from a London surgeon was read, in which he wrote:

> In my experience all these places have been started by medical men solely for their own benefit ... they have often done harm ... by curtailing their Subscriptions to the more valuable General Hospitals ... The Public is ruled by Sentiment, and give their money to any new Fad ... [They] give their money to Cancer Hospitals and the improvement of Idiots ... I have never yet heard of the Public founding a Hospital ...

Eventually (possibly because Dr Jabez Thomas had come down in favour of having a Throat and Ear Department within the general hospital), negotiations between the hospital authorities and those interested in the new institution were started on condition that Mr Brook would automatically become the surgeon in charge of that department. As there was some doubt as to whether this could legally occur without advertising the post, the Recorder of Swansea and the hospital's solicitor were asked for their opinion. The discussions were not nearly as acrimonious as they had been in the case of the Eye Hospital; nevertheless, when the talks were at their height, Colonel Morgan was inspired to comment at a meeting of the Providential Dispensary, 'amid laughter, that he was "pleased to come down to the Institution where everything was peace and quietness".'[24]

No separate hospital was formed and when the post for a Visiting Throat and Ear Surgeon to the general hospital was advertised, Mr Brook was appointed, but two months afterwards, he became a Visiting General Surgeon. The new department should have opened in August 1893, but Mr Brook's successor, Dr Elsworth, who also eventually became a general surgeon, found that there were no instruments or facilities there for holding out-patient clinics. He then decided to hold the hospital's first Throat and Ear Clinic at his own home, which, he rather laconically declared, 'was not altogether convenient'. In spite of his protestations, the new department was not functioning until August 1894.

With the exception of Dr Jabez Thomas's resolution opposing any further attempts 'to curtail the accommodation and usefulness of the Eye Hospital', the medical staff had not disturbed the general tranquillity for some considerable time. In fact, when complaints were received about the hospital's management, and the medical staff in particular, they were ignored because of the 'entire confidence' which was such a feature of the coalition between management and medical staff. This new-found friendliness coincided with a revision of the rules in 1891, which ended badly for Dr Rawlings. His continuing efforts to create new and specialized departments were agreed to in that year. With his personal interest in the field he had obviously hoped to be appointed as an Obstetric Physician, and his colleagues had agreed that:

> the officer appointed should have the advantage of a Consultant in cases of special difficulty.

The title of *consultant* had not been used previously in the hospital's history. Because of the nature of obstetric practice at that time, many doctors who worked in that field did not have wide surgical experience and the new consultant was meant to provide such a service. In suggesting the creation of an Obstetrics Department, and especially as he had put forward the name of Dr Griffiths ('who has extensive experience in abdominal surgery', which seemingly was only equalled by the extent of his irritability), Dr Rawlings narrowly lost an opportunity to move to work in that specialty. The Chairman at the meeting when the election took place gave his casting vote to Dr Nelson Jones, thereby ignoring the fact that Dr Rawlings had been the original advocate of the scheme and that the extent of his experience was far greater than that of his opponent. It seems that the strongest feelings were aroused on both sides as a result of the decision and many feared that the hospital would suffer as a result. It was also finally agreed that every member of the visiting medical staff who had held an appointment in the Indoor Department for twenty years should retire.

In October 1898, the resident doctors were instructed not to sell any more 'goods' to the honorary staff (presumably at the lower prices at which the material had been bought), and the Outdoor Staff were reminded that only two beds each were at their disposal for the admission of in-patients.

Still the calm lasted until 1899, with the reception of the first application for a post (as House Physician) from a woman doctor. Although her qualifications were better than those of the only other (male) applicant, it was resolved 'that the lady's application be not entertained'. Again, in 1900, three of the six applicants for the same post were women but none of them were invited for interview. This situation was not in any way unusual at that time. The first woman doctor, Elizabeth Blackwell, had graduated in America in 1849 and Elizabeth Garrett Anderson was the first to qualify from a medical school in Britain, in 1865. The opposition which women faced persisted for many years and in Swansea, even when there were difficulties in filling the resident posts, the policy was to readvertise in the hope of attracting male applicants.

The twentieth century opened quietly enough for the hospital and the agenda for its first committee meeting, held on 3 January 1900, gave no indication of the troublesome and exciting times that were to follow. The Poor Law Guardians asked if their probationer nurses could attend the medical staff's lectures and the resident doctors were asked to discharge as many in-patients as possible so that the new heating system could be installed. Finally, Dr Jabez Thomas gave notice that he would move that twenty beds should be placed at the disposal of the War Office for the treatment of soldiers wounded in the Boer War, a move of which no more was heard. Some months before he resigned later that year, Dr Jabez Thomas asked if his son, Mr Frank Thomas, could undertake his work as he had to be away from Swansea for a period. The medical staff refused that request but when Dr Thomas and Dr Davidson both resigned within two months of each other, Mr Thomas was appointed to replace his father in October 1900 at the age of 27; he remained the only Ophthalmic Surgeon for eleven years.

It became necessary to ask the senior doctors to provide a detailed report on the manner in which the two resident medical staff appointments should be made. They were clearly of the opinion that women should be barred from taking such posts but went on to show that some of the work expected of the junior medical staff was being ineffectively performed or even neglected. The 1901 edition of the *Rules for the Resident Medical Officers* shows that, in addition to his main duties in the medical department, the House Physician (or more properly, the Assistant House Surgeon as he was known) was also expected to help the Pathologist, to administer anaesthetics and to work in

Mr Frank Thomas.

Dr Florence Price, the first woman doctor to be appointed to the hospital. (*Pictures by kind permission of Mr Trevelyan Thomas.*)

the Eye Department. In the Out-patient Department, he examined all the new out-patients initially and, if there were more than 15 to be dealt with during any one session, he was to select the 15 most urgent cases for referral to the Out-patient Medical Officer. The House Surgeon worked in the Surgical, Gynaecology and Obstetrics Departments and was responsible for the care of the equipment and for discipline in the operating theatres.

With the erection of the new Children's Ward in 1901, the senior doctors reversed the position held by them and their predecessors for more than sixty years by advocating the appointment of a third honorary surgeon. This move was resisted by the Board for the same reason that the medical staff had previously given for refusing to sanction the change, namely that each surgeon would then have too few beds available to him. In spite of these differences, it was agreed to implement the senior staff's proposal that a third resident doctor (or House Surgeon) was urgently required. The new doctor, they thought, should have the title of Registrar, and his functions were to include the keeping of records on all indoor patients. His salary would be £20 a year with board and lodging and the post was thought to be suitable for recently qualified doctors or fourth-year medical students of either sex. Before that post had been advertised, the resident doctors had both resigned because of overwork, insufficient off-duty time and unnecessary interference with their work 'in minor matters and details'. At once, a rule was made that all sisters and nurses were to take their instructions from the medical officers, and eventually the resident doctors' salaries were raised to £75 and £50 respectively.

After the interviews for the new resident doctors, the honorary staff recommended 'the trial of a lady for . . . the post of House Physician' in December 1904. Since 1899, 9 applications had been received from 8 women doctors and they, together with one male Indian doctor in 1902, had all been refused interviews. In December 1904, 3 of the 9 applications for the 2 vacant posts were from women and Miss Florence Price of Carmarthen, who was 25 years of age and who had graduated in medicine at Edinburgh, was appointed by 27 votes to 4.

It had become apparent that a more extensive reorganization was called for in the workings of the medical department. The four members of the Outdoor Staff became Assistants to the Indoor Staff, but the Surgeon to the Throat, Nose and Ear Department was to remain as an Assistant Surgeon for some years yet. With two whole days in the week devoted to operating sessions, the Pathologist and Anaesthetist, Dr Daniel Evans, could no longer be expected to fulfil both functions, and he was invited—and he agreed—to become the hospital's first Honorary Pathologist. Until then, pathologists (and indeed anaesthetists for many years afterwards) were expected to tolerate working in what were then regarded as being unimportant branches of medicine in the hope that when a vacancy arose in a more prestigious specialty, they would have an advantage over any outsiders who might apply. In the seventeen years in which the post of Pathologist and Anaesthetist was in being, of the seven doctors who held it, five were appointed to other specialties, usually within three years. The pathologist's work carried a higher status than that of an anaesthetist and included an important teaching function. It was provided in the hospital rules that local doctors were to be informed whenever post-mortem examinations were to be performed so that they might attend. Of the three honorary Pathologists, Dr Evans became a Physician, Dr Cameron an Assistant Physician and then an Assistant Surgeon, and Dr D. R. Edwards, the Medical Officer to the Electro-Therapeutic Department, became, in effect, the hospital's first Radiologist, in addition to being Pathologist until 1911.

This separation of functions did not occur because of the belief that each field was becoming increasingly more specialized. 'The urgency for this change', recorded the Secretary, 'is created by the forthcoming visit to Swansea of the British Medical Association.' While the smallpox was raging in Swansea in 1902, the *South Wales Daily Post* of 18 July must have perplexed many of its readers by the curious headline 'doctors not afraid of smallpox'. This was a reference to the small deputation of medical men from the town who waited on the Corporation when the smallpox epidemic was at its height to ask for their help in inviting the Annual Meeting of the BMA to visit Swansea. The Association's only previous visit to the town had occurred in 1853 when a member of the hospital's honorary staff, Dr Bird, had been elected to the Presidency. In 1903, Dr T. D. Griffiths, twice previously one of the honorary staff, became the second Swansea doctor to hold the high office of President of the BMA. More than 600 doctors and their guests attended the meeting and the hospital staff were closely involved in the preparations.[25] The committee had asked them to invite as many BMA members as possible to the hospital so that they might make suggestions 'for its improvement'. Dr Blagdon Richards, the Ear, Nose and Throat Surgeon, asked for permission for 'a few patients' who had been brought over by Professor Gluck of Berlin, to sleep at the hospital during that week.

There were no suggestions for 'improvement' and the meeting made virtually no impression on the hospital. That was certainly not true of the activities of the Swansea Division of the BMA, and their minutes provide an interesting insight into the gradually expanding world of Swansea medicine. While they continued to agitate about the unfairness of colliery schemes which employed their own doctors and the increased work that the Notification of Births Act (which they otherwise welcomed) would bring with it, their clinical curriculum was being widened.[26] Twice in 1907, lectures and demonstrations were given on recent advances in bacteriology and it was fairly generally accepted that family doctors should become more involved in that work. Great interest was taken in the demonstration, using a microscope, of the organism *Spirochaeta pallida* which causes syphilis.[27] Mr Brook was able to discuss a patient with tetanus whom he had treated successfully with anti-tetanus serum. He had also gained some experience of removing the prostate gland (prostatectomy).[28] He had been practising plastic surgery and had grafted the skin from the neck of one patient on to his face after first removing a tumour and with another had constructed a new eyelid from the skin of the face.[29] The whole impression left is that it was a period of great excitement and innovation for the hospital in spite of the deplorably poor resources available.

An interesting reference was made in the hospital committee minutes in 1894 which suggests that the pattern as well as the extent of the clinical work was changing. There had been in force for many years a rule which prohibited the admission of mentally ill people. The more severe psychiatric disorders, the psychoses, would have required treatment in an asylum rather than a general hospital at that time. It seems, though, that towards the turn of the century, there was no objection to the acceptance of patients suffering from neurotic conditions. In 1894, Dr Rawlings asked for permission to admit, as a paying patient, the daughter of a newspaper proprietor so that she could have the Weir Mitchell treatment which 'could not well be applied in Swansea except at the hospital'. This method had been devised by Weir Mitchell for the treatment of gross hysterical symptoms after his experience as an army surgeon during the American Civil War. It consisted of an expensive combination of isolation, bedrest, overfeeding, and vigorous rubbing of the whole body twice daily.[30] No particular skill was required (although the hospital's nurses were 'partially trained in massage') and it was later alleged that any beneficial effects arose from the removal of the patient from the home surroundings.

Most of the diagnoses concerned less exotic (and frequently more dangerous) conditions. Dr Ebenezer Davies's advice was still sought whenever severe infections occurred in the wards, and in March 1899, the House Surgeon was asked to confer with him before fumigating the Talbot Ward, as a 'hose and spray' would be required. Colonel Morgan (still Chairman of the hospital committee) and he were then appointed to inquire into the outbreak of enteric fever in the hospital and were given powers to act to remedy defects in the hospital's drains. With the coming of the severe smallpox epidemic in January 1902,

Colonel Morgan was given further powers to close the hospital to visitors and to take any other steps which he thought were appropriate in order to protect the in-patients. The out-patient department was closed, except for the most urgent referrals, on two separate occasions that year and no communication was allowed between the clinic and the in-patient departments. No gifts except flowers were accepted, but by August:

> in consequence of the depression prevailing in the wards through the exclusion of visitors, [they] may be admitted and . . . the Resident Medical Officer is to insist as far as possible on the revaccination of patients if there exists no medical or physical objection.

Any patient who refused vaccination was liable to be totally isolated or was not accepted for admission, and this situation continued for six months.

It had already been agreed that some form of policy was necessary on the arrangements for dealing with established cases of epidemic disease. Broadly speaking, the hospital did not accept any responsibility for coping with the common infectious conditions which occurred in the community. Nor, because of the grave risks involved to other people who were already ill, were patients who developed those conditions after being admitted to their wards kept there. It was believed that their only responsibility lay in dealing with those whose wounds became infected after operations and who sometimes presented such a grave risk that they had to be nursed in isolation. When a conference to discuss the problem was arranged, the representatives of the Board of Guardians, although invited, did not attend, but something resembling a modern approach to the problem was decided on by the hospital's representatives and the Medical Officer of Health, Dr Morgan. There were certainly inconsistencies in the procedure agreed to, but they arose largely because it was finally decided that the problem must be shared between the authorities concerned. All patients with a contagious disorder would have to be notified to the Medical Officer of Health and those with scarlet fever 'whether Surgical or not' were to be sent to the town's isolation hospital. Those with erysipelas were to be sent only under the most exceptional circumstances because of the risks to others (which were equally severe if they were to remain in the general hospital, of course), and anyone developing measles was to be discharged home. When typhoid fever occurred in the general hospital, those infected with that condition were to remain there. Under the pretence of creating a new policy (and in the absence of the Guardians), the conference decided that 'all mental cases and attempted suicides' were to be transferred to the Workhouse Infirmary, as they had been previously.

Having achieved a great deal of agreement on those issues, the Swansea Corporation then instructed the Borough Estate Agent to write to the Medical Officer of Health to ask if he could meet the hospital committee to discuss a proposal for treating patients with tuberculosis of the lungs. It was said to be 'the most widespread of all diseases' at the time and very few attempts had been made in Wales to provide treatment facilities. The hospital committee had already decided that no one with that diagnosis should ever be sent to the Convalescent Home because of the fearful risks involved. They were therefore uncertain as to whether they ought to accept what was obviously an attractive offer from the Swansea Corporation to build a series of chalets on the hill behind the Convalescent Home, whose staff would need to be involved in the care of those nursed there. Having been asked if she would approve of the plan, 'X', the mysterious benefactor, sought the opinion of Sir Henry Burdett of the British Hospitals Association. He believed that:

> it would be manifestly improper to entertain the suggestion of the Municipality of Swansea so far as the Convalescent Home is concerned

and the plan did not proceed.

In 1905, the National Association for the Prevention of Consumption and other forms of Tuberculosis had invited a member of the medical staff as a delegate to a congress on that disease in Paris. One of the retired physicians, Dr. D. A. Davies, had attended and he later lectured on the subjects discussed there at a local BMA meeting. From then onwards, Dr Lancaster, who was one of the honorary physicians, took a great deal of interest in what were viewed as being exciting new advances in the treatment of tuberculosis. He attempted to treat patients with this disease by inoculation with tuberculin (which is a protein that can be extracted from the organism which causes the condition). It was essential that this treatment should only be undertaken where facilities were available to measure the ability of patients to combat the infection (in the form of a test called the Opsonic Index).[31] Dr Lancaster had trained the House Physicians for this work and Miss Price was thought to be particularly skilled in that sphere. While, in the other laboratory specialties, specimens were sent to the Clinical Research Association for analysis, bacteriology became the first of those specialties to become established as an independent discipline within the hospital.

Part of the newly acquired isolation hospital was equipped as a Bacteriology Laboratory. Although the honorary staff were adamant that they would not have women doctors taking the surgical house posts, they were 'much pleased' with Dr Florence Price's performance as a House Physician and recommended that she should be allowed to continue for a further year. In 1907, impressed with the increasing importance of bacteriology and its bearing on their clinical practice, they were eager to augment the work already started at the hospital in that field. Miss Price was eventually appointed an Assistant Bacteriologist for a period of six months. Her salary of £30 a year was paid by Colonel Morgan and Mr John Aeron Thomas and after that period, she offered to serve in an unpaid capacity while steps were being taken to establish a permanent post in that specialty.

Dr Florence Price's career as a bacteriologist was short-lived. She resigned after two months on getting engaged to Mr Frank Thomas, the Ophthalmic Surgeon.[32] For more than two years afterwards, the work of the Bacteriology Department, thought to have been of prime importance before her appointment, was not discussed again. It continued, however, and it is probable that Dr Lancaster and his House Physician shared the burden. In 1908, there occurred a severe outbreak of spotted fever, or meningococcal meningitis, in Swansea when sixty-three people were taken ill with the condition. The epidemic was admirably dealt with by the Medical Officer of Health and his staff in the town's Isolation (or Fever) Hospital and it was never suggested that those patients should have been admitted to the general hospital. In the following year, a patient who was found to have diphtheria after being accepted into Dyer Ward was refused admission to the Borough Hospital 'as Swansea Hospital was supposed to have an Isolation Hospital of its own' (which had already been used for some time in order to relieve the pressure on the other wards).

Clinically, the institution was taking on more of a semblance to a modern hospital, and much that happened then gave the clinical work a new impetus. In 1905, the Royal Colleges of Physicians and Surgeons recognized the hospital as providing clinical teaching facilities for their qualifying examinations (L.R.C.P., M.R.C.S.) but that did not lead to a rejuvenation of the movement to found an undergraduate medical school. The amount of activity in the surgical department had increased greatly by the time of the 1908 Annual Report which stated that 1,739 surgical operations had been performed and that the Chairman's Appeal (greatly helped by Mr John Aeron Thomas's readiness to devote a whole week to soliciting contributions) had eventually produced more than £8,000. The Works Governors asked all their contributors to donate a further one and a quarter per cent of their earnings during any four weeks in 1911 but so many demands were being made on the scarce resources available that those efforts did little to ease the situation.

Such matters as the refusal of the house doctors to accept the appointment of another woman colleague and difficulties in transporting patients by means of the 'hand-ambulance', and later the cab and horse-drawn ambulance, were overshadowed by graver problems. About twelve women died in Swansea each year from 'the accidents of childbirth'. These were thought by the senior doctors to be often preventable if only facilities could be made available for the admission of pregnant women. In addition, during the twenty years that the Department for Diseases of Women had been open, far more of the serious gynaecological conditions had been made treatable by surgery and they were anxious that this change in emphasis should be recognized. So, for a period of seven years from 1912, the hospital had its own 'Physician-Accoucheur' (as well as another gynaecologist) who was solely concerned with treating the abnormalities associated with pregnancy. (It was then that the operation of Caesarean section—not mentioned in the hospital records and previously avoided by many doctors because of the dangers from haemorrhage and sepsis—was first performed in the hospital). In 1919, on the death of Dr Knight, the Physician-Accoucheur, he was not replaced and there is no evidence that the gynaecologist took over his work at that time.

All these events served to emphasize the need for more laboratory facilities. When it seemed that the differences between the hospital and borough authorities were as great as they had ever been, the honorary staff suggested in June 1910 that a Bacteriology and Pathology Department should be set up in conjunction with the Borough Council, with the Medical Officer of Health acting as Honorary Bacteriologist and Pathologist to the hospital and as Director of the laboratory. It was also hoped to appoint another doctor as a full-time assistant who would be responsible for most of the day-to-day work, except for the Vaccine Therapy. By then, that was an integral part of the clinical work which was used in treating a variety of established infectious conditions including those which had developed after surgical operations, and was to remain the responsibility of one of the physicians.[33] The laboratory should be sited at the hospital and by allowing it to serve the whole of west and mid-Wales, it was thought possible that it could become 'in part self-supporting'. It had been established by the BMA that as many as 117 doctors were prepared to submit clinical material to a new laboratory for investigation and it was hoped that, if a series of meetings to deal with the matter could be called, that number would prove to be sufficiently impressive for the Corporation to wish to co-operate.

The scheme was not received with great enthusiasm and it was decided to delay opening negotiations with the Council, almost certainly because the financial burden would have been too great. They had been unable even to afford a more efficient means of disinfecting their blankets and soiled clothing so that the Sanitary Authorities had been asked to undertake that work. It had certainly never been the Governors' intention in accepting the building from Cray as an isolation hospital that they should treat the whole range of common contagious disorders and yet, it seems as though they were at times under pressure to do so. Any further discussions between the two bodies, it was felt, would only serve further to emphasize the hospital's indebtedness to the Council (who, in fact, had only given away a building for which they had no further use).

The issue was complicated by Dr Edwards's decision to resign as Pathologist in order to devote his time at the hospital solely to electro-therapeutic work. The German physicist, Röntgen had produced X-ray pictures of human bones in December 1895 for the first time. It was in January 1897 (by which time the first reports of tissue injuries following exposure to radiation had been recorded elsewhere) that Mr Brook recommended that 'the Rontgen Rays apparatus be ordered' at a price which was not to exceed £30. The few references made to the use of the X-ray machine in those early years refer only to providing facilities for its use in the operating theatre, to supplying a couch for patients to lie on while they were being X-rayed, to 'recharging the xray battery' and to the use of alternative power supplies (from other batteries) at times of emergency. By 1905, the apparatus was to be used only by the medical staff, the Theatre Sister and the Theatre Nurse. Attempts were to be made to ensure that all X-ray photographs were carefully preserved and catalogued for future reference. In 1906, work of this kind was given a great stimulus with the presentation by the High Sheriff, Mr Herbert Eccles of Neath, of 'xray and other appliances' worth £92. 9s. 3d.

With the introduction of these expensive improvements in the service and the greatly increased amount of work being done in the Casualty Department, even more economies were necessary. In desperation, the doctors were asked to impress on the nurses the need for economy in the use of dressings and the Swansea Tramways Company were asked for the right to place collecting boxes on the town's tramcars.

Dr Edwards was 'instructed' to write to an expert on X-ray work for advice on the equipment in his new department and when the walls had been lined with lead and wooden shutters provided for the windows 'to keep out every ray of light', his colleagues from Birmingham, who advised him, believed that the hospital would have 'a most complete X-ray department'.

Such self-sufficiency had certainly not been achieved in the field of pathology. In June 1911, dismayed at the Borough Council's failure to respond to the possibility of opening a joint Pathology and Bacteriology Department, Mr Roger Beck wrote to the Secretary:

> I today open a Brook and Beck account ... to enable the immediate starting at the Hospital of a Pathology and Bacteriology department. Mr Brook and I undertake, if need be, to contribute £500 for one year's working. We hope that by that time the Corporation will have awakened to the discreditable fact that a town of the importance of Swansea should have to send elsewhere for information it ought to possess on the spot ...

It had even been maintained that some of the deaths which had recently occurred among in-patients were attributable to the lack of facilities in that specialty but in spite of that, by April 1912, all hopes of an agreement between the two bodies had been lost. Because of a threat that the extent of the work done in the new department would be limited, Mr Brook later withdrew his offer until some assurances for which he had asked were provided. It so happened that there were other issues which had directed attention from the development of the pathology services.

CHAPTER SEVEN

Crisis and the War: 1909–1919

> Social health is not a matter for the individual alone, nor for the Government alone, but depends essentially on the joint responsibility of the individual and the community for the maintenance of a definite minimum of civilised life.[1]

> No man in the prime of his life knew what war was like. All imagined that it would be quickly decided.[2]

THE arguments concerning the use of the services provided showed no signs of lessening. Eventually, in November 1909, it was irrevocably decided that after out-patients had been treated for periods of more than two months, an enquiry would be made into their financial circumstances. No medicines were to be dispensed to patients who were members of Clubs or Friendly Societies and so great was the concern that the hospital was not getting all its dues that the words 'Not to be used for begging purposes' were printed on all the insurance and other certificates issued to patients. But other people's attitudes were also stiffening. Already, *The Cambrian* had issued a timely warning that 'in these democratic days it won't do to run counter to the working man'. The working people in Swansea (or at least, their representatives on the Works Governors' committees) were showing even clearer signs of dissatisfaction with the extent of their say in the hospital's affairs. They were able to show that in Cardiff, the hospital authorities had to beg the Trades Council to come to their assistance only a short while after they had refused a similar request for greater representation.

Another, possibly more impressive, sign of change was that from 1909 onwards, it became apparent that Lloyd George (as Chancellor of the Exchequer) intended making some form of provision for insurance against sickness. It was in Swansea in that year that he made a pronouncement that has since been seen as opening up the way for the National Insurance Act two years later:

> There are those who through no fault of their own are unable to earn their daily bread... the sick, the infirm, the unemployed, the widows and the orphans. No country can lay any real claim to civilization that allows them to starve.[3]

It is quite unlikely that the significance of those words was appreciated by those who managed the hospital. As it happened, when the Act was finally passed, it was not concerned with general hospital treatment and, as the dependants of those insured were not catered for (apart from maternity benefit), the impact of the National Insurance Act of 1911 on the hospitals was expected to be relatively small.

The British Hospitals Association believed differently. They were sufficiently concerned to organize a conference in 1911 to discuss the possible effects of the Insurance Bill on the voluntary hospitals, and the Swansea Hospital was represented there by a Catholic priest, the Reverend R. B. Gwydir.[4] The main concern locally was that the new measure would not relieve their financial burdens. As both employees and employers (who between them in Swansea contributed about three-quarters of the ordinary income) were to be subjected to increased levels of taxation to pay for the benefits provided, it was feared that their contributions to the hospital would be lessened. Sir Henry Burdett predicted that the extent of the reduction would be as much as a half of the revenue previously available, and that half a million of the fifteen million people insured would need hospital treatment each year, although the extent of his concern was not known to the hospital's Board at that time. The views of the speakers at that conference strengthened the belief that some form of intervention was necessary if they were not to suffer badly as a result of the new legislation. Ultimately, their fears proved to be groundless as the Swansea work-force continued with their support in spite of the changes that had been brought about. It has been claimed that once the new services were operating properly, the burden on out-patient clinics was reduced. Under the new system it was said of the old systems of medical practice that:

> the bottle of medicine was just about to settle down on its death bed [when] the Act rejuvenated it....[5]

The extent of that rejuvenation reflected the changes in the organization of medical practice in Britain rather than any differences in the pattern of illness. None of that was known to the 200 or more people (of whom the Reverend Mr Gwydir was one) who heard at the conference that a deputation had already met Mr Lloyd George to voice their fears about the possible impact of the Act on the voluntary hospitals. They were not at all certain that they had been able to influence him to the extent where he would be prepared to amend his Bill. Equally

The Hospital, c. 1911. (*By kind permission of Mr and Mrs G. Jones.*)

Swansea motor ambulance, 1908. (*By kind permission of Mr W. R. Stock.*)

worrying was the possibility that the voluntary hospitals would be 'thrown upon the municipalities' so that patients from surrounding rural districts would no longer be admitted to them. In keeping with the wish expressed at the conference, the attention of the local Members of Parliament was drawn to the position of the Swansea Hospital. Later, a proposal to the hospital committee that the hospital should be able to receive payments in the same way that was proposed for the sanatoriums was defeated, possibly because of the fears of government interference in their affairs. Finally, it was decided by the hospital's Board that a committee be appointed:

> to confer with the Swansea Branch of the BMA with a view to joint action... to carry out the spirit of the British Hospitals Association resolution.

No support seems to have come from the Members of Parliament but the doctors' opposition to the Act became more apparent at that meeting.

The BMA had already drawn attention to the need for new provisions of the kind brought about by the Act but had obviously hoped for better terms for the doctors involved. Once those conditions became known, the extent of the grievances seemed to be severe enough to threaten its operation. An outburst in *The Times* accused Lloyd George of being 'content with an antiquated notion of medicine and of medical service [based on] a notion built of some vague knowledge of village clubs.'[6]

Not all the doctors were as greatly opposed to the measures. That was true even in Swansea, as is known from the autobiography of Dr Urban Marks, who joined the hospital's staff in 1912 (first as Anaesthetist, and later as Assistant Physician), but who had worked in the town for some time before that.[7] Even by December 1912, a British Hospitals Association meeting in London heard that almost half the total number of patients dealt with in the voluntary hospitals throughout England and Wales were insured and, although this may have been interpreted as a sign of success by those who supported the new law, the news was received with a great deal of gloom by those present. In the discussions on the plans which ought to be considered for dealing with the situation as it worsened, the Association's Chairman said:

> If the Act is properly worked, hospitals should be relieved of the treatment of insured persons... the Act will [then become] a distinct boon to the voluntary hospitals.

That was a view that was not generally held. A policy was agreed on that when medical benefits became available under the terms of the Act, insured patients should only be admitted to hospital at times of emergency and out-patients were only to be examined if the patient bore a letter from a doctor.

The honorary staff's next course of action was of greater importance. Already suspicious to the extreme of the effects which the new Act might have on their own practice, they submitted a resolution in which they expressed their sympathy with other Swansea doctors in their attempt to obtain better pay for their work with insured patients. The fact that they did not confine themselves to uttering condolences led to difficulties. They took to signing the pledge which the BMA had issued to its members and vowed that after that part of the Act which dealt with medical benefit came into force, they would refuse to deal with insured patients (except where there was an emergency) through 'the service of any voluntary medical charity'. Nor would they co-operate with other doctors who had accepted a contract to treat such patients. The House Committee referred the matter to the Board without discussing it and there is no record of their reaction at that time. The doctors themselves seem to have felt confident of achieving their aims without difficulty. In October 1912, an anonymous letter was received by the *South Wales Daily Post*[8] saying that a patient had been placed on the operating table at mid-day, was then given the option of going home at 6 p.m., before finally having his operation at 8 p.m. The reason for the surgeon's failure to attend is not known but as the matter was again referred to the Board for their consideration, it seems possible that his action took the form of a protest. No record was made of any discussions that might have taken place concerning the matter. It may not be altogether coincidental that some of the honorary staff chose that time to provide one of their periodic reminders of the large numbers of schoolchildren who continued to be sent for ear, nose, throat and eye examinations. This again was not discussed but the recommendation made by them that a large and centrally placed clinic should be built to deal with those problems was sent to the local authority for their opinion. (In spite of their strained relationships, the honorary staff continued to make recommendations concerning their work throughout this difficult period including the suggestion that a fourth resident doctor was necessary.)

The Number One Branch of the Dockers' Union wrote to ask if a round-table conference could be set up 'even now at the eleventh hour' in the hope that some form of satisfactory arrangement could be reached between them before the date of the deadline set by the doctors. The Mayor organized a meeting between six of the medical staff and six representatives from the Friendly Societies and Trade

Unions but nothing came of that. An abortive attempt was also made by the visiting staff to meet the House Committee but that failed with the formation of a Medical Aid Society in the town. Many doctors were opposed to the formation of such societies as they found their terms of service to be unrewarding; nor would they subject themselves to the authority of the societies' committees. Under those circumstances, it was inevitable that the medical men's attitude should harden further and they decided to restrict their services from April 1913. It is apparent that the medical profession in Swansea was not as united on this issue as they might have wished to be. In 1911, in a House of Commons debate on the National Insurance Bill, it had been said that 'no Friendly Society has ever had any difficulty in getting all the doctors it wants'.[9] The local Branch of the BMA had quite independently confirmed that view. They anticipated, quite correctly, that such a Society, once formed, would have no problems in recruiting doctors to work for them. Nevertheless, the honorary staff were slow to yield.

Their threat not to co-operate with colleagues of theirs who undertook such work, except in an emergency, caused concern but may not have been as powerful a weapon as had been anticipated. The Joint Conference that had been arranged ended without a solution having been agreed. Relationships with the Board were not improved after twenty-seven children were sent away from an Ophthalmic Clinic without being examined. Circumstances of that kind only served to exaggerate the differences between both sides. A plea from the ever-observant Burdett in his journal, *The Hospital*, that 'the honorary staff and the general committee [at Swansea] should confer'[10] produced no response. The Board was then forced to issue an appeal to the working men of the district, many of whom had threatened to withhold their annual subscriptions.

If that were to happen, it was believed that the debt of £15,000 could be increased to £20,000. Curiously, the first sign of a change in attitude came when the Swansea Division of the BMA decided in June 1913 (by 18 votes to 9) to ask the honorary staff to delay putting into operation their resolution until the end of that year as they were anxious to ensure the success of the new negotiations that were to be held. No explanation has survived for this volte-face by the Swansea doctors but it certainly seems that, in the end, they were far less complacent than were many members of the hospital's Board. Within weeks, the dispute between the hospital's medical staff and the workmen's representatives was over. The doctors accepted a lower fee than they had originally asked (ten shillings and six pence for caring for a family with children who were under sixteen years of age, instead of thirteen shillings). The only condition laid down by them may well offer an explanation for their willingness to accept the new terms so readily. They insisted that:

> the labour organisations guarantee to oppose the formation of any Medical Aid Society in the distict and to use their influence to break up those already formed.

With the acceptance of that principle, it seems that the medical men lost far less than had seemed likely.

It was later alleged by Mr Brook that the maladministration of the new Act in Glamorgan had a great bearing on the original cause of the dispute. He claimed that two of the most important principles agreed to, namely freedom of choice of doctor for each patient and liberation of the medical profession from lay control, were being interfered with by the commissioners responsible for administering the Act in Wales. His proposition that the commissioners should be censured was not put to a meeting of the hospital's Board and the matter was never again recorded as having been discussed. The only probable effect that the dispute had was to help to consolidate the Works Governors' view that they were under-represented on the Board and to encourage them in their attempts to correct what they regarded as being a serious fault.

Eventually, the working of the new Act led to a gradual fall-off in the number of out-patients being sent to the hospital. Before advantage could be taken of the decreased work-load, there were signs that problems of a more severe and lasting kind were soon to appear. In November 1911, the Matron, Miss Scovell, had been invited to become Matron of the Number Four General Hospital of the Territorial Service. Almost simultaneously, the War Office had asked for an undertaking that four nurses could be supplied to them 'in time of war'. In September 1912, one of the physicians, Dr le Cronier Lancaster, submitted a request that the Matron should be granted an extra week's leave every third year to enable her to take a course of training with the military services. By 1913, the medical staff and Matron were asked for assistance in training members of the Voluntary Aid Detachments (or VADs—'these ignorant amateurs' as they were called in the *Nursing Times*).[11] It was agreed that three women could attend the Casualty Department for two hours each day for a month and witness minor operations on Saturday mornings. In less than a year, that number had doubled and they were given elementary instruction in ward work at the request of the British Red Cross Society.

There is no indication that the nine different approaches made by the military authorities for help over the previous three years were ever construed by the Governors as having any serious or lasting effect for the hospital. It was not until four days after war had been declared in 1914 that the honorary medical staff met the House Committee 'to consider... working the Hospital in connection with the present crisis'. It was recommended to the Board that, with the exception of the North Wing, the hospital should be closed. All clinics were to cease and only ten beds would remain in the Convalescent Home. The Matron was asked to impress on the staff the need for the strictest economies and she was to obtain an extra month's supply of provisions at once. It was to be the Reception Committee's function to reduce as far as possible the number of beds in use and the wards emptied were to be placed at once 'at the disposal of the War Authorities'. Finally, the Red Cross Society was allowed 'all possible space at the hospital to store their war supplies'.

The announcement that all the honorary staff had been called up for military service was received with a surprising degree of calm. The Matron was ordered to report to a military hospital in London, Dr Clarke Begg the Vaccine Therapist took over the Red Cross Hospital at Sketty (which had fifty-three beds in 1917),[12] and the surgeon, Mr Isaac (who had replaced Mr Brook in 1913), became the Senior Medical Officer to the Swansea Defences. He at once asked for permission to admit a number of men suffering from 'minor maladies' for treatment and was given the use of the Isolation Hospital.

There were 114 other (civilian) patients waiting for admission and with 111 in-patients already there, the 90 beds which had been promised to the Army's Medical Department had to be reduced to 66 for the time being. The anger and frustration of both sides in the dispute over workmen's representation on the hospital committees were now channelled into making preparations to fight the common enemy, encouraged by the histrionic war-cries which regularly appeared in the local press. Denuded of virtually all its senior medical staff and with the use of the St Paul's Congregational Church schoolroom 'as a temporary hospital if it should be required', the Swansea Hospital was ready for a war that hardly affected many of its functions at all in the end.

By early September, a number of German prisoners had been accepted at the hospital for treatment and their eventual disposal 'was left to the discretion of the Chairman', Colonel Morgan. Much of the work continued uninterrupted. Tenders for the painting of the outside of the building were asked for and, for a time, the numbers waiting for admission continued to rise. The greatest inconvenience came because of the absence of the honorary staff and this was particularly true of the Eye Department as Mr Frank Thomas was required to spend much of his time in Cardiff.

From 1903 onwards, it had been estimated that in the event of a war, the military authorities would require 50,000 hospital beds to be made available for their use throughout Britain. Less than two months after the outbreak of war, it was realized that the great efforts made to reduce the number of in-patients had been largely unnecessary. The Deputy Director of Medical Services for the Western Command was asked if the facilities that had been offered to him were likely to be needed soon. His reply only served to confuse the issue even further; it had never been anticipated, he said, that all the beds offered should be kept empty until they were required by his unit, and they should be used whenever that was necessary to obviate any hardship on civilian patients.

On 19 October 1914, seventy-four wounded Belgian soldiers were transferred from the military hospital at Cardiff and it was realized that the remaining medical staff could not cope with the amount of work that was accumulating. Advertisements for temporary anaesthetists were prepared, and a request was made for the transfer of those members of the honorary staff stationed at Cardiff back to Swansea so that they could resume their normal work. Although this was thought unlikely to be permitted, it did ultimately come about through the willingness of the senior doctors to offer their services whenever they were available and in the locality. Before long, the prevalent view was that both the government and the hospital authorities had over-reacted with their preparations, and that steps should be taken to restart the civilian work on a peacetime scale. Some disquiet was expressed 'with regard to the class of patients' being sent from the military hospitals and Sir Alfred Mond, MP for Swansea (who later became Minister of Health), was asked if he could help to ensure that 'a better use [was] made of the beds at the disposal of the War Office'. By December, the Colonel at the Cardiff Military Hospital had agreed to the temporary withdrawal of patients referred by him so that the civilian waiting list might be reduced. At the same time, when the Matron returned to her duties at King's College Hospital, London, the committee informed her that she 'should choose our way or the other during the war'. The remaining members of the honorary staff were asked to reopen the out-patient department 'as a purely consultative department' with no active therapeutic role and with a very limited facility for dispensing drugs. The Christmas festivities were allowed to continue as usual except that they were not to extend beyond one day. Apart from occasional reminders, such as the offer of food sent by the Sydney Chamber of Commerce, the war and the problems it had threatened to bring already seemed more remote.

While the committee were anxious to continue offering as much help as possible to the government, the presence of infectious disease made it necessary for the Isolation Hospital to be made available at once. A later compromise provided for fifty beds to be placed at the disposal of the War Department on condition that they would provide 'reasonable notice'. The War Department was therefore informed by the hospital's Secretary that all the beds were required for the civilian population but that 'we recognize that the soldiers have the first claim'. By March 1915, the Board of Education had written to the Mayor of Swansea with a request from Lord Kitchener, then Secretary for War, that as many local school buildings as possible should be made available for use as military hospitals. Mr Brook raised this matter with the hospital committee and asked if it would be possible for the hospital itself to provide the nucleus of a military hospital of 100 beds. For this, additional ground to allow for the erection of new wards would be necessary. In order to allow for a fifty-per-cent increase in the number of beds already there, the medical staff recommended that, wherever possible, the wards should be divided down the centre by a partition so that more efficient use could be made of the already existing space. A shed was erected on the flat roof of one of the wards to take twenty beds. Between the South Wing, the Isolation Hospital and the Out-patients Department 140 extra beds were made ready for use. The offer was made only on condition that the new military hospital would accept the wounded 'direct from the front'. In spite of the problems which had accrued from staff shortages and large waiting-lists (neither of which were all that foreign to those who had worked there in peacetime), and although there were other far more important issues to be faced, it was thought that a Union Jack should be bought before the arrangements were considered to be complete. The Convalescent Home would now need to be used to its fullest possible extent and would have to take twenty-five beds. The Langland Bay Home and the Assembly Hall of the Swansea Working Men's Club were offered for use as an annexe as only twelve beds could be vacated within twenty-four hours at the hospital itself although in a grave emergency, they would take 'as many soldiers as possible'.

Not even any ladies could be found to take the House Physician's post even though the salary had been raised from £125 to £200. A student from the Middlesex Hospital, Mr J. W. Tudor Thomas, who later achieved great eminence as an ophthalmologist, attended as a 'dresser' (a term used in teaching hospitals for medical students undertaking surgical training) at a salary of £30. Mrs Frank Thomas offered her services to work in the mornings and this, together with the comings and goings of the honorary staff (when they were not required at the military hospitals), ensured that the civilian part of the hospital's work was maintained.

Claims by doctors for exemption from war service were dealt with by the local Medical War Emergency Committee. Although two of the Assistant Physicians were officials of that committee, applications on behalf of the resident medical staff were not accepted and they were asked to withdraw their requests to remain at the hospital. That decision brought a quick reaction from the Miners' Agent in the Swansea Valley who asked for, but did not get, an assurance that the 16,000 men represented by him could be told that there was available adequate medical cover. 'It was', wrote a member of Swansea's Medical War Emergency Committee, 'a question of supplying the army and letting the public take care of itself.'[13] Early in 1917, the two House Surgeons were told that they were first and second on the list of local doctors who were due to be called up for service with the Royal Army Medical Corps. Yet, during the year that had just ended, more than 8,000 out-patients had been attended to and there were more than 150 patients in the hospital at any one time. (It seems that there was no shortage of dentists. A deputation of qualified dentists asked for at least three dental surgeons to be appointed in order to cope with the increased need for the early treatment and prevention of disorders of the teeth.)

Of the serious problems facing the hospital, the extent of the money worries had continued to raise difficulties. In November 1913, the Capital and Counties Bank wrote to complain that there was 'no tendency to reductions' in the extent of the debt, which amounted to about £11,900. There was little that could be promised except the launch at the first available opportunity of that most unsuccessful of panaceas, a public appeal. By the Annual Meeting of 1916, however, it could be stated:

> The grave national trial has taught the public to give on a scale which was not thought possible a year and a half ago.

Indeed, the annual income for 1915 was almost £17,000 with the result that the ordinary debt had almost been wiped off (although the amount owing on the Building Account still exceeded £6,000).

Never at any time were the contrasts in attitude towards the other problems faced more marked or perplexing. As the effect that the war had on the hospital was never as great as had been anticipated, activities that were better suited to peacetime occurred frequently. In July 1916, a subcommittee was formed to consider a proposal to establish a Medical School within the University of Wales. (After considering the implications of that move, it was decided not to continue to involve the hospital in those discussions.)

Miss Scovell attended to discuss a scheme involving the acceptance of probationer nurses from Victoria Park Chest Hospital, London, as second-year probationers on the understanding that Swansea nurses should be sent to Victoria Park for six months' experience in thoracic medicine.

At the height of the problems concerning bed shortages, Principal Salmon of the Training College and Mrs Elsworth, who was the wife of one of the hospital's surgeons, were asked to prepare a report on the admission, training and examination of nurses. Their completed work took no account of the chaos that had been caused by the war. Of its recommendations, the only one accepted at the time concerned the lack of general education among new nurses. This, it was thought, could be corrected by their being required to read a simple textbook of anatomy and physiology before being accepted. If candidates were found to be seriously lacking in education, intelligence or in application, their services should not be retained. Should the deficit be in education only, the appointment should be postponed 'till she has made the necessary improvement'. From November 1917, enamelled metal badges were to be presented to nurses who completed their training.[14] Mr Beck suggested that the words *Amicus Humani Generis* ('Friend of the human race') would be suitable as a hospital motto, and that the badge should have those words inscribed on it, with the Borough Coat of Arms and an outline of the front of the hospital building.

One of the other great (and very real) concerns was that hospital staff other than nurses and doctors might leave, as far higher wages were available at the munitions factory at Pembrey. It was decided that it would not be possible to offer better pay to the ancillary staff as the debt on one of the accounts had grown to nearly £6,400. The promise of salary increases for the nursing staff had to be postponed. (At the same time, as a concession, the laundry staff's working hours were reduced to 7.30 a.m. to 6 p.m. on weekdays, while they were allowed to finish at 3 p.m. on Saturdays, except when there was 'lost time' to be made up.)

At times, the committee seems to have had difficulty in distinguishing between the most severe difficulties that faced them and the slightest of trials which barely called for comment. Trivial sources of irritation were dealt with as though they were of the greatest importance. At the height of the war, the Matron found time to complain about the conduct of the House Surgeon. He was one of the few remaining members of the medical staff and his work had been greatly increased in the absence of many of the visiting staff. When he asked for a late breakfast after being kept at his work for most of the previous night, the Matron asked that he should be severely castigated. Much was made of the fact that two of the male resident doctors had attended a farewell tea-party for the nurses in their sitting-room without having been invited, and although they were fully aware of the effect of the Medical War Committee's decisions, a horrified committee asked one of them to leave as soon as he could find another post. The Sunday services held in the hospital square continued to disturb the more seriously ill patients and it was asked that they should either be held elsewhere or that no band should be used.

Not all the problems faced were of such a trivial kind. When the house Cae Parc was bought from Mr C. H. Glascodine in order to provide living accommodation for twelve nurses, it was not realized that this would involve the hospital in a wrangle which would draw much undesirable publicity and take up more of the honorary solicitor's time than many of the other seemingly more substantial problems. The argument concerned the right of access to a garage which had been converted into an Ironing Room that was connected to the laundry by a covered passage. With the construction of another entrance from the laundry into the lane, the freeholders (who were the heirs of the person from whom the land for the hospital had been bought) objected, and much time was spent on both sides in removing and replacing the padlock put there by the freeholders. An offer of £400 for the freehold was refused and the arguments continued privately and in the press until 1916 when by sheer persistence, the hospital won its right to regard the lane as theirs to use.

Occasionally, there occurred a reminder that the war was still continuing when fifty beds were suddenly needed for seriously ill soldiers in July 1916.

On 25 April 1914, *The Times* recorded:

> A number of gentlemen interested in Swansea Hospital have decided to purchase £1,500 worth of radium and present it to the hospital.

It had been thought wise to take steps for the treatment of patients by radium or radium emanation and a Charitable Company was formed for that purpose. The initial aim was to buy 100 milligrams of radium at a cost of £14 a milligram. This would then be available free of charge to patients being treated in hospital but it could also be hired for those being treated elsewhere, at prices lower than those charged by the Radium Institute. After each shareholder's initial investment, with four per cent interest, had been repaid, the radium would then become the property of the hospital.

The original shareholders were Mr Elsworth, the senior surgeon, Mr Brook, Colonel Morgan and Mr John Aeron Thomas. Mr Brook wrote to the newspapers appealing for support and, within a month, £1,070 had been promised. After signing a receipt, doctors using the radium would not be held legally responsible for its safety providing that they exercised all possible care while it was on loan to them. Over the following two years alone, its use saved the hospital more than £200 in hiring costs.

The amount of clinical work to be done within the hospital fluctuated greatly from time to time. At one stage, the most junior of the four resident medical officers considered resigning because there was insufficient work for him to do. By contrast, Mr Frank Thomas was the only ophthalmic surgeon left in south Wales for most of the war. He had asked that Dr Tudor Thomas should be allowed to look after the Eye Department at Swansea, but in April 1917, Mrs Frank Thomas was appointed medical officer there at a salary of two guineas a week. In July, the two House Surgeons were given permission to perform any operations which they considered did not need the attention of a more senior doctor, and Mr Brook's offer to restart work at the hospital was accepted.

Of the civilian work at that time, little is known. One of the most distressing effects of the war on the civilian population occurred in the munitions factory at Pembrey, where the women workers occasionally developed TNT poisoning. It was arranged that they were to be admitted to hospital without delay.

Early in 1916, two separate clinical problems caused a great deal of concern in the town. There occurred an outbreak of septicaemia following childbirth in the Brynhyfryd district. Under peacetime conditions, this would probably have been dealt with in the hospital but with the war-time shortage of beds that was not possible. Of far greater concern in the long term was the increasing incidence of venereal disease. The Local Government Board had already instructed all councils to prepare schemes immediately for providing treatment. After a meeting with the Borough and County Council representatives, it was decided that such a plan could only be considered for one year in the first instance because of the shortage of doctors. The Board of Guardians were asked to continue to treat 'seafaring men and women of loose character [whereas] ordinary civilian, army and navy cases' would be dealt with in the hospital clinics, which were to be held three times a week. Four beds (two for each sex) were set up in the Casualty Block (which had been opened in 1913 by Sir Alfred and Lady Mond). There, the new Salvarsan (arsenic) treatment was to be administered under Dr Clarke Begg's temporary supervision.[15] In accordance with the Local Government rules, he was paid £2. 12s. 6d. for each session of work undertaken by him. The hospital's first male nurse, Mr Tuckett, was later appointed to help him, at a wage of £2. 10s. a week. The extent of the work can be gauged from the fact that, as patients were accepted from outside Swansea, claims amounting to £1,850 a year were made to the other local authorities concerned.

It had been hoped that it would be possible to build an extension to the hospital in an attempt to reduce the length of the waiting lists. An approach was made to the Ministry of Munitions, who decided that 'owing to urgent national requirements', they could not grant a building licence. Although discharged soldiers and sailors were not meant to be referred for treatment to civilian voluntary hospitals, a request was made by the War Pensions Committee asking for suggestions as to what steps could be taken to provide accommodation for those who had left the Forces and who required in-patient treatment. The Ministry of Pensions was prepared to provide money for any scheme which met its needs, and it was decided to take advantage of this offer. A hundred additional beds were thought to be required, and would be provided if the Ministry were to pay for the building and equipment, and pay five shillings a day for each in-patient and a shilling for each out-patient visit.

Mr John Aeron Thomas, the Chairman of the House Committee, held negotiations with the Ministry of Pensions. Although he was not given any definite indication that the scheme had been accepted, the committee felt confident enough to ask the architect to prepare the plans. It was estimated that the cost of the new building, which was to be placed on the south side of the Penllergaer Ward, would be £4,000. When the War Pensions Inspector, Dr Webb, visited, he accepted the proposals together with the suggestion that the Ministry should provide a further £3,500 for equipment, although part of the money would have to come from the British Red Cross Society and the Welsh National Fund.[16] The St Paul's Congregational Church schoolroom and some additional premises in Castle Street were to be used temporarily until the annexe was built, and tenders from builders were asked for. Within weeks, £3,500 of government money was made available and the balance of £4,000 was guaranteed by Mr Charles E. Cleeves. The tender submitted by J. and F. Weaver of Manselton was the lowest (£4,064) and was accepted, although, before the building was finished, they admitted that they had underestimated the cost of the materials that would be required. The building was opened in April 1919.

Three weeks before the end of the war, the out-patient department had to be closed because of the great epidemic of influenza that swept across Europe. The Armistice was therefore ushered in quietly at the Swansea Hospital, with the shortening of the laundry workers' working day by half an hour and, a week later, with an application for the return to civilian duties of the only three absent members of the medical staff.

Some months before the war had finished, the Works Governors, with whom there had not been any disagreements for many years, revived their attempts to gain more representation on the House Committee. This was severely opposed by those senior doctors still in Swansea, who promised to use every means in their power to prevent it happening. A requistion was signed by twelve Board members asking for a Governors' meeting to consider the changes in the rules that would be necessary to increase the number of workers' representatives to twenty-four on the Board and to eight on the House Committee.

Peace had been declared between the nations, but there were already signs that hostilities were about to recommence within the hospital.

CHAPTER EIGHT

Post-war Developments

> A hospital is a living organism, made up of many different parts... Its work is never done, its equipment is never complete... it is to try all things and hold fast to that which is good.[1]

THE hospital to which Dr Gabe, and his two more senior colleagues, Dr Quick and Mr Isaac, returned on being demobilized had changed. It had not treated as many front-line casualties as it had planned for at the beginning of the war but the staff who worked there had been subjected to stresses and uncertainty. With the increased complexity of life in the post-war period, the transition to providing a peacetime service was not an easy one. As an institution, it was increasingly affected at this time by the changes that had occurred in society in general and in medicine too.

The death of Dr Jabez Thomas coincided more or less with the resignation of Mr Elsworth as senior Visiting Surgeon in January 1919, and those events, as much as the end of the war, marked the closing of an era. Encumbered with a debt that would have been greater had it not been for the war and a waiting list that might have been smaller,[2] it now included women porters and a lady pharmacist among its staff, and soon an engineer 'with a knowledge of Electricity and steam' would be needed. In spite of the overcrowded wards that had once been fit for heroes to die in, the hospital now boasted a 'Carter's lifting bed' and a 'whirlpool water bath'—indications that the slow evolution of medical practice was even affecting Swansea.

Dr Jabez Thomas's last crusade had been at a Special General Meeting in September 1918 when he protested with some vigour against the proposal (which was ultimately successful) to increase the number of Works Governors on the Board of Management and on the House Committee, in the absence of several members of the honorary staff and the Board who were still on war service. Twenty years previously, his views would have mattered, but the twentieth century had brought with it new ways and although he cared little for them, they were firmly established.

In this new atmosphere, there was a general expectation that administrative changes would occur. The most surprising proposal came from a section of the Great Western Railway employees who asked that the Outdoor Honorary Medical Staff should be paid retaining fees for their work. This was refused as being 'entirely contrary to the principles which had led to the opening of the hospital', although due to extraordinary circumstances an exception had been made during the war years. The Works Governors decided to ask all their subscribers to raise their contributions to 2d. a week and at the same time, they arranged a meeting to discuss the 'Nationalization of Hospitals' at which the representatives of 100,000 men sent resolutions to the Prime Minister asking that the voluntary hospitals should be taken over by the state and 'supported by Imperial Funds'.

Not everyone concerned with the hospital was agreed on that issue. It was apparent to most of the Governors that there could be no return to pre-war days, but the ambitious ideas cherished by some of them might be viewed as being muddle-headed. There were those who wished to extend both the hospital and the Nurses' Home and it was suggested that the town's War Memorial Committee might usefully consider providing a Swansea War Memorial in the form of a new Nurses' Home. In spite of having raised this possibility, the committee made plans to buy another house in nearby Brunswick Street for £300. It was also hoped that another large building in Walter Road might be available at a price that was not to exceed £1,800, in addition to the two houses already bought for the home.

There were also other demands being made. Apart from the need for more beds in all specialties, there was an urgent request for a properly equipped isolation unit for septic surgical problems, the want of which was said seriously to have hampered the clinical work. The isolation unit eventually had to take the form of an army hut, while a temporary building on the roof of the Graham Vivian Ward was set aside for other infectious diseases. Extensions to the X-ray, Massage and Electrical Departments were asked for and agreed to. The Nursing Institute, with Sir John Talbot Dillwyn Llewelyn as its spokesman, believed that, with the changing needs of the locality, it was the hospital's responsibility to undertake to replace or rehouse the Institute (which had been based at a nearby house) quickly so as not to interfere with its work in the community.

As part of this general haste, it was suggested in August 1919 that Parc Wern, which had been occupied during the war as a Red Cross Hospital, and the adjoining land should be bought so that a new hospital could be built. The owner, Miss Vivian, was approached and was asked for the right to the first refusal on the property (even though the debt had risen to £15,000).[3] The first problem encountered was Mr Dyer's objection to the removal of the Dyer Ward from the old hospital which, he maintained, would contravene the terms of the Endowment Deed. He was told that it was intended only to transfer sixty beds there and that Parc Wern would merely be an auxiliary hospital. A compromise was eventually reached with the suggestion by the doctors that the Ophthalmic and Ear, Nose and Throat Departments[4] should be moved so that more space would then be made available at the main hospital for medical and possibly general surgical work. Even then, there was still an apparent lack of direction in planning for the future. The stables at the back of the hospital in Brunswick Lane had been bought for £600 and then leased for five shillings a week.

The generosity of Mr Roger Beck, director of a local steel works,[5] reached its height in March 1920 when he offered to buy Parc Wern together with about eighteen acres of land for the hospital. It was later renamed Parc Beck as a token of gratitude to him. The main house was thought to be suitable for use as an in-patient unit for fifty-three patients with staff quarters for nine nurses and at least five servants. The outbuilding, which had been used as a billiard room, would become an Ophthalmic Out-patient Department. In this way, there would be no immediate need for a new building. Mr Beck's benevolence was not altogether an unmixed blessing at first though. Various people who were concerned with the hospital continued to believe that they could make good use of the building. There was a slight threat to the original plan when one of the surgeons suggested that its best use would be as a post-operative surgical centre. Once that slight disagreement was resolved, the tenants of the two lodges were given notice to quit and a proposal to form a Garden Allotment Society on the spare land was approved. In May 1923, Dr Woods, the Resident Surgical Officer (who later became an honorary Visiting Surgeon and the first Orthopaedic Surgeon) asked that the possibility of having ten extra beds at Parc Wern should be considered to enable him 'to materially reduce the waiting list'. This suggestion led to the revival of the plans for a new hospital there, and a scheme was evolved for laying out the estate so that there would eventually be 500 beds available. A competition for architects who would be prepared to design the new building was organized and a prize of £500 was offered.

Matters were considerably complicated when a Swansea resident who was not connected with the hospital gave the impression that he was in a position to arrange for the sale of the existing hospital for £100,000, which would have more than paid for the new building at Parc Wern. Fortunately, no action was taken as a result of that, but, in October 1924, the subcommittee that had visited other hospitals to inspect the facilities provided by them submitted its report. The Ministry of Health recommendations that one acre of land should be available for every fifty beds were no longer considered to be adequate, but there was sufficient land at Parc Wern for something more ambitious to be considered. Although the actual wards at the old hospital were thought to be equal to the best of the places visited, the 'very inadequate accessories' on that site made it essential to plan for 400 beds which would be increased to 600 as means permitted. Those plans were made in spite of the fact that the debt had risen to almost £22,000.

To confuse matters (although it was not seen in that light at the time), a deputation from the Ammanford and Llandybïe Trades and Labour Council had already asked for support in setting up a cottage hospital in the Amman Valley. It was intended that it would have about twenty-five beds and would be affiliated with the Swansea Hospital. The committee of inspection appointed reported that the YMCA premises at Ammanford would be suitable for adaptation for use as a branch hospital. Interest was later transferred to Pontamman House, which it was believed could be bought for use as an annexe to the main hospital. The owners, Mr and Mrs Folland, not only offered the house for that purpose when they were told of the plans, but agreed to endow it almost totally when the conversion was being undertaken.

In December 1922, the Clydach Works Governors met to consider the possibility of opening a small hospital there. Eventually it became established practice for some of the smaller cottage hospitals which catered for the same area as the larger hospital to assert that they were entitled to a part of the contributions made by workmen from their own districts. Even though there was some doubt as to whether they relieved the main hospital of a proportionate amount of work, by October 1925, the Clydach Hospital authorities had set a new pattern by issuing an apparently unsuccessful public appeal asking that their hospital should be entitled to a share of such contributions.

Following the industrial depression, the debt had risen to nearly £29,000 in 1922. The Works Governors, always anxious to increase the income whenever that was possible, suggested in April of that year that the large numbers of shop assistants, teachers, clerks and any other people who were employed in small businesses but who had never contributed regularly, should be invited to join the Contributory Scheme and their delegates eventually became known as the 'Group B Governors'. Consequently, it was believed that the darker days were over. Even though the average cost per bed was £176. 1s. 9d., with about 210 beds occupied constantly, the income for 1922 at last exceeded the ordinary expenditure by just under £200.

The attitude of the Governors to private practice was complex and bewildering. In October 1926, the South Wales Nursing Institute asked for permission to build a new nursing home on land at Parc Wern. The Institute later withdrew its application but it was the view of the honorary staff that the pattern established in many voluntary hospitals by then would have to be followed in order to provide an additional source of income and that:

> the Swansea General Hospital will, at no distant date, be compelled by circumstances to cater for paying patients.

The reluctance to take this step did not, apparently, stem from any objection on the part of the Works Governors. They, presumably, realized that if it were not for the private practice which was the mainstay of the senior staff's income, they would not have been in a position to work unpaid at the hospital. It was the fact that it would have violated the principle laid down in the early nineteenth century that its services were to be made available to all who needed them but were unable to pay, that was responsible for the persistent objections to the acceptance of private patients at that time. By and large, that early principle had been adhered to but there was no universal agreement as to what constituted financial hardship. The Reception Committee still reserved the right to enquire into patients' circumstances and to discharge anyone where it was thought appropriate to do so, providing that there were no overriding medical reasons produced by the medical staff.

It was of some help that the attitude of the Friendly (or Approved) Societies had changed, with the proposal to turn over any surplus money from Societies that had been disbanded with the passing of the 1911 Act to the voluntary hospitals. It had been estimated that about a half of those medically insured throughout the land were members of Approved Societies so that the decision made by them to hand over a proportion of their disposable funds to the voluntary hospitals was greatly welcomed. With the passing of the new Act, the Joint Committee of Approved Societies had estimated that there were fifteen million people in Britain who were already insured and they made it known to the British Hospitals Association that there was available an average surplus of about a pound per member. Of that, about thirty per cent could be spent on benefits in kind spread over five years, of which hospital treatment could be regarded as one. So, by December 1921, the attitude of the Friendly Societies had altered greatly with their recognition of the need to contribute regularly to the voluntary hospitals for 'the services which have been rendered gratuitously to their members for many years'. More than £200,000 was made available throughout Britain of which the Swansea Hospital was to receive a proportion on the understanding that it must be used to meet the deficit on ordinary maintenance and expenditure.[6] The hospital found some of the conditions laid down by the Joint Committee to be unacceptable; these may have concerned the giving of priority to the Societies' members. Nevertheless, the money was acceptable and was accepted. There were, however, some doubts about the wisdom of such a course of action. On 18 March 1921, the *Pall Mall and Globe* published a warning which echoed the thoughts of many who concerned themselves with the voluntary hospitals. They were 'in hearty agreement' with the proposal to dispose of the surplus funds in this way, as the voluntary hospitals had borne so much of the brunt of treating insured patients. They feared, though, that the acceptance of money from semi-public funds would need to be closely scrutinized as this might be followed by increased public control (which is exactly what the Works Governors at Swansea had proposed).

It became known in November 1924 that appeals for funds from some English hospitals were being circulated in south Wales. It was decided, therefore, that a series of advertisements appealing for money for the Parc Wern project should be prepared, in the hope that the ambitious nature of the new venture would divert attention (and money) to the local undertaking. It was soon realized that the upsurge in unemployment in the 1920s was to bring about a sharp decrease in the hospital's income and it was slowly becoming obvious that the plans for the use of Parc Wern were too ambitious at a time when the hospital owed a large amount of money.

Irrespective of the size of the debt, new accommodation had to be found for the nursing staff. A new Nurses' Home at Parc Beck would have cost £12,000 and an effort was made to proceed by launching another special appeal. Such appeals sometimes produced fairly generous responses in the short term without ever providing a permanent solution to the money problems. All patients who were not members of a Workmen's Contributory Scheme were, in future, to be asked for a donation. Shortly afterwards, Lloyds Bank made one of its exceedingly rare and polite enquiries about the possibility of a reduction in the size of the overdraft. The Secretary produced a special report in which he recommended that extra office staff should be employed specifically to raise funds. His rather ambitious recommendations were not accepted in entirety. But it was agreed that an organizer should be appointed solely to be concerned with attempting to increase the voluntary subscriptions, and that a clerk was needed as payments from employers, insurance companies and Approved Societies were not being effectively dealt with. As the plans for the Amman Valley Hospital did not materialize (with Mrs Folland's decision that it was to become a maternity hospital run independently of the Swansea Hospital), £10,000 of the money bequeathed in her husband's will eventually formed the basis of the new appeal.

In 1926 a thorough investigation of the hospital's financial position was asked for, and this was undertaken by a local accountant. The main cause for concern was the continuing increase in the extent of the overdraft, which had grown from about £7,000 in 1916 to nearly £30,000 in 1925. There was no evidence of want of economy or lack of good management, and this was borne out by the fact that the cost per head for the previous year was £154. 2s. 6d. This was more than was spent by the infirmaries at Bristol and Cardiff but less than those at Newport and Gloucester and was therefore considered to be satisfactory. Much was made of the 'splendid support' which the people of the district gave to the hospital (with the exception of the Swansea Corporation which, in comparison with the Cardiff Town Council, was donating only a tenth of the money which might have been expected of it).

In spite of the apparently optimistic and almost euphoric tone of the 1926 report, the total excess of expenditure over income continued to thwart many developments that were necessary to keep up with advances in medical treatment. Any available means of making money had to be sought, and a great deal of energy was expended in producing relatively small sums. Collecting boxes taken around the local theatre, the Albert Hall (by nurses in uniform who had 'volunteered' for the task in their off-duty time) when Mr Lloyd George was given the Freedom of the Borough in 1923, raised a useful but still small sum. Thought to be of more value was the offer of the 1926 National Eisteddfod organizers to leave their pavilion on its site in Swansea in the hope that profit-making events could be arranged. Although that did not succeed, the Executive Committee of the Eisteddfod donated £1,000 for which they were entitled to have a commemorative plaque placed above a bed in one of the wards. Again, it provided no permanent solution to the problem of providing an ever-increasingly expensive service at a time of industrial depression. In April 1926, with the aid of the Red Cross Society, the Works Governors and the nursing staff, the first 'Egg Week' was organized when 106,410 eggs were received by the hospital. They were meant for use in the hospital and became a most valuable annual source of income up until the time of the Second World War (when often egg-powder was donated instead).[7]

Although almost half the subscriptions came from those employed locally, annual subscribers were still able to claim privileges under the antiquated system that had been in operation for more than a century whereby a ten-shilling subscriber was entitled to nominate one out-patient for treatment at any time. The only significant difference that had occurred since 1818 was that the privileges allowed had become more generous in some instances as the demands on the services had increased.

In October 1921, the Voluntary Hospitals Association came into being in order to administer the government grant of half a million pounds to the voluntary hospitals. The Association proposed setting up a committee for Glamorgan, and Swansea was to be allowed one member. It later became known through the Borough Health Committee that £13,000 would be made available for the whole of the county's voluntary hospitals of which more than £4,000 would be for the Swansea Hospital with a distinct possibility that another £2,000 would be added later.[8]

More and more often, the hospital was finding that it no longer had a monopoly on the provision of specialized treatments in the locality. The challenging of its rights by the smaller hospitals was already proving to be a great problem. There was much confusion in the Governors' attitude to other bodies which had a statutory duty to provide medical services. Later, these bodies (particularly the local authorities) were to become formidable opponents and were viewed as (and frequently were) intruders. Sometimes though, outside intervention was acceptable and some of the newly-acquired functions of such bodies were welcomed. The gradual expansion of the Schools Medical Service had been hampered by the war and while some of its work was still done at the hospital, it was considered best that no further assessment of throat, nose and ear problems in children should be undertaken, as that was supposed to be the sole responsibility of the Medical Officers of Health. The decision by the Borough Council to form such a clinic led to a letter from the hospital being sent to all local authorities in south-west Wales urging them to organize similar services. The Corporation had still not fulfilled its obligations in that field a year later. A new arrangement was then made whereby the hospital undertook this work but the local education authority became responsible for paying the medical staff.

The Glamorgan County Council attempted to form its own specialized services for schoolchildren in 1921 and appointed a School Oculist and Medical Inspector. The hospital committee's response to that appointment was swift. From then on, each child referred to the hospital would be charged on an individual basis and the most basic of the rules, namely that free treatment was to be made available to those who could not afford it otherwise, was temporarily forgotten in the desire to take advantage of the money which was available from education authorities. (The Breconshire County Council, with its smaller population, made no attempt to provide such a service although they complained that the fee of one and a half guineas charged by the hospital for each patient was 'very high'.)

In the adult specialties, they were also difficult times. Dr Quick, whose release from the army in order to take over the work in the Venereal Diseases Department had not been allowed during the war, returned to the department and found by May 1919 that he was unable to cope with the increasing numbers of patients referred there. It was not unusual for him to have to deal with eighteen new patients and to have to administer as many as forty intravenous injections in a clinic that was meant to be of two hours' duration. As he had already been given the status of a full ophthalmic surgeon on condition that he undertook out-patient work on two whole days in the week, he complained that it was 'manifestly impossible to carry on like this without degenerating into a sixpenny dispensary type of clinic'. It was then agreed to appoint another doctor so that six clinics could be held each week. Later, as the diminishing number of attendances at the hospital's VD clinics had been discussed at a meeting of the town's Health Committee, the Town Clerk was informed that this decrease had only occurred since the Corporation had established its own clinic for females in the upper part of the town. At the same time, the Ministry had expressed a great deal of concern that gonorrhoea was not being treated sufficiently effectively (largely because women tended not to continue with treatment for as long as was necessary).

The Ministry of Pensions had asked for permission to increase the number of beds allocated to them but this was refused as they were not thought to be making full use of the beds already available. Their request to borrow facilities to set up an orthopaedic clinic which would be organized by them was also refused. In other towns, the Ministry had made their own arrangements in the setting up of such clinics, and as no agreement had been reached with the hospital by April 1920, they were prepared to follow the same plan in Swansea.

A greater degree of agreement was reached with the Corporation at a conference to discuss the treatment of the war pensioners' children who suffered from orthopaedic disabilities. Relationships with that body, often precarious, were further damaged soon afterwards when the Medical Officer of Health went on record as saying that it was not possible for children with orthopaedic disabilities to be treated in Swansea and that they had to be sent to Cardiff at great expense to the ratepayer. The reply sent to the Mayor was more restrained than might have been expected:

> [the statements made] are absolutely untrue, misleading [and]

detrimental to the prestige of our town and the Hospital and particularly the Honorary Medical staff... Orthorpaedic (sic) Surgery is and always has been a very important feature of the surgical work of the Hospital...[9]

Since orthopaedics then involved a sharing of responsibility (between the hospital, the education authority and the Ministry of Pensions), it was virtually guaranteed that disagreements should occur about the management of orthopaedic problems. When the new Orthopaedic Centre was opened at Victoria Park in the autumn of 1921, no notification was sent to the hospital of the Ministry's intention to transfer their work to the new unit. Their plans were ambitious and included the setting up of a special orthopaedic surgical centre in Swansea with a number of affiliated clinics which would be supervised by an orthopaedic surgeon. The Victoria Park Centre was to be a sub-centre specializing in electrical and massage treatment and run by the Order of St John, who would be given a grant for that purpose.

By June 1921, the Ministry was being accused of not settling its accounts in accordance with the agreement originally made for the treatment of war pensioners. It owed £1,565 and was told that if it did not pay within some weeks, its patients would no longer be accepted. Five years after their erection, under the arrangement with the government authorities, the temporary buildings should have been demolished, but as those wards were fully occupied, a year's extension on their use was allowed by the Borough Council. At the same time, the Ministry of Pensions made it known that it would no longer require the facilities there.

It was a stimulating time for those in clinical practice. No further mention of the possibility of forming a medical school had been made for a considerable time. In March 1922, the Examining Board in England, representing the Royal Colleges of Physicians and Surgeons, confirmed that the hospital was still recognized as providing the experience necessary for their examinations but that only six months (either in Medicine or Surgery) could be spent there. The senior medical staff were convinced that students would gain greatly from spending more time at the hospital 'on account of the excellence of the clinical material to be seen there', but the maximum period allowed was not extended. Later in that year, the Dean of the Faculty of Medicine at the Welsh National School of Medicine at Cardiff wrote asking numerous questions:

> with a view to submitting the whole matter of the relationship of Swansea General Hospital with the School, to the University.

The medical and nursing staff in 1919. In the second row are Mr Brook (fourth from the left, seated), the Matron, Miss Scovell (fifth from left) and Dr le Cronier Lancaster (sixth from left). The lady holding the dog is probably Dr Florence Price. (*By kind permission of Miss Mair Davies.*)

The honorary staff had already revised the regulations regarding the acceptance of students. Medical students were expected to offer some service in return for their tuition, should attend on six days in every week and, in spite of the Royal Colleges' ruling, must spend at least a year working there.

The increasing importance of the pathology services had become more apparent. Since Dr Edwards had relinquished his responsibilities in that field in 1911, there had been no one to replace him, partly because the negotiations with the Borough Council had been fruitless. That fact, together with the coming of the war, had very considerably delayed the development of pathology as a separate specialty in Swansea.

In February 1919, it was recommended to the Governors that, for three years in the first instance, a full-time Pathologist should be appointed at a salary of £750. The post was offered to Dr Arthur F. S. Sladden, who was the hospital's first properly trained pathologist and who shortly transformed the practice of his specialty in the locality.[10] A new, fully-equipped laboratory was to be constructed and an application was made to the Home Office for a licence to inoculate animals. Dr Sladden also submitted a scale of charges which he proposed should be made known to doctors and public health authorities who might wish to make use of his department's services. It was not long before the extent of the new pathologist's activities were widened. He became the first Home Office Specialist Medical Referee in Swansea and had the responsibility for investigating the incidence and cause of pitch cancer among patent fuel workers, again at the express wish of the Home Office.

The new laboratory, opened in May 1920 by the President of the Royal College of Surgeons, Sir George Makins, was named the Beck Laboratory to commemorate Mr Roger Beck's donation of the building and equipment, and his undertaking to guarantee it financially for the first three years. Mr Brook's contribution was recognized by naming a room in the laboratory after him. The opening was a spectacular occasion. At 3.30 p.m., Dr Lancaster, who had retired as senior Visiting Physician some months before, took the chair and after Mr Beck had presented Sir George with a gold key, an address was given by Professor Hepburn, the Professor of Anatomy at University College, Cardiff. That evening a dinner was arranged by the medical staff at the Hotel Metropole to mark what was the beginning of yet another new era.

Dr Sladden's first annual report had been described as 'highly gratifying' and his application for an increase in salary of £250 with the creation of a new position of Assistant Pathologist at a salary of £500 was unanimously recommended to the Board.[11] In that year (1919–20), 3,820 different examinations had been carried out in his department. Three years after his appointment, half of the in-patients were being investigated by the Pathology Department. Of those, 100 patients had investigations for anaemia, 150 cases of cancer had been confirmed and 80 samples of cerebro-spinal fluid had been analysed where 'meningitis or Nervous Diseases' were suspected. Dr Sladden was already working on the use of a new method of testing whether diphtheria carriers needed to be isolated or not. He also found time to complete for the Home Office his preliminary report on the examination of patent fuel workers. The 'cordial spirit of cooperation' that existed with the Swansea Public Health Authority was noteworthy, and at that time, between eighty and ninety per cent of the laboratory work undertaken for them was concerned with the diagnosis of diphtheria.

One of the most exciting innovations in the history of medicine occurred in 1921 with the discovery of insulin. It became available in Swansea for the treatment of diabetes mellitus about two years later. After he had been using it for eight months, Dr Clarke Begg, by then a Visiting Physician, wrote a book based on his experience of treating more than seventy diabetics by this means.[12] It had been, he wrote, 'one of the epoch-making events in the treatment of disease'. He was convinced that it was now possible to treat patients with that condition with hope and confidence, 'knowing that we can usually restore them to health'. Later, there was to be a great deal of argument about payment for this expensive form of treatment. Those catered for under the provisions of the National Insurance Act were entitled to have their treatment free, and on being discharged from the hospital, non-insured patients were provided with insulin if the physician regarded them as being 'suitable cases' (but that state was never defined). Although 'many lives were saved', the expense incurred was considerable. A special plea was made to the government asking that the manufacturers of insulin should be provided with duty-free alcohol so that the cost of extraction of the product was lessened. Ultimately, it was the Borough's Medical Officer of Health, Dr Thomas Evans, who made it possible by the most ingenious means for needy patients who lived in the town to be given their insulin without payment. He discovered that Section 133 of the 1875 Public Health Act, which became law long before insulin had been discovered, allowed any local authority to 'provide a temporary supply of medicine and medical assistance for the poorer inhabitants of their district'. The Town Council accepted his argument that, as that act had not been repealed, they were still entitled to take advantage of its benefits.

There were also other important developments occurring at that time. In May 1925, Swansea's first known blood donor was mentioned in the committee minutes, when the members wished to:

> convey to Mr John Williams of 4 Annexe Terrace, the thanks of the committee for his kind attention in giving blood for the transfusion of a patient.

Six months after that, the Secretary was:

> instructed to take steps to form a panel of persons willing to give blood to patients at the hospital. The Resident Surgical Officer [was] to consult the Secretary in cases where remuneration might be given.

The Swansea Radium Company had continued to allow its stocks to be used according to the original agreement. In November 1927, however, the hospital committee accepted responsibility for insuring the radium and later attempted to buy the company's shares in the hope that it could provide a rental service for use in private practice. This was refused by the shareholders. Having had the matter drawn to their attention, the shareholders asked that from then onwards, all patients who were prescribed this treatment should have an enquiry made into the circumstances so that a charge might be made whenever appropriate. The House Committee refused the request whereupon they were told that the radium would be withdrawn from use unless they accepted the new terms. It was the Managing Director of the *South Wales Daily Post*, Mr David Davies, who resolved the situation by offering to buy the radium for the hospital for £1,000. At least £2,000 were needed and an appeal was launched for the remainder of the money. Three offers were received from people who were prepared to donate their investments in the concern to the hospital but the company's articles prohibited the transfer of shares to anyone other than shareholders. The appeal produced more than £2,700 and stocks of radium worth £3,000 were bought. It became apparent that no patients had been neglected as a result of the Board's decision and work in the Radiology Department was able to proceed undeterred.

Indeed, the Radiology Department was so busy that requests from the education authority to treat ring-worm had to be refused. The prison authorities had to be told that if they were prepared to pay for X-ray work, they should refer their problems to the radiologists privately and not to the hospital. By that time (in 1929), the first casualty from the use of X-rays had occurred in the hospital when a member of the staff developed dermatitis as a result of his duties in that department. It was uncertain as to whether occupational dermatitis was a scheduled industrial disease or not at that time. Consequently, when a claim was made against the hospital, it was not known if it should be dealt with under the provisions of the Workmen's

Compensation Act of 1906 or the common law. (Although the condition was to come within the scope of that Act shortly afterwards, at that time it was not a scheduled industrial disease. Presumably, the committee's attempt to ensure that such matters should be dealt with under the workings of the Act stemmed from a fear that if a legal action were to occur under the common law, it might be inferred that neglect on their part had occurred.)

In 1923, Dr Edwards became sufficiently concerned about the dangers connected with using the X-ray machine that he suggested that an expert from the National Physical Laboratory should be invited to inspect the apparatus. With the appointment of two Honorary Assistant Radiologists, an X-ray Therapy Room was set up and £1,500 was spent on an electrocautery, diathermy and new X-ray equipment to coincide with the change-over from the use of Direct to Alternating Current.

In December 1925, a circular was sent to all the doctors in the district calling their attention to the abuse that had been made of the use of the X-ray Department and asking for their co-operation to prevent it recurring. The fact that the number of X-rays taken had increased from 4,141 to 8,274 in one year was actually probably more a reflection of changing trends in medical practice than of any actual abuse. That idea had not occurred to the hospital authorities and, because of the exceedingly heavy cost of maintaining that department, a contribution box was 'placed in the care of the Sister and patients given an opportunity of contributing'. In September 1925, attention was drawn to the fact that special privileges (of an unspecified kind) were being extended to doctors who represented insurance companies where X-ray sciagrams were taken at the hospital for their use. This led to further fears that the hospital was being greatly abused as the facilities were being made use of for compensation purposes, and this in turn helped to widen the rift between the workmen and the honorary staff.

Not a great deal is known of the practice of dental surgery in the hospital from the time of the appointment of the first Surgeon-Dentist, Mr F. J. Clouston Scott in 1869. His successor, Mr H. J. Thomas, took up his work in 1891, and in 1910, it was suggested that the department should be considerably enlarged 'so as to include conservative dentistry' (although that recommendation was not accepted). Two honorary Dental Surgeons were appointed in 1920 for a period of two years and they were expected to attend on one day a week and to be available for emergency work.[13]

Legal actions against the hospital were uncommon. In May 1924, a difficult situation arose when the Ammanford District Collieries Joint Committee complained that an X-ray report received on one of their members was not considered to be satisfactory. Their doctors had asked for a report from another source and had found the difference between the two to be 'terrible'. It was alleged that the hospital's Radiologist had failed to diagnose a fracture of the ribs but an independent examination by two radiologists from the Royal Gwent Hospital at Newport confirmed the original findings and both sets of X-ray films were to be sent to the President of the British Radiological Society for him to arbitrate. No more was heard of the matter.

In 1919, Judge Rowland Rowlands had severely criticized the medical staff in a court of law (in an action that was never mentioned in the hospital records) for failing to keep clinical notes. He refused to accept a submission that a severe shortage of doctors justified this:

> Not one of the doctors made a single note of what was done at the time... [I] have to conclude that one or the other is telling a lie... of the very thing that is the cause of death there is not a single mention... doctors cannot defend themselves [without notes] against the charge of falsehood, which was made on the present occasion.[14]

In spite of that, it was not until November 1925 that the honorary staff asked for a revision in the existing antiquated system for the registration of patients. They recommended that an experienced doctor should be appointed as Registrar to supervise the duties of the other resident staff and to deputize for the visiting surgeons in their absence. He would be required to be a Fellow of one of the Royal Colleges of Surgeons and would be paid £350 a year, rising to £450 after two years. A full-time clerk would be required to assist him and as forty new beds were being planned, an additional junior resident doctor would be required. Mr C. J. Cellan-Jones was appointed as the first Registrar, and from the outset he made his presence felt. Soon, he was able to demonstrate that increasing attempts were being made to examine closely all the facets of patients' lives in order to give them more effective treatment. It was, for example, unusual for the medical staff to take any interest in the means by which their patients travelled to the hospital, but in spite of the great energy with which he performed his clinical work, he was not too busy to draw attention to the unsuitability of the town's ambulance for carrying seriously ill patients. He had seen as his first major task the clearing of the surgical waiting list. A year after being appointed, he had reduced the number waiting for admission from 523 to 359 and there had been an increase in the number of admissions of more than 500. In March 1927, his title was changed to that of Medical Superintendent and he was the only doctor in the history of the hospital to have held that office.

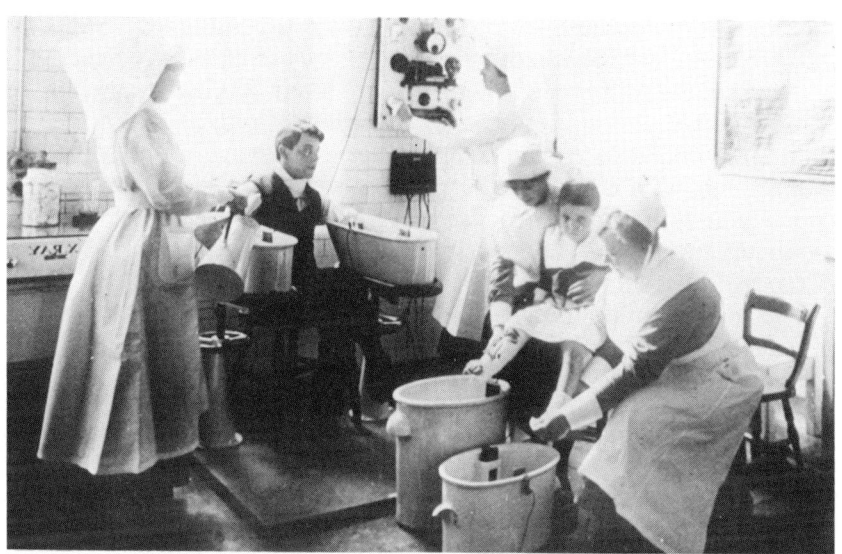

Treatment room in the Out-patients Department.

Domestic staff, 1924. (*Pictures by kind permission of Mr Rowley Davies.*)

There were also signs that the rules were old-fashioned and inadequate for the changing needs of the times. After twenty years, the honorary staff were required to resign. Even though he was still a comparatively young man, Mr Frank Thomas's term of office (with four years added to take account of his war service) came to an end and brought to a close in 1924 two generations of his family's direct connection with the hospital. He was made a Life Vice-President with a seat on the Board and was given the permanent use of two beds in the Eye Department.

The general uneasiness that was so much a sign of the times had manifested itself in the sphere of nursing by then. During the war, the Chairman of the British Red Cross Society's Joint War Committee had written to ask for support in establishing a College of Nursing. The hospital committee had been 'in sympathy' but preferred that the matter should be referred to the British Hospitals Association. There had already been attempts to pass bills which were concerned with the registration of nurses, although members of the nursing profession themselves were far from being united in their views. The College was eventually formed in March 1916 and in December 1919 an Act was passed which set up the General Nursing Council and was concerned with the formation of a Register of Nurses. Until 1923, applications to be admitted to the Register could be made by nurses with a minimum of a year's experience at a recognized hospital.[15]

Mr Brook expressed his uneasiness at the criteria that would be used in deciding whether nurses already trained would be accepted or not. He believed that membership of the College of Nursing, which was quite a separate body from the General Nursing Council, might prove to be an unfair advantage. As that College had refused to admit nurses from hospitals of less than forty beds, he claimed that the new criteria were:

> unjust and unwarrantable and calculated to seriously jeopardise the means of livelihood of a very large deserving body of women among whom are many with nursing credentials of the highest order.

At his request, a meeting was arranged between six members of the House Committee and the representatives of the College of Nursing. There, some concern was expressed not only that experienced nurses might be unjustly excluded from the Register but that those trained in Cottage Hospitals would not be allowed to attempt the new examination even though they might not have been aware of the new regulations when they accepted posts there.

As might be anticipated, local discussions of the kind led by Mr Brook were not likely to be particularly effective. Undaunted, he continued to take an active part in attempting to resist the efforts of the

College of Nursing to set itself up as a somewhat élitist organization by excluding some nurses who had been trained before the College's formation. He also made another, more serious accusation against the College of:

> seeking their ruin by stigmatising them in print as semi-trained or untrained persons from whom the public must be protected... and... refusing them assistance from the 'Nation's Fund for Nurses', a fund raised by the public for the benefit of all Nurses in old age, sickness or distress.[16]

His spirited attempt to persuade the hospital's Board to sever its connection with the College of Nursing caused a stir, and a greatly diluted version of his proposal called on them to modify their rules so that those large numbers of nurses trained in previous years could become members. The hospital's Board approved of the College's attempts to elevate standards of nurse training and to produce a more uniform system of instruction throughout the land. In spite of that, there seems to have been a certain amount of confusion in their minds between the College's role and that of the General Nursing Council. (In the middle of this confusion, Miss Scovell resigned as the College's local representative, having already condemned the long hours and small salaries which nurses had to endure. She gave no reason for this and it is not known if it occurred as a result of pressure from her employers or from Mr Brook himself.)

By March 1921, a draft version of the new syllabus of lectures and demonstrations had been prepared by the General Nursing Council. The Matron was requested to attend as an informal observer a conference at which the new course was discussed. Following that, the hospital was invited to adopt the curriculum of training laid down so that it might become a nurse training school. The closing date set for the registration of existing nurses was 14 July 1923. Mr Brook feared that any nurses who had not been accepted by the College of Nursing well before that date would minimize their chances of being accepted by the General Nursing Council unless they sat the new examination. But the debate with the College of Nursing was not allowed to hold up the General Nursing Council's plans. The subcommittee formed in Swansea to consider the new syllabus recommended that it should be accepted in its entirety. Each new nurse would in future have to pay ten shillings a week towards her maintenance (the money would be returned at the end of six months' service), and would be required to spend three months at the Parc Wern Preliminary Training School before starting on her three-year training period. There was to be a minimum age of entry of nineteen, with an examination before any candidate was allowed to start work at the hospital.[17]

Dr Lancaster represented the hospital at the conference that had been arranged to discuss the new examination. On his return, he was convinced that too much would be expected of those hoping to take up nursing as a career. No discussion had been allowed on the principles involved in what was to be the greatest change in nursing education ever brought about in Britain. He voiced his doubts at the conference and believed that his views were shared by many of those present; he thought that the new syllabus was too wide in scope and required too much detailed knowledge about subjects which were irrelevant to the practice of nursing at that time. His concern was that a shortage of candidates for nursing posts in places such as Swansea might be the result. The reaction among the Governors varied widely. On the one hand, the Works Governors asked that a letter of protest should be sent to the Ministry of Health. At the other extreme, the Nursing Subcommittee went as far as to ask the Principal of University College, Swansea to attempt to arrange for the new nurses to attend science classes at the College.

The intention was that there should be a voluntary examination held in 1924 for nurses who had started their training in 1921, and the first compulsory examinations would be held in 1925. In spite of the protests, the hospital gained recognition as a Nurse Training School in October 1922 and Swansea and Cardiff were designated as examination centres alternately. The honorary staff accepted invitations to become examiners and the first examinations at Parc Beck were held in October 1924.[18] The Matron and the teaching sister were complimented on the excellent results that were obtained in the first examinations for the new nursing qualification, but this success was rather short-lived. By April 1928, the results were thought to be 'most unsatisfactory' and means were sought of inducing those in training to pay more attention to their studies. Those who passed their examinations would be offered five pounds, or two pounds if they passed the hospital examinations but failed those set by the General Nursing Council. The relevance of Dr Lancaster's warnings had become apparent, and a great deal of concern was expressed at the general standard of education of the examinees. At that stage, the science classes were left in abeyance, and a simple preliminary examination in 'General Education, Reading, Writing and Arithmetic' was substituted. In spite of that, the success of the new examination system was confirmed when the Nursing Subcommittee was asked to consider the possibility that nurses could also be trained for a Midwifery Certificate. Dr Lloyd Davies, the newly appointed Gynaecologist, was very keen to establish midwifery training courses at the hospital. He was asked to visit the Central Midwives' Board to discuss this matter but it was not taken any further because he did not think that it would be possible to provide midwives in training with the necessary supervised experience of working in the community.

Already, other hospitals had been allowed to send their nurses to Swansea for part of their training and the number of applications for affiliation in order to conform with the new requirements increased considerably. The smaller hospitals at Maesteg, Pontypridd, Pembroke and those maintained by the Metropolitan Asylums Board had all been accepted in this manner by 1925, on condition that each nurse seconded had a minimum amount of experience already.

As the number of large hospitals recognized for training was not great, the Swansea Hospital received more applications for affiliation than it could accept. At the end of that decade, the Matron reported that she had great difficulty in arranging for nurses to get experience on the medical wards as the committee had agreed to accept trainee nurses from four other hospitals to the detriment of their own nurses' training. By May 1923, the Swansea Guardians too had become aware that a new era had opened up in nurses' training. They were unable to offer their nursing staff at Tawe Lodge sufficient experience in surgical nursing, and they too suggested that a scheme for interchanging nurses should be set up. This was not accepted because the Poor Law institution would have had little to offer Swansea Hospital nurses in any exchange scheme. That led the Guardians to consider asking the Ministry of Health for permission to open a surgical ward for paying patients at the Poor Law hospital.[19]

The need for new accommodation for nursing staff was greater than ever, but, with the introduction of the new training scheme, premises had to be found for a new Preliminary Training School. This was formally opened at Parc Wern (Parc Beck) in May 1922 by Mr Beck himself. There was also accommodation there for the sixteen members of the night nursing staff, the twelve Training School pupils, the three masseuses, the new Sister Tutor and the domestic staff. (With the failure of the plan to undertake part of the out-patient work there, the Reverend Mr Mander and Dr Quick made an application on behalf of a committee who wished to establish a school for young children in the outbuildings. This was agreed to at a rental of £30 a year and there were to be thirty scholars.)

With the opening of the new Nurses' Home at Parc Beck, accommodation for 132 nurses was available. With the intended increase in the number of beds and the longer off-duty hours that had been hoped for, it was envisaged that 100 nurses would be required to staff the hospital. To introduce an eight-hour working day with a three-shift system, a total of 149 nurses would be needed, and that system was adopted 'for trial' in 1926.

By October 1926, all was not well in the Nursing Department. Some members of the staff had received anonymous letters and, although the Matron had been commended for the steps taken by her to enforce discipline, the committee refused to ask one of the sisters to resign. As a result, Miss Scovell offered her resignation as she believed that she did not enjoy the full confidence of the committee. She was, however, asked to withdraw her resignation; she requested a period of three months to consider her position. She was given a fortnight and decided to stay.

Few of their own nurses applied for senior posts in the hospital, apparently because there were few fully trained nurses on the staff and the new nursing school had not yet been in existence for sufficiently long for the hospital to be able to fulfil its own need for qualified staff.

The Matron's explanation for the increased incidence of sickness among her nurses was accepted without question. It was attributed to overcrowding in some of the wards, and, to some extent, to poor ventilation, although the committee members themselves believed that patients' visitors carried infections into the building (which seemed to affect the nursing staff to a greater extent than the patients). For that reason, for three months, the number of visitors allowed at each bed on visiting days was restricted to three close relatives (apparently more in order to protect the staff than those who were under their care). In addition, the Sanitary Tower at the end of the Talbot Ward balcony was closed and sites for erecting tents for the nursing staff to be able to take advantage of the sea air were hired at Langland Bay for the duration of the summer.

Since 1921, it had been commonplace for staff members who were ill to be paid during periods of sickness, particularly if it could be shown that the illness was directly related to circumstances at work. The granting of individual pensions, especially to those who retired after many years of service, was well established but it was not until December 1925 that a draft pensions scheme for hospital officers and nurses was prepared. After consultation with several professional bodies, the Housekeeper at the Walter Road Nurses' Hostel was granted a pension of five shillings a week on her retirement, but when Mr Hughes retired as Secretary because of ill health, he was given his full salary for three months and then a pension of £300 a year. An attempt by the Transport and General Workers Union to reverse that decision failed. By December 1930, a new voluntary superannuation scheme for staff had been brought in and thirty-four employees had taken advantage of its benefits.

Life for the in-patients had altered from the time when they were expected to be partly responsible for the running of the wards as soon as they were well enough to do so. A great deal of consideration was

SWANSEA GENERAL & EYE HOSPITAL.

Ward....*Llewelyn*........ Bed No............

Name....*Nellie Roach*..........................

Date....*15--5--26*....

Admit ONE VISITOR only.

This Card to be produced on entering Hospital, and to be returned when Patient leaves.

Visiting Days—Wednesdays, 2 to 3-30; Saturdays, 2 to 3-30; Sundays, 2 to 3.

Not more than Two Visitors allowed at a bed at the same time

This Ticket will be cancelled if above regulations are infringed.

NOTICE.

Patients' friends are allowed, with the permission and subject to the inspection of the Ward Sister, to bring in the under-mentioned goods:—

- Fresh Eggs.
- Fruit.
- Cocoa (in tins)
- Plain Biscuits.
- Jam.

By Order,
W. D. Hughes,
Secretary.

VERY IMPORTANT.

This Ticket will be forfeited if any goods, other than those mentioned above, are brought in

Visitor's ticket from 1926. (*By kind permission of Mr and Mrs G. Jones.*)

given to the comfort of the illest among them. All were treated with a level of dignity which, although not extravagant by modern standards, would certainly have surprised the patients and staff of an earlier age. More attention was paid to minor details concerning their welfare. While there was little that could be done about the lack of privacy in the large open wards, when such implements as an electrically operated automatic gramophone were offered to the surgical wards, they were refused on the grounds that their use might impede the recovery of some patients. The attempt to maintain an appropriate level of silence in the hospital square, which had been a gathering place for the more audible of Swansea's amateur musicians for decades past on Sunday afternoons, continued, and a proposition by a local band that they should play selections in the grounds each week was quickly rejected. On the other hand, the presentation of a wireless set by the Radio Guild was received with some enthusiasm. Had there not been great opposition, the Board's Chairman, Mr Gilbertson, would have arranged for the transmission throughout the hospital by means of a loudspeaker system of the presentation ceremony at the BBC studio. By 1927, there was valid evidence that a far more concerted effort was being made to meet patients' other psychological and social needs more adequately. The Swansea Labour Association asked if nursing mothers whose children were in-patients could be allowed to sleep at the hospitals at weekends and that was arranged whenever possible. The Matron suggested in 1929 that children should continue to be educated while they were in-patients and with the help of the Samaritans' Committee, facilities were provided.[20]

By the end of that decade, new advances were commonplace and medical practice was rarely static for long. Even greater changes were soon to occur and of all those associated with the hospital, perhaps it was the admirable Dr Sladden who best caught the spirit of the age when he wrote:

> There is in all branches of medical work, a growing demand for the greatest possible exactitude in diagnosis.

That exactitude could only be bought at a price and with almost 175,000 out-patient attendances and 5,000 admissions having occurred during the year, the price had reached a level that was almost beyond the scope of a voluntary hospital.

CHAPTER NINE

The Depression: 1929–1939

> The whole conception of hospitals as self-contained institutions, placed as local generosity has dictated, each doing its bit to apply local skill to local suffering within a horse-transport radius, is outworn...[1]

THE organization of hospital services on a more rational and less fragmented basis had taken up the attention of many people throughout the land. Since the passing of the 1911 National Insurance Act and particularly from the time that the Ministry of Health was formed in 1919, state intervention in the provision of medical care had increased. By the 1930s, this process was accelerated with the passing of new legislation.

The Local Government Act of 1929 charged local authorities with a responsibility for providing additional hospital accommodation. Under the terms of the Act, they were to consult with the voluntary hospitals when they made provision for hospital services, but there was no set procedure by which this was to be accomplished. The hospital's House Committee was apprehensive about the Borough Council's new-found powers which, they feared, might signify an invasion of a province that had hitherto been theirs. With the abolition of the Boards of Guardians, the intention of the new law was to provide a more unified approach to the work of the health services. Although it cannot be said to have been a stirring success in Swansea at that time, it was felt that the various councils concerned should be contacted to seek their views on ways in which co-operation could occur.

Before that had been done, a suggestion was made by the Chairman of the Governors of the Cardiff Royal Infirmary that the voluntary hospitals in south Wales should be provided with a forum to protect their interests. It was thought that such a committee ought to seek recognition from the various councils concerned. An initial meeting held at Cardiff decided that four lay members and four doctors from Swansea should represent the hospital in any discussions.[2]

The Town Clerk's reply to the request that was made for information about any proposed consultation procedures held out little hope of amelioration in relations between the Borough Council and the Swansea Hospital. As the Borough Council had not yet considered their new responsibilities concerning hospitals, the Town Clerk saw no occasion to hold consultations at that stage. The attitude of the Glamorgan County Council was a little different; they did not suggest any joint meetings but asked what charges would be made for patients sent to the hospital by their Public Assistance Committee (which had taken over the functions of the Guardians). This was considered by the hospital to be a matter for the representatives of the voluntary hospitals in Glamorgan to discuss and that individual hospitals should be discouraged from setting up their own scales of fees for this type of work. As neither council had made any plans for broadening the scope of their hospital work, they refused to meet a deputation from the voluntary hospitals and denied them any official recognition.

The situation was complicated by the fact that increasing numbers of subscribers from the eastern end of the area covered by the hospital were being admitted to the Penrhiwtyn Infirmary at Neath because there were no beds available for them at Swansea and were being compelled to pay for private treatment there. Threats were made that workmen's contributions would be discontinued unless some satisfactory solution could be reached. But the House Committee refused to consider accepting the principle that they should reimburse patients whose names were on their waiting list but who had to accept treatment elsewhere. The first attempt to break the deadlock with the local authorities was made by the Medical Officer of Health for Carmarthenshire in April 1932. He arranged a conference to which voluntary associations were invited in order to consider the best means available to them for discharging their functions in the field of health care.

Dr R. Bruce Low had visited the hospital on behalf of the Ministry of Health in 1931 in connection with the survey he was conducting of the health services provided by the Swansea Borough Council. He was eager to investigate the extent to which the council was co-operating with the hospital. No record of the hospital's replies to his questions has survived. But in December 1934, Dr Thomas Evans, the Medical Officer of Health to the Borough, published his survey on the development and co-ordination of health services in Swansea, and from this document, it is apparent that the Ministry held the view that there was a need for further hospital accommodation in the locality.[3]

The abolition of the Boards of Guardians had been carried out under the terms of the Local Government Act of 1929, and the medical branch of the Poor Law service was transferred to the County and County Borough Councils. The Swansea Guardians, it seems, had not used the extensive powers which would have allowed them to provide a rate-aided hospital service. They:

> had only... converted Tawe Lodge into an inadequate and ill-adapted workhouse infirmary.

Although Tawe Lodge had largely served as a hospital with minimal use for non-medical indoor relief, doubts had been raised as to whether it could ever be properly adapted and developed as a modern hospital. Even then, no sick person could be admitted without the authority of a relieving officer, who was an untrained lay official whose work was largely concerned with the payments that were made to the poor. Neither was the Medical Officer to the workhouse to arrange urgent admissions there without the permission of the workhouse manager, the Master.

The only hospitals satisfactorily maintained by the Borough Council were Fairwood and Hill House (which were isolation hospitals and were run under the terms of the Public Health Acts). The Welsh National Memorial Association was said to be interested in opening a new hospital for the treatment of tuberculosis in the town. By far the best developed services maintained by the Health Committee were those concerned with maternity and child welfare work. Dr Evans was somewhat hard pressed to suggest a long-term plan for the increasing role which his Committee ought to have been playing in the development of health care services. He raised the possibility of appointing members of the Swansea Hospital's visiting staff to similar (paid) positions at Tawe Lodge. That might lead to a better co-ordination of services and less chance of duplicating the buying of equipment. There was, he thought, a deep-rooted prejudice against the Poor Law institutional medical services in the town. But, in spite of pressure from the Welsh Board of Health, the representatives of the Ministry, there was no measure of agreement between the Council and the hospital authorities on the co-ordination which the new law demanded. The Council particularly chose to ignore the advice of the Minister of Health at the annual meeting of the Hospital Savings Association. He stressed that:

> a practical and unified system of cooperation between [local authorities and voluntary hospitals] was the sensible and practical course [and that] they must be marshalled together in a joint war against disease and death.[4]

The hospital's proposal that the Corporation should provide money for the building and partial maintenance of a maternity unit at Parc Beck had not been accepted, as the Council preferred to assume total responsibility for work in that field. When the Welsh Board of Health asked for an explanation for the delays in starting negotiations between the two bodies, the Town Clerk's reply was that 'present financial conditions [had] militated against the progress of consultation'. They had already spent almost half a million pounds on their new psychiatric hospital, which the *Daily Express* had claimed would be the most up-to-date in the world.[5] It seemed unlikely that they could meet the requirements of the 1929 Act easily. Nevertheless, the Welsh Board insisted that there should be no delay in starting discussions. The fact that the hospital dealt with a wider catchment area than the Borough led to further difficulties.

Dr Evans reminded the members of his Council that they had no power to make capital grants to voluntary hospitals and were likely to be limited to providing annual contributions in payment for services. He thought it desirable that the hospital's position as the centre for specialized services for Swansea and south-west Wales should be maintained, possibly with the help of an increased rate-aided annual contribution if that could be legally justified. Having committed himself firmly to such a proposal, he then made it known that he himself favoured the erection of a municipal hospital of 150 or 200 beds which would include maternity accommodation. The total number of municipally controlled beds in Swansea (including those at the psychiatric hospital) already exceeded that at Swansea Hospital but the municipal total (which amounted to 4.2 per 1,000 of the town's population) was considerably less than that available in many other towns such as Cardiff (6.4) and Liverpool (9.08). It eventually became obvious to the hospital Governors, who had hoped for Council support without increased intrusion, that there was indeed to be no more interference than previously but that there might in practice be less help available.

At this time there came a flurry of published reports of various kinds which carried no legal weight but each of which emphasized deficiencies and suggested remedies for one aspect or another of the hospital services in Britain. In varying degrees, they all had some relevance for the hospital. In 1921, the Cave Committee's deliberations had led to the creation of a Voluntary Hospitals Association which had, to a large extent, failed to gain the support of the hospitals themselves. The British Hospitals Association, with its Sankey Commission,[6] and the BMA, through its *Essentials of a National Health Service*,[7] drew attention to matters which should have taken the Governors a considerable time to discuss but which were never mentioned at their meetings.

The report on nursing commissioned by *The Lancet* and published in 1932[8] (the year in which Miss Scovell died after 22 years' service) apparently went unnoticed, probably because the staff shortages and bad general conditions that were common elsewhere were less of a problem in Swansea. There was, of course, much in that report that was relevant. The committee had decided to take no action concerning the Bill that was before Parliament in 1931 intended to limit the working hours of nurses and to ensure them a minimum wage. A year later, all the proposals put forward by the College of Nursing had still not been accepted. In July 1937, ward sisters still worked $45\frac{1}{2}$ hours a week and night nurses $56\frac{1}{4}$ hours. As any alteration would have called for an increase in the number of staff employed, the matter was deferred. At the same time, the entrance examination for student nurses was becoming more difficult. From January 1936, a matriculation certificate or school certificate examination would exempt candidates for nursing training from any further tests.

There was a great deal that happened in the Nursing Department that diverted the committee's attention from their nurses' working conditions and more serious problems. In 1935, when a lady of 'Indian Nationality' was accepted as a probationer, some form of explanation was evidently considered to be necessary. She was described as being 'a very refined and well educated girl', which was more than was said of some of her colleagues. One nurse was discharged for 'continually inhaling the Ether Meth'. Four others who went with members of the resident medical staff to a dance at Carmarthen and failed to return until 6 a.m. were severely dealt with. One of them resigned immediately rather than face what was to follow. The Matron suggested that the other two staff nurses should be given an opportunity to do so. The final year nurse was allowed to continue with her training but was 'deprived of the privilege of wearing a blue belt'. (One of the doctors concerned also resigned, one was reprimanded and, curiously, one was able to give a satisfactory explanation.) The first sign that this tyrannical era might possibly be drawing to a close occurred when a (totally ineffective) Nurses' Representative Council was formed in 1938, at which the probationer nurses' problems were discussed. During the first year of its existence, only one matter raised by that Council was ever discussed at the House Committee, and that was a request that nurses should be allowed to remain out until 10.30 p.m. on their half-day off duty. One of the most remarkable features of the Nursing Department's work at that time was that it was intended to start postgraduate courses of seven to fourteen days' duration for nurses each autumn 'in return for part-time services' on the wards.

In October 1929, the Paying Patients' Subcommittee was anxious to find out from other hospitals what procedures were commonly followed in the case of patients able to pay for treatment. They asked for information on the system of enquiry into the financial circumstances of those referred to hospital, the basis on which charges were made, and the operation of Contributory Schemes. As a result, the

SWANSEA GENERAL AND EYE HOSPITAL

NURSE'S CERTIFICATE.

This is to Certify that Doris Elizabeth Davies has received practical and theoretical training at this Hospital during a period of three years from 1-2-32 to 1-2-35 Both in the wards, and at the examinations she has acquitted herself to the satisfaction of the Medical Staff and has proved herself to be fully qualified to perform efficiently the duties of a Nurse.

Howell _____ Chairman of the Hon. Medical Staff
G. W. Peacock _____ Chairman of the House Committee.
Agnes Duncan _____ Matron.
_____ Secretary.

Dated 20-2-1935

Nurse's certificate from 1935. (*By kind permission of Miss Doris Davies.*)

hospital's first (qualified) Lady Almoner, Miss Kathleen Jones Richmond, was appointed in December 1930 (at £225 a year with lunch and tea provided), and she took over most of the work of the Reception Committee. By the time she had started on her work, a registration fee of sixpence, which was sometimes 'remitted', was being charged to all out-patients on their first visit. Diabetics who were thought to be able to afford the cost of their insulin were having to pay, and a fee of five shillings was being charged for each X-ray taken in many cases.

Later, the editor of the *British Medical Journal* was to list the main faults of the National Insurance scheme as the exclusion of dependants of insured people from any benefits, the omission of hospital treatment and the fact that it was almost completely divorced from the other branches of the public health service.[9] This meant that little help could ever be obtained from that source for many Swansea families requiring hospital care, and alternative methods of financing the treatment of the more seriously ill had to be sought. Efforts to persuade all contributors who worked locally, and were already subscribing, to pay twopence a week had not been successful; many contributors gave less than was asked for.

In May 1929, a circular letter was sent to doctors in the district asking for their co-operation in preventing the continuing abuse which occurred when patients who could afford to pay for treatment were sent to the hospital. It had been suggested in 1932 that a Visiting Staff Fund should be formed so that the senior doctors could be paid in part for their services. But the overdraft was almost £50,000 and, with 7 resident doctors, 127 nurses and 174 other members of staff already on the payroll, such a scheme was not acceptable. Instead, new and stringent economies (including the re-collection of warm water from sterilizers, from radiators that had been switched off, and from calorifiers into a storage tank in order to reduce the amount of coal used in heating water) had to be introduced.

There was also a perpetual fear that the hospital's rights might be infringed by the setting up of money-collecting schemes for other hospitals. Strong objections were made to St Bartholomew's Hospital, London, about their use of a canvasser in the locality to collect on their behalf who was thought to be diverting money away from the local hospital. In September 1931, an announcement that a Hospital Association at Neath was to be formed caused some alarm. Its function would be to encourage the inhabitants of the town to pay weekly sums that would enable them to be treated at the County Hospital at Penrhiwtyn and it was feared that this would lead to a substantial reduction in the contributions received from the eastern end of the hospital area. At the same time, it became apparent that some of the smaller hospitals were no longer prepared to accept without argument the authority of the Swansea Hospital committee on all matters and it was feared that they might succeed in channelling contributions from the main hospital into their own funds. The collection of money from workmen was still a haphazard business, and the door-to-door collections had not produced satisfactory returns for some years.

A subcommittee was therefore formed to consider the possibility of creating a properly organized Contributory Scheme. The Secretary submitted suggestions for their consideration. They included the possibility that all those insured under the National Insurance Acts, together with their dependants and other people whose income did not exceed a maximum figure (that would be determined by the number of dependants but which would be £300 a year for a married man with a family of at least one), would be eligible for its benefits on payment of a predetermined weekly sum. The plans for the scheme were completed by May 1932 although there was a long delay before it was actually introduced. The options offered to contributors were to be that they should pay at least twopence a week or a penny on each pound of their weekly wages. If the sum were paid annually in advance, a discount would be given and the full benefits made available for eight shillings a year. It had been hoped to ask for threepence a week (as was already happening at the Llanelli Hospital) but, because of the industrial depression, this was not thought to be wise. Those who failed to join the scheme within three months of its inception would be expected to wait for three months after their first payment before being eligible for the benefits.

A great deal of publicity by means of press announcements, posters and cinema slides was given to the meeting planned in November 1932 to introduce the Contributory Scheme, and the three local Members of Parliament were asked to speak there. The house-to-house collectors' services were dispensed with. A male organizer, with previous experience of such a scheme, was advertised for at a salary of £400 a year (£100 a year more than the Matron's salary although hers was a resident post) and £120 car allowance. Mr Llewelyn B. Dart of Liverpool was appointed to the post and two offices were built for him at a cost of £75. He pressed the hospital's case with such vigour that, within three months of his appointment, there were sixty-four District Committees formed. At these, some of the honorary staff spoke on behalf of the hospital and Dr Clarke Begg broadcast an appeal on the radio on Sunday, 11 June 1933. Several alterations in the laws of the hospital were necessary with the adoption of the scheme and it was accepted that thirty-two representatives should be elected from among the Contributory Scheme Governors for membership of the Board.

By the end of 1934, reciprocal arrangements had been agreed with ten English hospitals and one in Monmouthshire that each would treat the other's patients as the need arose. No such special consideration could be given to the cottage hospitals in the locality:

> and if the people of Port Talbot [want the privileges the hospital has to offer] . . . they must accept the conditions laid down.

The relationship with the surrounding smaller hospitals was not made easier with the introduction of the Contributory Scheme. The Swansea Hospital committee pressed for the introduction of a general scheme in 1934. Had it been accepted, it would have meant that for each threepence claimed by the peripheral hospitals, the Swansea Hospital would have been entitled to a penny. However, at Port Talbot and Llanelli no conditions were made when their contributors requested treatment, whereas at Swansea those who contributed were not automatically entitled to treatment, and income limits were set above which additional payments were required from contributors. It was almost inevitable that, once this difference between the schemes was brought to light, accusations would be made that the Swansea Hospital operated a means test. Attempts were made to show that many were deeply dissatisfied with this state of affairs, but it seems that the vast majority recognized the need to distinguish between the better-off contributors and the others. It was the more deprived section of the community who benefited from the use of this scheme.

The Port Talbot Hospital offered to accept full financial responsibility for patients from that town treated at Swansea rather than risk having the new Swansea Scheme operating in their area at great detriment to them. This was refused as the Swansea Hospital Board was not empowered (and probably did not wish) to enter into reciprocal arrangements of that kind with other hospitals. In fact, such a contract, which consisted of an agreement to treat the other hospital's patients free of charge when that was required, was later introduced in 1934, but this agreement usually involved other hospitals of comparable size in distant places. By September 1934, 94 contributory schemes were affiliated to the British Hospitals Association's Contributory Schemes Association, which had a total membership of 4 million.

They were uneasy times for the hospital generally. The dissensions continued and became more pronounced as house doctors, the Works Governors and the honorary staff all became more dissatisfied with their lot. In 1930, two conflicting moves of some importance had occurred. The surgeons suggested that a possible means of lessening the pressure on the hospital would be to place a notice in the Casualty Department showing the number of patients on the waiting list for admission and providing information about the number of beds vacant each day at Nursing Homes in the immediate vicinity. Proposals were also made that people should be admitted as in-patients if they were able to pay the hospital some of the cost of their treatment (but never if they were able to pay fully). When payment was made, it was maintained that the honorary staff should be entitled to claim a fee for their services.

There had been much unrest among the visiting staff over the question of payment. Since the publication of the Cave Committee's report in 1921, that principle had been accepted in some quarters but it was not seriously considered at the Swansea Hospital. In the next decade, the senior doctors claimed (though without justification) that it had never been intended that they should provide their services free of charge for anyone other than those totally without the means to pay. With the passage of time, it was argued, the financial status of many of the patients accepted had altered. The abuse of the hospital's services, which had been confined to the out-patient department in the nineteenth century, had by then been allowed to spread to the indoor department. The honorary staff had made their feelings of resentment over this known but on the whole had not had a sympathetic hearing. Once the principle of payment was accepted to a limited extent during the war and later with the development of the Schools Medical Service, the issue at once became more difficult and contentious. The visiting staff insisted that new conditions called for a revision in their terms of service. The whole matter had to be deferred. It would not have been a viable proposition without an increase in the rate of the workmen's contributions to threepence a week. That could not be considered because of the economic conditions.

A section of the workmen's representatives were unable to accept what they regarded as the unphilanthropic attitude of the doctors. They proposed that the Swansea municipal authorities should be informed of the urgent need for additional hospital accommodation. This would have helped to diminish the in-patient waiting list of 1,670 patients but would have defeated their purpose in that the consulting staff appointed to a municipal hospital would have been paid. The uneasiness felt by the remaining lay Governors at the possibility that the Swansea Borough would at last build its own municipal general hospital was apparent and the motion was defeated. Instead, a committee of nine was appointed to examine the needs of south-west Wales and they were asked to provide a report by the summer of 1935. Angry scenes followed when it became known that the details of that report had been released to the press by one of the Swansea Works Governors before being presented to the Board itself. Accusations were made of a gross breach of confidence which would have a deleterious effect on future developments.

The report had been carefully prepared. The Swansea Council and the Welsh Board of Health were consulted, and surveys of available accommodation elsewhere were conducted. The Welsh Board of Health approved of the principle of developing regional hospitals but they were not prepared to offer advice on the optimum number of beds needed in Swansea. It was found difficult to estimate with any accuracy the extent of the shortage of beds in the region because there was no definite basis on which it could be calculated, particularly as it was believed that many people in need of in-patient treatment were no longer applying for admission because of the long periods of time for which they would be kept waiting. Neither was it known if the smaller voluntary hospitals were being used to their full capacity. Eventually it was decided that 410 more beds were needed to cope effectively with Swansea's population with an additional 50 for more specialized use as Swansea's contribution to the future needs of the outlying areas. Other hospitals throughout the region were contemplating an addition of 152 beds to their numbers. This would have left a shortage of 1,266 beds in the peripheral districts if the agreed figure of 4 beds per 1,000 of the population was to be reached.

The committee's attitude to the prospects of interference from the local authorities was that 'The voluntary system stands supreme'. Any attempts to undermine that system were forcefully resisted. Yet, apart from occasional attempts to increase the number of Swansea councillors entitled to places on the Board, there is not a great deal of evidence that the local authorities in west Glamorgan were inclined to intrude in the hospital's affairs. The Glamorgan County Council had its own county hospital at Penrhiwtyn in Neath (which later became the West Glamorgan County Hospital). In Swansea, it seems probable that the Borough Council would have erected their own hospital had there been money available, but they had certainly shown no great enthusiasm for undertaking negotiations in order to promote a jointly run service.

By August 1935, the hospital committee itself was considering the possibility of building a new hospital of 250 beds at Parc Wern, which would have brought about an actual increase of 180 beds as the Folland and Griffith Thomas Wards on the old site would eventually have to be removed. The cost was estimated at a quarter of a million pounds which it was thought could be raised by various means. An increase of a penny a week from those who gave to the Contributory Scheme would have produced £75,000 over the following five years. It was thought that a public appeal would produce a similar sum over the same period and that the Swansea Corporation would be prepared to donate £100,000.

The Joint Committee, where the Borough Council representatives finally met the hospital representatives in September 1935, showed more enthusiasm than had been hoped for.[10] Of the possibilities considered, it was decided that one where local authorities would donate on the basis of rateable value would be effective. It was even suggested that the Swansea Corporation might be prepared to raise a loan of £250,000, which should be repaid over forty years. As there were more than 1,700 names on the waiting lists, the Joint Committee decided to make its recommendations known within three months. The trend towards developing Public Assistance Hospitals, apparent elsewhere, served to emphasize the need for the voluntary hospitals to decide on their future policy. The Governors' views that, with the progress of medicine, large regional hospitals offering a specialized service to a wide area were necessary coincided with those of the Ministry of Health. The Joint Committee agreed with the Swansea Hospital's report that, though the extent of the hospital bed shortage was difficult to estimate, more beds were needed in Swansea—possibly 250 extra beds. The Ministry was not prepared to offer guidance on the appropriate ratio of beds to population in any one area. Its sanctioning of local authority schemes would, apparently, only be governed by the length of the hospital's waiting list.

The smaller hospitals were to be asked about their future plans as it was thought that they might possibly cope with at least some of the demand from their own localities. Of far greater significance was the agreement reached that it was essential that some form of reciprocity should occur between the Swansea Hospital, the peripheral hospitals, and the municipal hospitals so that all the facilities could be used to their fullest possible extent.

It was universally accepted as impracticable that the 250 extra beds required for Swansea could be provided by enlarging the old hospital building. The plan for a new hospital at Parc Beck, first considered in the 1920s, was therefore revived. In the absence of any representation from the west Wales counties and Glamorgan, it was decided that an appropriate basis for negotiation would be to suggest that Swansea should provide fifty-five per cent of the Councils' share of the burden, with the remainder being shared proportionately between the various counties involved, but an additional sum of £30,000 would be required to implement this plan. The whole matter was confused by the Llanelli Hospital, which favoured a system whereby payment was made for each patient from its catchment area treated at Swansea, and a sum of ten pounds a head for in-patient treatment was named. A similar arrangement was then offered to the hospitals at Port Talbot, Carmarthen and Haverfordwest.

This new spirit of co-operation with the Swansea Council produced signs that the hospital authorities were prepared to hand over some of their responsibilities to the local authority. Their solicitors, after examining the conveyance deeds, were of the opinion that it was within the power of the Trustees, if directed to do so by the hospital's Board, to grant to the Swansea Borough Council a lease of land for the building of a municipal hospital. It could be shown that co-operation of that kind was in the interest of the people for whom the hospital had been intended and was within the intention of the donor of Parc Beck. There was, therefore, some confusion at one stage as to the ownership of the new hospital that had been proposed. (The Glamorgan County Council had eventually decided that it must commit itself to developing the site at Penrhiwtyn as a county hospital although agreeing to consult with the Swansea Hospital Board before embarking on any extensions.)[11]

Meanwhile, the negotiations with the Swansea Council were continuing. At those meetings it was suggested to the Board that they should consider asking the Glamorgan and Carmarthen County Councils to join with them in building a new hospital under the Councils' control. But the Charity Commissioners did not consider that they could give their consent to such a proposal. Discussions were also complicated by the eventual formation of the Penrhiwtyn Hospital Association at Neath and the hospital's refusal to accept an offer from the Llanelli Hospital of six shillings a day for treating its in-patients (although an identical arrangement had been made with the Pembrokeshire War Memorial Hospital).

The after-care of patients had assumed a greater significance and the After-care Subcommittee sought a closer level of co-operation with the Samaritan Committee and the Lady Almoner. In 1934, 90 patients were offered some form of after-care, and by 1935 that number had increased to 158. The Convalescent Home was by then too small, although 479 patients used its facilities during 1936. The possibility of renting the orphanage at Killay, the Cottage Homes at Cockett, or a building at Llangennith were all eventually turned down. Patients were sent to convalesce either to the Porthcawl or Southerndown Homes, with 'only the very necessitous cases' being offered a period at Builth or Llandrindod. An arrangement whereby children were able to go to Weston-super-Mare or Devon failed, not because of lack of money but because many parents did not approve.

Travelling to Swansea from the more distant areas was not easy and many patients preferred to have treatment at the hospital nearest to their homes. Within the town, Tawe Lodge, because of its use as a workhouse was less popular than the general hospital. The decision as to where the contributors were to be admitted was to be made by the hospital's Reception Committee, the Resident Medical Officer and the Almoner (but not the patient). If patients should be admitted without authority, the hospital would expect them to pay the costs, although arrangements for them to be reimbursed were introduced later. There was some opposition from the County Council to the acceptance of Swansea Hospital patients at Penrhiwtyn and it was obvious that some form of agreement must be reached quickly.

The Swansea town Group A (Works) Governors had caused sufficient ill feeling for the other members of the hospital committee to declare in December 1935 that they would only attend meetings if they could be given an assurance that only matters listed on the agenda for that day would be discussed. That group (which did not include Group A Governors from outside Swansea) had been accused of allowing 'literature detrimental to the welfare of the hospital' to be circulated at one of its meetings. This took the form of a letter from them to the Town Clerk asking the Council to reject the approaches being made by the hospital for financial help and pressing on them the need to provide a municipal hospital. Their attitude, which was far from being typical of the other workmen's representatives, did nothing to help improve the standard of care for patients, nor did it advance the emancipation of working-class people's rights in the voluntary hospital movement. (The Group A Governors as a whole rarely hesitated before raising contentious issues, such as the allegation that favouritism was being shown by one of the visiting staff to compensation cases, and they invariably got a fair hearing.)

At the 1938 Annual Meeting, the Secretary of the Swansea Group A representatives criticized the Board's decision to pay £5,000 to the Visiting Medical Staff Fund. He proposed that the Visiting Medical Staff should only retain their twenty-four representatives on the Board as long as they gave their services gratuitously. For every £1,000 paid to them, he further proposed that the number of their representatives should be reduced by one. It was later accepted that a reduction of one for every £3,000 paid should be made. The complaints made by this small group often seemed to be an assertion of political power; however, the acceptance of money by the 'honorary' staff for work that had been carried out entirely without charge for well over a century, at a time when unemployment had reached exceedingly high levels locally, was certain to anger many workmen, who had been told on joining the Contributory Scheme that their subscriptions would not be used for payments of that kind.

The new Contributory Scheme introduced in 1937 should have produced between £12,000 and £15,000 in additional income but several months elapsed before the majority of the contributors accepted the new conditions. Some groups at Clydach, Gorseinon and Neath left the scheme at this time because of the demands being made on them by their local hospitals. In spite of that, an increase of £4,300 in income was brought about. It was thought that, if only 5,000 subscribers of a guinea each could be found, the financial difficulties could be lessened and the future faced with confidence.

The Board argued strongly against the creation of a multiplicity of contributory schemes each offering different benefits, on the grounds that this must surely militate against the creation of an effective and unified service for the region. The only solution, they felt, would be the setting up of a comprehensive scheme covering the whole region. After several meetings with the other hospitals concerned, the principle had been accepted but no detailed agreement had been reached.

By that time, the Ministry's Inter-Departmental Committee on Nursing Services had issued its interim report. As a result, among other matters, a 96-hour fortnight for all nurses was urgently introduced. The financial implications for the hospital were only too apparent. Soon, the new salary scales recommended by the College of Nursing were to be brought in. In 1935, the British Hospitals Association (which had been likened 'to a schoolmaster without a cane trying to keep order among 1,000 mischievous boys'[12]) had set up the Sankey Commission to consider the most effective way of safeguarding the interests of the voluntary hospitals in the light of current legislative and social changes. The Commission had overwhelmingly decided that some form of federation among the hospitals was inevitable. All services should be organized on a regional basis. In spite of that, there were many who seemed to have made the tacit assumption that the hospital system as it was then being operated was efficient and sufficient to meet the country's needs. In the House of Commons in May 1937, Sir Kingsley Wood, the Minister of Health was asked if he considered that state aid should be given to all hospitals; he simply replied 'no'. The matter was not discussed in any more detail than that.[13]

In 1937, at the time that the BMA was drafting its *Proposals for a General Medical Service for the Nation* (which was finally published in April 1938),[14] *The Times* published a 'national Health Number'.[15] The intention was to commemorate the government's 'Call to the Nation' National Health Campaign, and in this number, the Chairman of the Welsh Board of Health, Sir John Rowland, wrote that in Wales:

> the comparatively small administrative units increase the difficulties of organising health services.

Of greater significance, as the Contributory Schemes had by then attracted many members from among income groups which had not formerly made use of them (represented in Swansea by the Group B governors), the BMA made it clear in February 1938 that wherever Contributory Schemes existed, some form of remuneration must be agreed on for the honorary staff, and a Staff Fund was to be created for that purpose. Such a fund was established at the Swansea Hospital in that year, as we have seen.

In October 1937, the government's National Health Campaign was launched by the Prime Minister in a radio broadcast. The object was to encourage a wider use of the existing health services and to bring home the need for increased physical fitness. Yet, although the aim of the undertaking was admirable, the fact still remained that during that year, one person in every thirty-seven in the British Isles was likely to become an in-patient in a voluntary hospital and one in eight would attend an out-patient department.

The assumption was that the voluntary hospitals would somehow or other muddle their way through crisis after crisis. The formation of the Ministry of Health had been enough of a concession by the State. Arising out of the report of the Sankey (Voluntary Hospitals) Commission, the Ministry accepted the need for a regional hospital system. Meetings between the three principal hospitals in south Wales (Swansea, Cardiff and Newport) were held in Cardiff. It was decided that, in the new region, the western area covered by the Swansea Hospital would begin at Port Talbot and would include the hospitals at Brecon, Llandrindod and Aberystwyth as well as those in west Wales. Representatives from all the hospitals concerned were invited to produce a scheme for co-ordinating the existing services.

In January 1938, after a series of press statements concerning the Contributory Scheme, which were seen as a further effort on the part of some of the Group A Works Governors to undermine the administration of the hospital, the Secretary was authorized to issue a statement. Anyone who discontinued payment would be deprived of his privileges and an attempt by a group to set up an independent central fund was thwarted. Had that attempt succeeded and had the new fund been formed, there would have occurred an escalating number of threats to the committee's work and to the hospital's efficiency.

There was still some hope that several (unnamed) councils were prepared to discuss the possibility of co-operating in the setting up of a regional service. It this was found to be impracticable, it was decided that the discussions with the Swansea Borough authorities must proceed. By late 1938, it had become obvious that the power of the Ministry of Health to control the activities of local authorities in the sphere of health care was far less than its power in the sphere of social welfare. There was little hope of having any practical help from the direction of the central government.

Relationships with the Borough Council had improved sufficiently for an agreement to be reached by the end of 1938 that patients would be accepted at Tawe Lodge for the payment of a small fee. One of the main difficulties had been that many unemployed people who had been members of the hospital's Contributory Scheme were admitted to the hospital without payment but that if they were sent to Tawe Lodge instead, the Council would be entitled to claim a fee from the hospital on the grounds that they were technically 'contributors'. Eventually, it was agreed that whenever any members of the scheme were treated at Tawe Lodge, the fee should be either forty-five shillings or two shillings and sixpence a day up to a maximum period of four weeks.

In February 1937, the visiting medical staff suggested that each member of the scheme should pay an extra halfpenny each a week (and there were 112,906 contributors at that time), in an attempt to ease the difficulties, but those who earned less than a pound a week would be exempted. The Group A and Group B representatives objected on the grounds that many of the contributors were unemployed (which was a curious objection as the unemployed were to be exempted). The two groups of Governors differed in their views on the payment of the visiting staff. Those from Group B (whose membership varied widely from non-manual unskilled workers to school teachers and other professional workers) were of the opinion that if such payments were arranged, this would involve a degree of control over the doctors which they did not wish to have. On the other hand, the Group A governors would have greatly welcomed this form of control but were opposed to having to achieve it by those means.

The creation of a reciprocal arrangement with the Gorseinon Hospital was thwarted in 1938 because of the schemes under consideration by the Ministry of Health for the regionalization of orthopaedic, radium, and deep X-ray treatment. It was also feared that such unilateral arrangements might prejudice the formation of a Regional Contributory Scheme. A meeting had already been held in March 1938 with the representatives of eight other hospitals in the locality and in west Wales to consider forming such a scheme. With the exception of the Cardigan Hospital, there were ten such schemes already in operation in the region which between them produced £74,250 a year, of which £40,000 belonged to the Swansea Hospital. Evidence was already available from several places in England of the advantages of changing from a flat-rate contribution to payments based on the 'penny in the pound' principle. It was believed that the only alternative would be to increase the flat rate to threepence a week which would ultimately bring the total revenue to £100,000. This was eventually accepted. Each small hospital would receive identical amounts to those under the existing scheme. The surplus would then be available for the Swansea Hospital, whose old scheme fell short of the cost of treating

Contributory Scheme members by more than £10,000 a year. Eventually, the Board decided that although such a scheme would have suited its purpose best, there would have been too many disadvantages involved in trying to implement it. The matter was dropped, although the increased local rate of contributions was brought about. Simultaneously, the difficult question of payment to other hospitals who treated their contributors as in-patients was settled with an offer of payment of six shillings a week up to a maximum of five weeks.

The Superannuation Scheme for staff which had been in existence since 1930 was extended. Those who earned more than £160 a year, as well as those employed before 1930, could benefit, although it was thought that many 'might not wish to join'.

In spite of the continuing wranglings about money, there was much else that happened in the 1930s that benefited patients generally. In 1932, the Medical Superintendent of the new psychiatric hospital (later named Cefn Coed Hospital), Dr Ian Skottowe, asked for permission to start a psychiatric clinic at the Swansea Hospital.[16] At that time psychiatric clinics in general hospitals were far from being widely accepted, yet the Swansea committee was progressive enough to invite him to join the honorary medical staff. The charitable organizations connected with the hospital continued to flourish and to do a great deal of excellent work. In their 46th Annual Report, the ladies of the Samaritan Fund were able to show that they had kept up their weekly visits to the more socially disadvantaged patients. The Linen Guild, the largest in the land, with 6,217 members and 50 branches, provided all the pillowcases, towels and calico at the hospital.

Clinically, 'encouraging results' were being obtained in the treatment of pernicious anaemia. Of the 49 patients admitted with diabetes, only 11 had died, which was considered to be a vast improvement. The blood transfusion service had also developed. Dr Sladden had access to between 100 and 200 potential donors and 25 to 30 transfusions a year took place, with relatives usually volunteering to give the necessary blood. There were only 8 suitable donors who could be called on at any time and it was thought that another 4 or 5 would be quite sufficient. If a transfusion was given outside the hospital, a fee of 3 guineas was received, of which 2 guineas were given to the donor. (When the Voluntary Blood Donors' Association had been formed in 1921, only one 'voluntary transfusion' occurred throughout Britain, but by 1935, more than 4,000 donors gave their blood without payment.)

A dermatologist was appointed to the honorary staff in 1931. But not all the specialties were able to claim that their work was an unqualified success. Of the 85 pregnant women admitted in the year covered by the 1930–31 Report, 28 suffered from the most severe complications (eclampsia), 70 had a 'complicated childbirth' and 3 had died of haemorrhage. The only consolation was that not one had developed puerperal sepsis. By 1934, the situation had deteriorated markedly. Following three deaths from puerperal sepsis, the gynaecologist (the title obstetrician was not used), Dr Lloyd Davies, ordered the ward to be closed. The Swansea Council, which had already started to develop its maternity care facilities, was asked if it would take over the whole responsibility for that work. Again it was suggested that it might be prepared to investigate the possibility of donating a sum of money towards the building of an Obstetrics Department at Parc Beck.

The medical staff had continued to draw attention to the need for more wards. The Matron had to seek permission to use the Visitors' Shelter, at first as a canteen for out-patients and then even as a room for the treatment of 'massage cases'. In November 1929, a proposal had been made that the X-ray department, which was in the basement and had been flooded from time to time, should be extended by excavating under the Dyer Ward to provide additional space. At times when the Parc Beck scheme was in abeyance, it was not unusual for somewhat unrealistic plans for extending the old hospital to gain some prominence. In May 1930, it was suggested that two further storeys should be built over the Penllergaer Wards, even though that would have put each of them out of commission for several months.

Within some months, Dr Iwan Davies, who was Dr Edwards's successor as Visiting Radiologist, was of the opinion that the X-ray apparatus was quite unsuitable for use in modern radiography. Dr Franklyn from King's College Hospital, London drew attention to the inadequate measures used to protect staff there. Apart from the case of severe dermatitis in 1929, several radiographers had been found to have low blood counts from being exposed to large doses of radiation. The hospital did not have to pay compensation and it was not thought necessary to arrange any special form of insurance for the radiographers. In spite of all the obvious hazards, it was still maintained that there was no real danger from this source until low blood counts were found to occur 'with disconcerting frequency'.

The dental staff had been given the use of two beds in 1934. By 1937 it was said that the attendance of out-patients in their department had doubled over the previous four years. As many as 43 'gas cases' were being dealt with in the course of a morning. By August 1933, it had been decided that 40 extra beds and new X-ray and Electrical Departments must be built at a cost of not more than £10,000. Within a year, this was altered to a new pavilion of 100 beds and a new laundry which was to be built at Parc Beck. A fortnight after that decision had been made, plans were approved for X-ray and VD units; with one small ward on the ground floor and two small wards on the first floor, at the old hospital. This was to cost £11,250 with an additional £3,000 for more modern X-ray apparatus. It was providential that Mr D. W. Davies of Ystalyfera should have offered the hospital £10,000 in 1935. The new block with its 36 beds was named after him and opened by him in May 1935. The hospital then had 13 wards named after various benefactors and 50 endowed beds.

With radium therapy, the possibility of hazards to the staff were totally overshadowed by the complex administrative arrangements. At Dr Iwan Davies's request it was decided in 1932 that the Radium Sister should not work in the room in which the radium was stored. Consequently, legal action had to be taken to try to gain possession of a house in Brunswick Street which was owned by the hospital. As the tenant's rights were protected by the Rent Restriction Act, no eviction order was made at the County Court and the radium was eventually stored in a cupboard which had been built in the Secretary's room. In 1925, the National Radium Centre had been asked for permission to establish a Radium Centre at Swansea as the use of that treatment had been well established there for many years. The Ministry of Health delayed taking any further action. Eventually, the newly-formed Radium Commission refused to grant the status of a Regional Centre to Swansea, even though, some three years later, the Swansea Hospital was the only institution in south Wales with a deep therapy unit. The Commission was only able to lend radium to medical schools although this did not affect the hospital's ability to use this treatment. When Mr Isaac reported on the use of radon as a substitute for radium,[17] some use was made of it in Swansea especially as it called for less in-patient accommodation.

By 1936, attention had again been diverted to the project for building on the Parc Beck site. The committee thought that 'with optimism as the key word [that project] should become a reality'. Previously the Linen Guild had decided to defray the cost of building a new mortuary and chapel there. Although work had been due to begin in July 1930 on those projects, they were never started. An interview was to be arranged with the local Members of Parliament to ask if a government grant could be obtained towards the cost of the new building. It was not considered that the time was opportune to launch another large appeal to the public for money. In spite of the previous refusals and the underlying legal difficulties, an approach was again made to the Swansea Corporation and the other local authorities whose areas were served.

It seemed unlikely that the financial difficulties could ever be forgotten. Press reports appeared in which it was said that the Glamorgan Public Health Committee proposed spending large sums of money on developing the hospital at Penrhiwtyn over the following four years.[18] That move had occurred without consultation and was therefore contrary to the intentions of the Local Government Act. Before any protests could be made, the BMA claimed that the South-West Wales Contributory Scheme was in direct opposition to its policy because no provision had been made in it for the use of income limits (the inclusion of which would only have served to anger the workmen's representatives). Undaunted by the intensity of the preparations for war that were going on around them, the rebels among the Swansea Works Governors attempted to prevent the Visiting Staff from voting at Board meetings. They believed that the doctors had too much influence already.

In July 1939, at discussions between the hospital and the Swansea Council representatives about a new jointly-run hospital, doubts expressed by the Charity Commissioners over the use of the Charitable Trust funds for such a hospital almost put an end to the negotiations there and then. But the Board wished to continue negotiating as long as it was to be allowed equal representation with the Council on the governing body if the hospital were to be built. That was not acceptable to the town's councillors, and both bodies approached the Welsh Board of Health for advice. That Board's Chairman, Sir John Rowland, decided that, if the new hospital were ever built, it could not be owned by both bodies; either one or the other must have a majority of the seats on its committee. He believed that by then local authorities were entitled to co-operate in the establishment and maintenance of new regional voluntary hospitals, but there was little evidence locally of a wish to implement such a policy. It appeared that most councils preferred to set up their own hospitals and the Welsh Board of Health had no power to intervene.

In the end, it was not the whims of the hospital's governors and local council, the stubbornness of the doctors or even the needs of the patients which determined the fate of the new hospital, but the political situation in Europe.

CHAPTER TEN

The Second World War: 1939–1945

> We are passing through a period unprecedented in the world's history.[1]

THAT august body, the Swansea Division of the BMA, was preparing itself for war. Although it later found time to indulge in far more civilized activities such as organizing the first Cellan-Jones golf tournament, together with several highly successful lunches at the Mackworth Hotel, there were other more serious matters to be considered in 1939. In February, a lecture by Swansea's Medical Officer of Health, Dr Tighe, on *The relation of medical services to ARP* (air-raid precautions)[2] gave some indication of the hard times that were expected. The topic chosen by Dr Tighe would not have surprised the honorary staff (one of whom, Mr Howell Gabe, later lectured to the Division on his experiences in organizing a casualty clearing station on the Western Front during the First World War). As early as 1932, Territorial Army units had 'encamped at Swansea and Neath' and permission had been asked for them to be treated at the hospital in the event of illness or injury. The exercises were repeated in 1934 and 1937. It was arranged for six non-commissioned officers from the 158th Welsh Field Ambulance Corps to attend twice a week for instruction in elementary nursing. At the same time, three of the hospital's sisters had joined the Military Nursing Reserve. Three staff nurses were to be released 'in time of a national emergency' but the remainder of the nursing staff were allowed to decide for themselves whether they wished to attend the ARP lectures provided. The Home Office had also written to local authorities in 1937:

> describing the scheme of medical instruction in anti-gas measures and inviting authorities to cooperate with the BMA to ensure that they are economical and effective.[3]

In July 1938, the Royal Army Medical Corps Reception Station at Cardiff asked the hospital what the charges would be for 'military patients'. They were told that they would be nine shillings a week, which was three shillings more than was expected of the local councils. The Matron complained that in most hospitals, the ARP lectures were compulsory. As a result, a course of six lectures was included in the nurses' syllabus.

In June 1938, when the Swansea Town Council was preparing an ARP scheme to submit to the Home Office, the Deputy Medical Officer of Health had asked if it would be possible to free 80 beds immediately they were required and 100 beds within a week of that time. By the autumn, the Ministry of Health 'required' 75 beds to be evacuated within 24 hours and also asked for facilities for 'decontamination' although no details were provided as to what exactly was needed. On 7 September 1939, the Prime Minister announced in the House of Commons that there were more than 200,000 hospital beds available for air raid casualties, 41,000 of them outside London.[4]

Six months before the outbreak of war, the Minister of Health travelled to Cardiff to review the arrangements made by the voluntary hospitals and the local authorities for the provision of hospital facilities in the event of war. At the same time, in the hospital itself, the possibility of taking out a war insurance policy was being discussed and a first aid post was set up. Two mobile first aid posts had also been organized in the town; the Medical Officer of Health's Department was allowed the use of the out-patient clinic on two evenings a week so that the 'personnel may meet the medical officers'. A fire extinguisher was bought for the Convalescent Home (at a cost of fifty-five shillings). Scoops, hoses, sand containers and stirrup pumps were bought for the hospital, where the staff had been attending classes in anti-gas measures and the treatment of fires caused by incendiary bombs.

The arguments about the Contributory Scheme continued after the outbreak of war, and the visiting medical staff continued to be objects of hostility for some time. Meanwhile, the majority of the London medical schools had closed and clinical facilities were made available for fifth and sixth-year medical students. Soon there were difficulties in replacing resident medical staff, and representatives from the Ministry of Health asked for permission to inspect the Griffith Thomas and Folland Wards, which, it was thought, might serve as ARP posts.

The Port Talbot Hospital had been provided with 8,000 more sandbags than they needed. Those were offered to and accepted by the hospital. Casualty hospitals were expected to have more operating theatre space than was available in relation to the number of beds. But the Ministry refused to pay for the conversion of the major operating theatre so that two operations could be performed simultaneously, as had been suggested by the Visiting Medical Staff.

While the government had clearly stated that it did not wish to interfere in the internal management of the hospital or take over its workings, it was essential that there should be available a mechanism for co-ordinating the work being done by each hospital. The Air Raid Precautions Act of 1937 had already made local councils responsible for setting up certain medical services in the event of war. In July 1939, proposals were put forward for the creation of an Emergency Hospital Medical Service and an emergency ambulance service. By December 1939, the arrangements for providing ambulances and cars at times of emergency were being discussed in detail. By February 1940, the local Medical War Committee had been formed. All those present were convinced that the recruitment of doctors should remain in the hands of local committees as they were best able to judge the order of priorities for any locality. At first, the hospital accepted their decisions without question. But the Swansea Group A governors were again determined to show their independence by applying to the Central War Committee for deferment for one of the medical staff without the knowledge of the House Committee. When the Emergency Medical Service (EMS) was established, the Swansea Hospital became one of the main casualty hospitals (Class 1A) for south Wales and almost immediately after war was declared, the service offered to the civilian population was curtailed, as it had been agreed that 100 beds would be set aside for possible air-raid casualties. By August 1940, the hospital took over the Workingmen's Club and Institute at Langland Bay so that 137 extra beds were made available. Annexes of this kind were largely intended to be used for the transfer of casualties from hospitals. In this case it was agreed by the Ministry that the Langland Annexe could be regarded as being part of the main hospital, so that it became possible to transfer large numbers of civilian patients there within a few days of having had surgical operations, as the town itself was regarded as being particularly vulnerable.

As many as 650,000 people had been evacuated from London early in September 1939. On the Ministry's instructions, mothers and children from bombed areas were to be admitted to 1A hospitals for forty-eight hours before being moved on to their new homes. During 1940, 314 healthy mothers and children were temporarily housed at Langland and by the autumn, the Ministry had taken over the running of the Annexe there.

The first air raids on Swansea occurred in June 1940. An ARP Subcommittee had been formed a month before the war started but it had not been particularly active at that stage. Five days before the first raid, wooden shutters had been fixed to the windows of the old X-ray room to provide a gas-proof refuge room for children. Later, special gas masks were provided for the telephonists. By 1941, the minimum number of fire-watchers necessary to maintain an effective service at the hospital was ten. Already, the basement of the hospital's property at Walter Road had been converted into a public air-raid shelter (at a rent of two shillings and sixpence a week).

The staff were required to carry certificates of employment as a means of identification 'at a time when freedom of movement may be denied to others'. On the night of 1 September 1940, one of the hospital houses adjacent to the hospital at Cae Parc was destroyed during an air raid. The fire was dealt with by the Matron, two porteresses and two men who had volunteered to help. During that year, ninety-eight patients were admitted to the hospital as a result of injuries sustained during air raids, although not all those injured in the town seem to have been sent to the hospital.

By September 1940, part of the stocks of drugs and chemicals were transferred to Langland Bay for safe keeping. Later, the use of the diathermy machine was causing problems as the waves which emitted from it were interfering with the use of short-wave radio apparatus. The Radio Branch of the Post Office was generally restricting the use of such machines but the hospital was allowed to retain theirs providing it was contained in a room that had been specially earthed and screened.

After the formation of the National Blood Transfusion Service, the hospital took an active part in banking blood from July 1940. Up until that time, donors had been called on at times of emergency. Six months after the hospital's first blood bank was formed, 132 donors gave blood which was then kept at the hospital for a week and was available for use. Any remaining supplies were sent to Cardiff. In return, the hospital was given plasma and serum which did not require refrigeration. Although the life-saving effect of immediate transfusion had become apparent, supplies were insufficient to meet the demand for civilian and military emergencies. It was hoped to attract at least 3,000 donors from the Swansea district alone.

The numbers of nurses available by then was quite insufficient. From June 1940 onwards, 494 Nursing Auxiliaries and members of the Civil Nursing Reserve underwent practical training at the hospital before being sent to other hospitals in the area or to work with the National Blood Transfusion Service. The WVS had already provided a great deal of help in making surgical dressings, towels, operating theatre garments and black-out curtains. Untold numbers of voluntary helpers gave their services unstintingly.

The courage and devoted service of the staff, stretcher bearers and auxiliary firemen during the heavy raids in February 1941 was all the more commendable considering the severity of the damage to the hospital itself. Several of the wards were left unfit for use. The laconic way in which the medical staff instructed the Secretary of their committee 'to submit a proposal for replacing the glass in the windows of the Theatre with Windolite' illustrates admirably the extent of the resolution with which all those employed at the hospital faced their work at that time. There was no loss of life or even injury to patients or staff but the hospital was evacuated for some weeks so that repairs could be properly carried out. It was during that period that the air raids on Swansea were at their worst, and 120 surgical beds had to be made available at Cefn Coed Hospital by the transfer of 70 of their patients to the psychiatric hospital at Bridgend. Although most of those 120 beds were taken by wounded soldiers, as many as 180 local residents were admitted to Cefn Coed Hospital within three days when the air raids were at their height.[5] It was the Swansea Hospital surgeons and nurses who manned the unit there, and 20 beds in the Cefn Coed Nurses' Home were released for the nursing staff.

After consultations with the Welsh Board of Health, it was decided that the number of beds at the main hospital must be reduced and far more use was to be made of the Langland Annexe. In that way, it was hoped to maintain a service that would be almost normal in its extent. It would certainly help to reduce the anxiety being experienced by patients and staff.

It seems surprising that in the midst of this agitation, there were other activities more remote from the care of patients and the protection of the buildings during air raids that took the attention of some of those connected with the hospital. The war had not drawn to a close the negotiations concerning the peacetime development of the hospital services, and they continued. In July 1940, a conference called at Cardiff decided in favour of forming a Regional Hospitals Council for south Wales and plans continued to be formulated for the post-war period. At the close of 1939, the Glamorgan County Council had finally made it known that it would be heavily committed to a policy of extending the hospital at Penrhiwtyn (which was by then the West Glamorgan County Hospital). The County Council could not therefore be relied on to support plans for a regional hospital at Swansea. Large numbers of subscribers to the Swansea scheme were being admitted at Penrhiwtyn for treatment. This posed an additional problem as the Council had to be paid for its services by the hospital. (At that time, payments of more than £2,100 in one year had to be made to other hospitals for the Swansea contributors being treated there.) The financial problems brought by the increased cost of surgical equipment and the migration of labour from non-essential industries as a result of the war were great. It became apparent even then that a radical change in organization would be necessary.

There were times when the rebel members of the Swansea Group A Governors behaved as though they were quite unaware of the privations being suffered as a result of the war. They continued to agitate for more representation (possibly urged on by the fact that some of the senior medical staff were not there to defend their point of view) as though this was the single most important issue to be resolved at that time. Noticeably absent whenever help was required at times of crisis, their militant attitude continued unabated in spite of the serious effects that the war was having on the population in general and on the life of the hospital in particular. In January 1941, and again in October, they resigned from membership of all the Standing Committees. Their resignations were not accepted, possibly more from a fear that the contributions would diminish rather than from any intense fraternal feelings towards them on the part of the remainder of the Board. It was not until May 1942 that they and the Board had 'resolved their differences' but the reason for the improvement in their relationships is not known.

In spite of the great reservations expressed about the Board's decision at the beginning of the war unconditionally to extend the benefits allowed to those members of the Contributory Scheme who were serving with the forces, the income for 1941 had increased. Payments from the Emergency Medical Service for that year amounted almost to £22,000. They did not represent the actual cost of the service offered and it had to be accepted that no final settlement could be reached until after the war. On the other hand, expenditure had increased between 1939 and 1943 from £70,345 to £101,157 while the total increase in income was only £26,690.

It was impossible to predict the nature of the changes likely to occur in post-war policy. The Ministry had requested that the development of Regional Councils should not proceed but that surveys of the work of the hospital service and its needs, which might be useful in planning for the future, should be undertaken. In October 1941, the Minister of Health, Mr Ernest Brown, made a statement in the House of Commons that the direction of the hospital service in peacetime had been engaging the attention of the government for some time.[6] It had been agreed in principle that as soon as possible after the war, a comprehensive hospital service should be provided and made available by some means or other to all those who needed it. At that time, it was still widely anticipated that the major local authorities ('in close co-operation with the voluntary agencies') would be responsible for its organization and that the partnership between those two agencies would be 'on a more regular footing'.[7] The *British Medical Journal* quickly saw the disadvantages of such a system. The Editor's words might have been written about Swansea:

> It is one thing to rejoice sentimentally over the happy partnership between the two systems which is so confidently foretold by those who ... are sure that the best of all possible worlds is on the doorstep. It is more salutary, perhaps, to recognise that there are sharp cleavages of opinion and conflicting vested interests ...[8]

In December 1941, an international gathering was organized in BMA House by the United Kingdom Council of the International Hospital Association 'to consider the positions of hospitals over the world at the dawn of peace.[9] In his speech Mr Ernest Brown was careful to emphasize that the Emergency Medical Service had not been designed as a prototype for a post-war service. In practice, however, its influence was felt in many localities for long after the war. Discussions had been taking place between the military authorities and the Borough Council on the setting up of a military hospital. Maesygwernen at Morriston was eventually chosen as the site which had the best facilities. The Morriston Hospital was not opened until November 1942 but in June, a deputation was received by the Swansea Hospital Board to discuss the Ministry's policy for the new hospital. It was promised by the Board that they would offer all the help possible in setting up the new service. The Welsh Board of Health made it known that the post-war role of the Maesygwernen (Morriston) Hospital had not yet been considered. A promise was made that, although the hospital was a military one, they would attempt to relieve the civilian waiting lists already in being.

The Emergency Medical Service Pathology Section set about establishing their own area laboratories and asked for permission to recognize the Beck Laboratory as the area laboratory in Swansea. This meant that the 'sideroom' laboratories at Morriston, Neath and the Carmarthen Public Assistance Institution would be supervised from Swansea.

The calmness with which much of the hospital's ordinary work went on was quite remarkable. Dr Esmond Rees requested permission in December 1941 to start a Speech Re-education Clinic, the Swansea Division of the BMA met there to hear Professor Mackintosh lecture on 'Modern Methods in Anaesthesia', the student nurses held a sale of work and those eternal optimists of the financial world, Lloyds Bank, sent yet another of their polite and mildly worded reminders concerning the overdraft.

The *British Medical Journal* had already issued a warning of the dangers that would follow air raids in districts where radium was being stored.[10] The effects of its release after bombing could not be precisely assessed. But it was thought necessary to store all radium supplies in specially constructed wells at a depth of fifty feet so that there was a covering layer of earth of thirty feet. The radium in use therefore had to be deposited for safe keeping in a well sunk at Cardiff. The heavy radioactive gas, radon, was more expensive and was not suitable for treating all the conditions for which radium therapy was provided, but had to be bought as a substitute.

The debate about the storage of radium continued seemingly for most of the war. The Welsh Board of Health had refused to consider bearing the cost of producing a bore hole at Swansea because the quantities kept at the hospital were so small that it would not be 'justified' to use this procedure during air raids. It was believed by those who were responsible for the radium at the hospital that if a specially made steel container were provided, the whole quantity in use could be safely removed and deposited when necessary in the container within ten minutes. At that stage, the unit at Cardiff asked if it would be possible for a specific number of beds at the hospital to be allocated for the treatment of malignant disease by radiation techniques. The visiting medical staff recommended that thirty beds should be released at once but, as there had been a severe air raid which had badly affected the hospital in the meantime, the whole stock was transferred to Cardiff. In the case of the few patients left who needed treatment of that kind, X-ray therapy was to be used. Part of the stock was apparently returned to Swansea at the time of the air raids in 1941 and it was then stored at Langland surrounded by a fourteen-inch blast wall.

In 1944, the Welsh Board of Health had no objection to the return of the radium from Cardiff 'as the hospital will serve as an Approved Sub-centre of the Institute of Radiotherapy'. Since the passing of the Cancer Act in 1939, the local authorities had reason to believe that they would have a major role to play in the development of the radiotherapy services. Even before that time, it had been agreed in principle that there should be a Radiotherapy Institute for South Wales, based at Cardiff, with sub-centres at Newport and Swansea. A conference of local authorities had approved the formation of a Joint Board which would concern itself with diagnosis and treatment. It seemed totally illogical to the Swansea Hospital Board that, whereas they had been providing specialized facilities in this sphere for many years before the outbreak of war, the Swansea Borough Council, which had neither the expertise nor the facilities was now to take over the organization of the service.

By December 1944, the Welsh Board of Health wished to reopen discussions on the arrangements for the diagnosis and treatment of cancer in south Wales. A growing demand and urgent need for new facilities had become apparent. No steps were to be taken to establish any new administrative machinery for a service until the government's intentions on any proposed new health service had been made known.

As the military hospital at Morriston was administered for the central authorities by the Town Council's Health Department, the possibility that the pre-war plans might come to fruition with that hospital, rather than with the older hospital at Swansea, as the new centre for the treatment for cancer caused some concern. When the House Committee were asked if they would enter into preliminary discussions with the Welsh Board of Health and the Town Council, their previous experience had shown them that any plans put forward by them would not necessarily be accepted by the local Council. Events proved them to be right. Later, the local authorities refused to accept the scheme which had been prepared on the basis that work in that sphere was entirely their responsibility and that the Welsh Board of Health had no authority to make approaches to the voluntary hospitals on this matter. In 1944, all those concerned with the matter were reminded that the possibility of a co-ordinated service for treating malignant disease had first been raised in 1936. That did little to improve relationships but the hospital eventually proceeded with the appointment of a radiotherapist (in 1945) quite independently of the Council.

The House Committee discussed the War Damage Bill in February 1942. It seemed to them that the best they could hope to gain from it would have been that the proposed War Damage Commission might ('if they think fit') make a payment for the damage that had been done. The committee had hoped for rather more and would not have found it easy to settle for less, as the debt would otherwise mount even higher. There were also fears that there were plans for the voluntary hospitals to be put under public (that is, local authority) control after the war. There was therefore a great deal of support for the demand that the government make an early declaration of intent. This would have been difficult as it was not known which political party would be in power after the war. It is highly likely that, in spite of the discussions that had occurred on the future of the service, no clearly designed policy had been developed at that stage.

After the air raid of February 1941, patients had been temporarily evacuated to Carmarthen, the Amman Valley Hospital and some of the smaller hospitals such as Fairwood. It had also been intended that the Community Centre at Townhill and the Tawe Lodge Hospital should be used as annexes. This intention was not carried out because of 'administrative difficulties' of an unspecified nature. It was then decided that the Griffith Thomas and Folland Wards should not be used as military annexes, as the Ministry had hoped, because one ward was required for 'massage' work and the other was to be kept in reserve. The first aid post at the hospital had needed several alterations after the first air raid. In March 1942, the Welsh Board of Health approved a plan submitted by the Town Council whereby that first aid post would be used to screen 'against an abnormal influx of lightly injured persons [and as] a sorting department for the hospital'. It would be manned by a sister and five nurses who would be paid by the local authority. To worsen their problems, there occurred an outbreak of diphtheria in the hospital and town in June 1942.

Before the outbreak of war, the BMA Council had decided that no new appointments must be made to the consultant staff of any hospital for one year after the end of the war in order to protect the position of those doctors who had joined the forces. Mr Woods had been asked to stay on as Honorary Surgeon for the duration of the war. In 1942, there was a move to increase the number of medical staff when it was recommended that two additional physicians and two surgeons should be appointed. This eventually led to a major disagreement between the House Committee and the honorary staff. It is possible that this gave an additional impetus to the demand (of some years' duration) to limit the number of medical staff on the Board and Standing Committees. As neither side would yield, BMA officials from London had to be asked to visit in an attempt to settle the dispute.

Long before that was achieved, the hospital was subjected to a great deal of damage (on the night of 16 February 1943). It may well be that the continuing stresses of working under wartime conditions and the bitterness of the dispute between the doctors and the committee were not entirely unrelated. During the air raid on that night, the Griffith Thomas Ward was so severely damaged that it had to be demolished. The old Out-patients' Department, the Folland Ward (previously used as a temporary clinic), and the Registration Office were also affected.[11] The total number of beds was reduced from 305 to 234, as the Talbot Ward had to be converted into a clinic and office. The work of the 'excellent' team of staff who undertook the clearing of the debris and the repairs enabled some of the wards to be reopened after some weeks.[12] Although there were sixteen per cent fewer beds available than in 1942, the reduction in the number of patients admitted was less than ten per cent of the previous year's figure. Sufficient confusion occurred over the arrangements on the night of the air raid for a 'Subcommittee re Raid incident' to be formed to investigate the matter. The Matron commented on the lack of leadership that had become apparent during the crisis but the extent of the chaos was far greater than had been anticipated. The operating theatres were out of action, there was overcrowding in the Casualty Department whose entrance was blocked because a time bomb had been discovered outside, and delays had occurred in providing ambulances to evacuate the hospital. Three hundred patients (including twenty-eight children) were eventually removed with surprisingly little delay. One of the House Surgeons had been accused of leaving his post but he had left

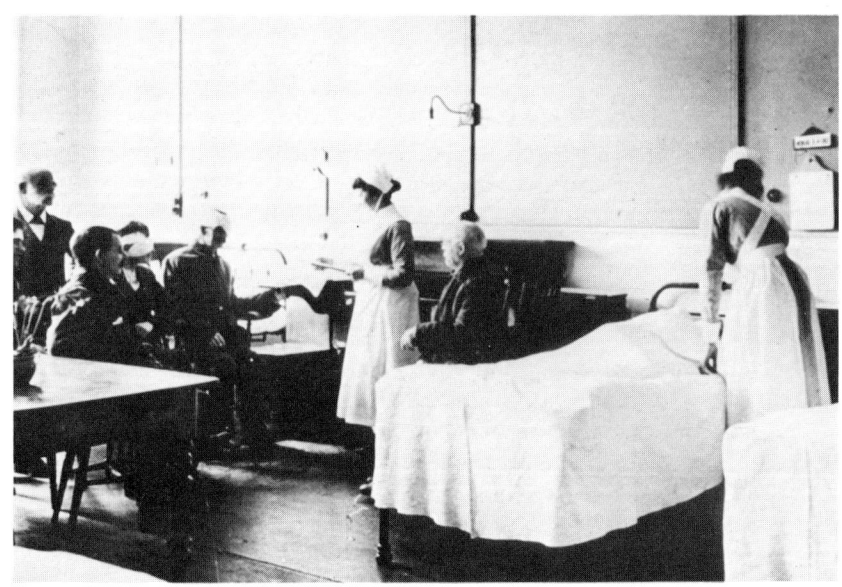

Soldiers in a ward during the Second World War.

Inspecting bomb damage in 1943. (*Pictures by kind permission of Mr Rowley Davies.*)

at 4 a.m. to take a convoy of people injured during the raid to Morriston Hospital. There, he was told to wait in case he should be required and did not return until the following afternoon. In the end, the staff were congratulated on their work which had enabled some of the wards to be made ready for use within a short space of time. Although no patients were killed during the air raid, it seems that some of them did die later, presumably as a result of their wounds. There later occurred an improvement in the arrangements made for such emergencies. But in any case the number of air raids on the town diminished from that time onwards and the hospital itself was not affected afterwards.

In spite of these hazards, many of the hospital's ordinary activities were able to continue. The police prosecuted a local dairy for supplying less milk to the hospital than had been paid for. The Matron, Miss E. A. Smith, made an authoritative pronouncement on the importance of practical training for nurses ('intelligence is not the only factor which should be taken into consideration in nursing'[13]). Three nurses developed tuberculosis and had to be sent to Craig-y-nos for treatment. Nursing staff were refused permission to wear their outdoor uniforms when they travelled by bus in the town. With only 148 nurses working, there was a shortage of 25. It was the Ministry of Labour that asked hospitals to suspend, for the duration of the war, the rules which forbade nurses from getting married.

The dispute with the senior medical staff continued. Great resentment was felt at the accusation made by the Secretary of the BMA, who said:

> there are influences at work which have as their object the perpetration (*sic*) of the dispute and the destruction of this spirit of good will which is essential to a satisfactory conclusion.[14]

That letter probably contained a great deal of truth. It was written, however, soon after a severe air raid which had taxed the patience of the ordinary workforce at the hospital to the limit. Although they themselves did not enter into the dispute, there were members of the Board (who had done nothing to help during the recent upheavals) who took umbrage at what they considered to be an attack on their integrity. The Board generally deprecated the attitude of those of their members who had already published statements in the press on matters which were regarded as being *sub judice*. It was a complex quarrel because of the divisions of opinion within the Board. The situation was not eased when the journal *Medical World* concluded in January 1943 that the House Committee had 'outsmarted' the doctors by making an honorary appointment without referring the matter to the medical staff who had been excluded from all the committees as a result of the dispute.[15] The BMA ban on increasing the number of doctors there was lifted as soon as the senior doctors were given back their places on the committees. The BMA was thought not to have made a strong enough stand. The staff were advised to take matters into their own hands rather than:

> submit to an inglorious defeat at the hands of the Chairman of the Board [one of the Swansea Group A governors] who is the local ringleader in this dispute.

A few days before that article appeared, the visiting staff had given notice that, as the Board had not carried out the agreement as had been arranged, they would withhold their services from 1 February apart from providing emergency cover. It was thought for a time that a settlement might be reached but again the medical staff had to threaten to withdraw. Their first request for an independent inquiry had been refused but was later agreed to, and the doctors were reinstated as committee members in June. No copy of the report of the inquiry has survived. Its terms, however, were accepted in October 1943 and eventually each unpaid member of the visiting staff was allowed to become a Governor. With the inclusion of the Langland Annexe, the number of beds had increased for much of the war and the numbers of visiting and resident staff had diminished. The Board had therefore decided to increase the numbers of honorary staff, which was against the BMA's policy. The Welsh Board of Health took the view that the BMA had interfered unnecessarily. As the needs of the area were urgent, the assistance of the Ministry of Health should be sought. The visiting staff continued to insist that they had taken issue with the hospital on a point of principle. Their arguments did not in any way concern any individuals who might be appointed to honorary medical posts.

In February 1944, the Welsh Board of Health confidentially requested all class 1A hospitals to restrict civilian admissions to those requiring immediate and urgent treatment from a date of which they were to be informed. It was intended that beds should be kept for wounded members of the forces and for civilians from hospitals in London. On 12 August 1944, 124 patients, most of whom were 'chronic civilian sick', arrived. Another smaller number was transferred to other hospitals locally on that day. It was then made known that they would not be required to take any more civilians but that between 50 and 60 beds must be kept for battle casualties. When 56 of them arrived later that month, in spite of all the preparations, some confusion arose. No one knew whether they were to be treated as civilian patients or to what extra privileges they might be entitled until the Military Registrar at Morriston was asked for advice.

Apart from the sound of heavy gunfire that occurred after midnight on Saturdays when a military unit did its practising, the war had less effect on the hospital by 1944 than in previous years. In spite of the general confusion about planning for the future, it was possible to extend the Beck Laboratory by using 10 Brunswick Street (which was owned by the hospital) for that purpose. The Welsh Board of Health agreed that the Out-patients' Department must be rebuilt at a cost of £2,557, the money to be provided by the War Damage Commission. Once that was completed, thirty-four extra beds would be brought back into use, as the Talbot Ward would also be reconditioned at the same time. On 1 February 1945, the first true indication that the war was almost over came with the announcement that beds no longer needed to be reserved for the Emergency Hospital Service unless fresh instructions should be given later.

With the withdrawal of the hospital from the Emergency Medical Service, there occurred a significant loss of revenue but a larger number of beds was made available to deal with the 'exceptionally high' waiting lists. The Welsh Board of Health was prepared to continue to maintain the Langland Annexe for civilian use for as long as the tenancy agreement would allow and the House Committee decided to take advantage of that offer. By then, the Working Men's Club and Institute had made it known (in August 1945) that they needed the building for use as a convalescent home. It was agreed that the last hospital patients should leave there in November 1945. That move marked the end of the hospital's association with the Swansea Volunteer Stretcher Bearer Corps, which had provided such superb service in transferring patients there each week and at times of emergency for most of the war.

The end of the war was marked within the hospital by the removal of the emergency water tanks from the tennis courts and the dismantling of the blast walls. Those who worked there were gradually able to adapt themselves once more to a peacetime existence with all its problems. The significance and extent of the changes that were to occur after the war had still not been realized. From 1 January 1945, the rate of contributions was increased from threepence to fourpence a week. The British Hospitals' Association policy concerning reciprocal arrangements with other voluntary hospitals throughout Britain was accepted. The Association itself had continued to work effectively in planning improvements in the voluntary sector throughout the war. The Swansea delegates to its conference in 1942 had been very much concerned with finding some means by which the Contributory Schemes could be made available to all sections of the community after the war.

Six days before the war was officially over, a request from the

National Union of Public Employees asking for permission to hold a meeting in an attempt to enrol members was refused. The cursory comment was added that, though the House Committee could not object to their employees joining a trade union, there was no obligation on them to grant facilities for meetings of that nature on hospital premises. However archaic that attitude may seem to be now, let it not be forgotten that it was the same committee who had already ushered in (from 1 January 1945) one of the most revolutionary changes in the history of the hospital with the abolition of Recommendation Letters. That move, which anticipated one of the most important features of the National Health Service, was introduced with the words:

> Henceforth the privilege of recommending a patient will rest with the General Medical Practitioners.[16]

CHAPTER ELEVEN

The Coming of the National Health Service: 1945–1948

> History has now shown clearly that Aneurin Bevan stuffed the mouths of the medical profession not with gold but with committee minutes.[1]

THAT there were to be changes in the administration of the hospital service after the war had been apparent for a considerable time. In 1940, the BMA had considered a plan for the future organization of medicine. Two years later, the Swansea Division (among others) had submitted a resolution to the Association's Annual Meeting that any new health service should:

> render available to every individual all necessary medical services, both general and specialist, and both domiciliary and institutional.[2]

In that year too, the Beveridge Report was published, and its basic principles reflected opinions commonly held by doctors throughout Britain. In 1943, the Labour Party produced its pamphlet *A National Service for Health*.[3] There were clearly apparent signs that alterations to the system were inevitable. The uncertainty about the nature of those developments caused grave concern to doctors and hospital governors alike. On 18 February 1944, *The Times* announced that the Chairman of the Council of the BMA intended sending a list of questions on the new White Paper for a National Health Service that the government of the day had produced to all doctors working in Britain. A week after the two-day debate on the subject in the House of Commons,[4] it was arranged for local doctors to discuss the issue and at that BMA meeting several points of view were put forward. They varied from wanting a 'showdown' with any possible future government to mistrust of the BMA itself. One family practitioner recalled the position in 1912 when the profession had originally opposed the new system but eventually agreed that it had brought only benefits.

There were fears that the voluntary hospitals would be 'squeezed out', the loss of the Contributory Schemes was regretted, and there was a feeling that the new consultant posts to be created would be unevenly distributed throughout the land.[5]

The general air of nervousness among the Governors about the hospital's future had become apparent from the early 1940s and increased in intensity with time. Before the end of the war, an answer had been sent to a questionnaire from the British Hospitals Association saying that 'subject to adequate safeguards', the committee was in favour of the principle of a National Health Service, although they had no conception at the time of the form that it would take and they believed that the voluntary hospitals would survive in some form or another. At first, it was thought that both the voluntary hospitals and the major local authorities would be asked to set up Regional Councils, but no information was made available about their intended function. The somewhat forlorn hope was that, apart from an influx of money, little else would alter. At the request of the Minister of Health, the plans for Regional Councils were later discontinued so that time could be spent on preparing for surveys of future needs. In 1942, the Minister announced that the responsibility for the new service would rest with the major local authorities 'in close co-operation with the Voluntary Bodies'. Both were asked to facilitate this partnership but this did not please the hospital's Board. They insisted that their system:

> has virtues which it is essential to retain and which flourish more freely under voluntary and independent management, but our aim should be to contribute to an efficient and economically administered scheme, co-ordinating Municipal and Voluntary Hospitals without losing the best characteristics of either.[6]

'We face the future', it was added, 'with confidence.' That confidence was largely lost as it became apparent that the voluntary system was doomed. At first it had been clearly said that no voluntary hospital would be compelled to become part of the new health service. That pronouncement served only to increase the concern that if voluntary and local authority hospitals were meant to coexist as part of the new system, the hospital at Morriston (already virtually in the hands of the Swansea Corporation, who administered it on behalf of the Ministry) might assume a more important role. In consequence, the Swansea Hospital might largely lose its freedom and independence.

In May 1946, the hospital's Secretary-Superintendent, Mr O. C. Howells, wrote a memorandum in which he summarized the salient points of the new Act as it affected the voluntary hospitals. The very fact that the document was allowed to lie on the table was an indication that the hospital committee had at last accepted the principle that the era of the voluntary hospitals was drawing to a close. Consequently, discussions about plans for the future were inclined to be confused and indecisive and were confined for a time to methods of restoring the bed complement to its former level.

With the publication of the National Health Service Bill, which led to the passing of the National Health Service Act of 1946, it finally became known that the voluntary hospitals would be taken over by the State by 1948. But a great deal was to happen before that time.

In October 1941, it had been announced in the House of Commons that the government intended to conduct a survey of hospital services (excluding psychiatric units). In 1943, the Welsh Board of Health commissioned a report on south Wales, which was published in 1945.[7] Its authors were quick to point out that the only successful attempt at co-operation between the local authorities and the voluntary hospitals had occurred during the war in the case of the Emergency Medical Services. But that was obligatory and took place under the direction of the Ministry of Health. Tawe Lodge was dismissed in the report as an 'out-of-date public assistance institution'. Swansea Hospital was found to offer an adequate service, although it was seriously overcrowded and considered too small. Removal to a new site was thought to be required as a matter of urgency. It was envisaged in the report that there should be local hospitals (already in existence to some extent in the form of the cottage hospitals), area hospitals, and group hospitals which should provide a more specialized service for a wider area but would also have to function as area hospitals. Throughout the district, 877 beds (including some of those at Morrison Hospital) needed to be discarded and at least 1,736 new ones were required. Of those, it was thought that about 1,000 should be at the new area hospital which was to replace Swansea Hospital. It would serve as the 'group centre' (or one of two such centres) for west Wales. It would also include a maternity unit to replace the two smaller local authority units which had been destroyed during the war, and some 'local beds' to avoid the unnecessary construction of smaller hospitals in nearby districts.

Meanwhile, with the rebuilding of the out-patient clinic and the reconditioning of the Talbot Ward at the hospital in July 1945, a further thirty-two beds were made ready for use. It had already been decided that the immediate post-war priority must be to restore the bed complement to its pre-war level. The Town Council's Health Committee had already sent delegates to inspect new hospitals that had been built at Oxford and Birmingham. The Welsh Board of Health was asked to support an application for rebuilding the Griffith Thomas and Folland Wards to enable in-patient facilities to be brought back to their pre-war level. The attitude of the Swansea Council was that their post-war planning programme for the town would involve the hospital site; consequently, they could not sanction any further building there. The hospital committee could hardly be blamed for believing that the true reason for the refusal was that the Council members hoped that they might yet be instructed to take over the entire responsibility for administering the hospital service. A vote of censure was passed on one of the Swansea Group A Governors:

> for his attitude towards this Hospital at the Council when the recommendation of the Highways Committee was under discussion.

With the loss of the Langland Bay Annexe by November 1945, the Council's refusal added greatly to the difficulties of coping with the waiting list. Also, increasing numbers of patients were being treated at other hospitals, which aggravated the financial problems. Counsel's opinion was sought on the legality of the decision and the Welsh Board of Health was asked for its advice. Having attempted to intervene, the Welsh Board and the Ministry of Health believed that there was no point in continuing with the negotiations.

Further bad feeling was caused by the fact that the major south Wales local authorities had not been prepared to accept the Interim Scheme for the diagnosis and treatment of malignant disease proposed by the three main voluntary hospitals which served the region. The local authorities maintained that, as the Cancer Act of 1939 had given them the right to prepare such projects, the Welsh Board of Health was not entitled even to seek the views of the hospitals on the matter. In June 1945, they prepared an interim scheme of their own and they later invited representatives from the voluntary hospitals (including two nominees from Swansea) to discuss the project. It was then envisaged that the scheme would start operating on 1 May 1946.

The early post-war period was beset with problems. The direction of labour that had occurred in wartime and from which nurses were not exempted, was being allowed to continue for what seemed to be unnecessarily long periods. All attempts to prevent the transfer of the night staff nurse in charge of the operating theatre to work elsewhere failed. The Ministry of Labour were unimpressed with the inconvenience caused by the failure of the hospital to attract qualified staff. During the war, unqualified nurses had been appointed as staff nurses because of the shortage and this had to continue for some time even after the regulations concerning the direction of labour had lapsed.

Having considered various means by which the shortage of beds might be eased, the Board eventually (in April 1947) decided to take a lease from Mrs Henry Folland on a large house called Llwynderw in Blackpill as an annexe. The house had been used as a Red Cross hospital and its tenancy was available until 1951, after which it was bought by the Ministry. It eventually housed 40 beds for patients having post-operative treatment, so that the total number of beds available to the hospital was still only 316. Not even all the patients who needed treatment urgently (and who included many with malignant disease) were being dealt with as quickly as would have been wished. In July 1945, therefore, the visiting medical staff invited an expert to Swansea to advise on the suitability of the Parc Beck site for building a new hospital. He was of the opinion that it would not be possible to place a building with a thousand beds there. Having visited two other sites on Gower Road, he concluded that one of them would be suitable if an arrangement could be made with the Town Council to acquire fifty or sixty acres of land. No more was heard of that plan.

The Ministry of Health had made approaches within a fortnight of the end of the war to ask if the hospital would participate in a scheme for providing postgraduate education and experience for doctors who were due to leave the forces. As their salaries would be paid, four such posts were asked for. Two medical students were employed at that time at half the House Physician's salary because of the shortage of doctors. The Swansea Committee for Medical Education (whose composition is not known) believed that the matter should be taken further and a Postgraduate School of Medicine for Wales, which would form part of the Welsh National School of Medicine, ought to be established in Swansea. Its function would be to make available training facilities for specialists and arrange refresher courses for family doctors 'and others requiring them'.[8] Never pursued with any vigour, this scheme suffered the same fate as the earlier attempts to create a medical school.

Medical advances of the greatest importance were rarely recorded in the hospital committee minutes. It is not even known when penicillin was first used locally. Only small quantities of the drug had been available for use in treating civilians but in September 1944, a list of diseases was published for which it could be requisitioned for use outside military circles.[9] In October 1945, the 'penicillin train' (which carried an exhibition on the use of the drug) was touring south Wales. Committee members and the honorary staff were invited to a preview at High Street Station before it was officially opened by the Mayor. Free supplies of penicillin would be discontinued in May 1946 and it was estimated that the cost of purchasing it subsequently might be about £2,000 a year. The hospital was the distributing centre for the whole area but since it was intended to prepare the drug in a more readily available form, there was no reason why other large hospitals should not in future buy their own supplies. This had occurred by June 1946. Then the pharmacist was able to prepare penicillin without restriction by government departments. Previously, it could only have been obtained from the pathologist with permission from the Ministry of Health. Once a 'Frigidaire' (which cost £126. 16s.) and a 'Drying Oven' (at £32) had been bought, penicillin became available to the visiting staff on the same terms as it was bought by other hospitals.

Uncertainty and confusion concerning the future of the hospital were reflected not only in the attitude of the hospital committee but also in that of the Town Council and even of the Ministry itself. In November 1945, Winston Churchill asked the Prime Minister in the House of Commons if he was then in a position to make known the position of the voluntary hospitals.[10] Five months afterwards, the Secretary had obtained copies of the White Paper which was eventually to form the basis of the new National Health Service Act. But at that time, there was still sufficient hope left that the voluntary hospitals would survive for the committee to concern itself with some aspects of planning for the future. It was anticipated that the Special Appeal organized in early 1946 would raise £35,000, but that sum would not clear the debt or pay for the massive redecorations that were necessary, let alone be available for new additions to the building. The proposals made by the British Hospitals' Contributory Scheme Association for the retention and reconstruction of Contributory Schemes were deferred because of doubts about the intentions of the new government. In fact, income from the hospital's own Contributory Scheme had increased in early 1946 because the rate of contributions was raised.

Even so, the financial difficulties were effectively highlighted by the refusal of the *Pharmaceutical Journal* to accept an advertisement for a post of Assistant Pharmacist because the salary which the hospital could afford to pay was too low.[11]

The recommendations made in May 1946 about the numbers of new medical staff to be appointed did not differ greatly from those already in existence. The visiting staff asked that three surgical units should be formed, each with a Surgeon, an Assistant Surgeon, an Anaesthetist and a House Surgeon. That scheme was vetoed but later, ambitious plans were prepared for a new, self-contained surgical block of 150 beds. It was hoped that between fifteen and twenty medical students could be accepted regularly during the summer months. That would add greatly to the hospital's prestige and would help form 'the nucleus of a teaching organisation which is visualised in the future'. Again, the possibility of creating a new Orthopaedic Unit was considered. In spite of the hospital's uneasy relationship with the Town Council's Health Committee, it was suggested that it might be feasible for the Swansea Hospital to share the services of a visiting surgeon in that specialty, either with the hospital at Morriston or at Neath.

The Welsh Board of Health were asked for advice as to how to proceed. It was also decided that a paediatrician should be appointed later. More immediately, the question of developing services in plastic surgery, thoracic surgery and neurosurgery should be discussed with the local authorities.

As no decision had yet been made on the future of Morriston Hospital, it was found impossible to start discussions on the sharing of facilities locally and an approach was made to the Glamorgan County Council. Having already used their statutory powers to develop their own hospitals to a considerable extent, the Council refused to help with the creation of an area Orthopaedic Department. As a result the visiting staff asked for the appointment of a full-time Orthopaedic Surgeon and a Medical Officer in Physical Medicine and Rehabilitation. By January 1947, the situation had altered again as the Welsh Board of Health had decided that if the Orthopaedic Department were formed, the surgeon's services could be used at Morriston Hospital for Emergency Medical Services' work, but that decision was later reversed. Equally uncertain was the fate of the new surgical block that had been intended to replace the wards lost during the war. At various times, permission seemed likely to be given for this to be built providing that the site was changed from the tennis court to one opening on to St Helen's Road, which would have involved the demolition of part of the hospital's property. But each demand for new facilities lessened the chance that any others might succeed. Under pressure from Dr Iwan Davies, who was concerned that the lack of sufficient beds for treating malignant disease would exclude the hospital (whoever would have the ultimate responsibility for administering it) from any new regional scheme for radiotherapy services, an increase of beds in the proposed surgical block (to provide thirty beds in all) was agreed to. It was thought that this would be best achieved by building additional balconies to the Talbot and Penllergaer Wards. Even with the imminent reorganization of hospitals into a state service, there still existed a lack of cohesiveness in planning for the future needs of the locality.

By April 1946, when the contents of the Bill which preceded the National Health Service Act of November 1946 were known, there was an upsurge in the concern felt by the hospital's supporters. This was allayed to some extent in April 1947 when a strictly confidential communication was received from the Welsh Board of Health in which they were prepared to recommend to the Treasury that Exchequer funds should be released to enable the hospital to continue providing the fullest service of which it was then capable. The conditions laid down were that an attempt must be made to maintain the present income from voluntary sources and that building operations of an exceptional nature must not be started without permission. Their accounts were to be made available for scrutiny if required and beds were to be reserved for the Emergency Medical Service when they were required. Increases of salary would not be taken into account and additional full-time staff should not be appointed without approval. As this offer meant that such block payments from government funds would prevent the overdraft from rising further, there was no option but to accept the offer. These terms were reasonable but that concerning the Emergency Medical Service must have caused some confusion. With a large hospital that had been opened for the use of that Service already functioning at the far end of the town, it is quite inconceivable that there could have been a further need for such facilities unless it was the Ministry's intention at that time to close Morriston Hospital. On the other hand, it may be that the possibility of using the Swansea Hospital for work in such fields as thoracic surgery or neurosurgery had not yet been excluded and that the Welsh Board of Health foresaw that some of their Morriston Hospital patients might need to make use of those facilities.

Within a year of the National Health Act, the hospital's Secretary recorded that:

> the imminence of the appointed day has already [had a] detrimental effect on income from voluntary sources.

Later, a conference was held with the local Members of Parliament as a shortage of materials and labour had made it unlikely that any additions to the building could be made. Yet another meeting with the Welsh Board and the Swansea Council was called for and permission was sought to erect temporary wards; that move was approved by the Ministry of Works Licensing Committee in February 1948. Since the hospital had failed in its attempt to take repossession of a ward at Cefn Coed Hospital because of the increasing need to re-establish the full use of that hospital as a psychiatric unit, and since the Ministry had issued instructions that no building projects were to be sponsored from government funds because of lack of money, this compromise had to be accepted. A press report in January 1948[12] that the plan for the extensions had been approved by the Council's Highways Committee was discussed by the House Committee although no official notification of the decision had been received at the hospital. (It so happened that the two wards were not completed until well after the hospital had been taken over by the State although the foundation stone was laid two days before the appointed day.)

The visiting staff continued to agitate over the question of payment for their services, and in 1946 they recommended that an attempt

The nursing staff at Swansea Hospital in 1960. The matron was Miss Smith. (*By kind permission of Miss Mair Davies.*)

should be made to interest the Glamorgan County in appointing specialists on an area basis in all specialties. The Council, however, refused, and it was widely agreed that it would be premature to take any further action at that stage and the matter was left until the new Hospital Board was formed. The same advice (put in a somewhat more forceful way) was offered by the town's Medical Officer of Health to his committee when they considered another request to share the cost of creating a new orthopaedic service.[13] By the end of 1946, there was therefore clear evidence that medical agencies outside the hospital were refusing to become involved in new projects at that time because of the uncertainties about the future of the health service as a whole.

Great relief was expressed when it was heard that the Joint Cancer Committee had designated the Swansea Hospital as a Class A Centre and would pay for the maintenance of patients with cancer treated there. The staff's satisfaction was diminished, however, when it was realized that peacetime conditions were not likely to return in all spheres of hospital administration for some considerable time. There were great difficulties experienced in obtaining adequate supplies of surgical dressings because the government gave priority to orders from foreign firms in order to promote exports. The control of hospitals by the Central War Committee was not discontinued until January 1947. After that, it was no longer necessary to have government approval before making changes in the medical staff establishment and it was decided to revert to the previous arrangement whereby two House Physicians were appointed. The principle of paying the visiting staff on a sessional basis was at last approved, providing that the Welsh Board of Health would make available the necessary money. The BMA had already decided that the fee should be no less than five guineas for a two-hour session but as the British Hospitals' Association had not been consulted, their advice was that payments should be deferred (and the fee was later reduced). It had been calculated that eighty-one consultant sessions a week would be necessary in the hospital, which would have cost nearly £18,000 but only two-thirds of that sum was obtainable from the Ministry of Health.

The Future Policy Subcommittee continued to meet but made no outstanding contributions in deciding how to increase the bed complement. The decisions that were made concerned the buying of a house in St James's Gardens as a nurses' hostel (at a cost of £2,500), and plans for re-equipping the Radiotherapy Department continued into 1947 with the purchase of new equipment and the conversion of the visitors' shelter in the forecourt into an X-ray room (for barium meal and chest X-ray examinations). A new syringe sterilization service employing two technicians was proposed by the medical staff and a Hearing Aid Clinic was started in December 1946. On a somewhat more ambitious (but unsuccessful) scale, the Orthopaedic and Fractures Subcommittee continued for a period to press for additional facilities but there was a general tendency to defer making decisions of any great importance. The Ministry's plans for postgraduate training for consultants resulted eventually in the appointment of a Neurosurgeon and he and the Thoracic and Plastic Surgeons (from Cardiff and Chepstow respectively) were invited to become members of the Medical Staff Committee before the initiation of the new service.

As more information about the form that the new Health Service would take became available, a change of attitude became apparent. When the House Committee considered a report from the South Wales committee of the British Hospitals' Association, the first priority was thought to be to ensure that the voluntary hospitals should be adequately represented on the new Welsh Regional Hospital Board which was to be formed. Four names were submitted for inclusion among that Board's members but only one (Alderman William Evans of Gowerton) was accepted. Later, the Welsh Hospital Board invited the hospital's Governors and members of the Contributory Scheme to submit nominations for membership of the Glantawe Hospital Management Committee which would be responsible for the day to day management of the general hospitals in the area. Eight names were submitted of which only two (Mr Philip Lewis of Ystradgynlais and Mr Cellan-Jones, who represented the medical staff) were accepted.[14] The new Management Committee of 17 members would be responsible for more than 2,000 beds in 16 hospitals and Mr O. C. Howells, the Swansea Hospital's Secretary-Superintendent, who had worked there since 1914, became the first Group Secretary and Alderman William Evans was appointed Chairman. In their first annual report, it was said that:

> The changes in administration during the transitional period have been carried out smoothly and without undue disturbance of the service generally.[15]

For the first time since its formation, the Swansea Hospital would now have to share the services of its House Committee with another hospital (Hill House Hospital).

At the final meeting of the House Committee for the Swansea Hospital, a requisition for supplying and laying linoleum for the Dental Department was presented and a memorandum was submitted from the Ministry of Health 'relating to the dissolution of the Governing Bodies of Voluntary Hospitals'. By sharp contrast, at the last meeting of the Board of Management, Mr Cellan-Jones, in what must have been a powerful final speech reviewed the development and progress of the hospital over the previous 130 years. He ended:

> by expressing the hope that whatever changes may be envisaged, those

responsible for the new service will remember that Swansea and its hospital have grown up together; that their traditions are inseparable, and that that which is noble in them should be preserved.[16]

Five days later, with the coming of the 'appointed day', the National Health Service came into being. The most successful begging exercise that the town of Swansea had ever known was over.

Appendix I Swansea Hospital Register[1]

\# appointed to a Consulting post on resigning.
* still in post in July 1948.

Honorary Staff

Physicians:

#Thomas Hobbes	1817–1818
J. C. Collins	1817–1818
#William Edwards	1818–1831
#James Gibbon	1822–1835
Edward Howell	1831–1855
Douglas Cohen	1835–1858
Prestwood Lucas	1839–1840
#G. G. Bird	1840–1855
Thomas Williams FRS	1855–1865
William Rowland	1855–1858
David Nicol	1858–1862
#George Padley	1863–1878
#John Paddon	1865–1881
George Mowat	1878–1881
#J. A. Rawlings	1881–1897
#D. A. Davies	1881–1892
#F. Knight	1891–1903
#J. S. H. Roberts	1897–1908
#E. le Cronier Lancaster	1903–1919
D. E. Evans	1908–1931
A. Clarke Begg	1920–1928
#A. Clarke Begg (resumed)	1931–1938
W. Macdonald	1928–1934
W. Esmond Rees	1934–*
D. Rhys Lewis	1938–*

Assistant Physicians:

D. E. Evans	1906–1908
A. W. Cameron	1906–1910
C. L. Isaac	1908–1912
Alban Evans	1912–1913
A. Clarke Begg	1913–1920
#Urban Marks	1913–1945
W. Macdonald	1927–1928
Rhys T. Lewis	1928–1933
W. Esmond Rees	1933–1934
D. Rhys Lewis	1934–1938
T. J. Evans	1938–*
H. W. Howell (temporary)	1943–1946
H. W. Howell	1946–*

Special Department for Diseases of Women:

R. Nelson Jones	1891–1911

Physician Accoucheur:

F. Knight	1912–1919

Physician to the Skin Department:

D. Rhys Lewis	1930–*

Surgeons:

H. J. Williams	1817–1828
Charles Sylvester	1817–1822
J. Davies	1818–1825
W. Terry	1823–1832
Edward Osler	1824–1827
G. G. Bird	1827–1840
William Rowland	1832–1843
William Bevan	1840–1845
W. Harris Long	1843–1857
Henry Wiglesworth	1845–1849
#T. A. Essery	1849–1864
#J. Griffith Hall	1857–1881
#Andrew Davies	1864–1875
#Jabez Thomas	1875–1892
#H. A. Latimer	1881–1893

APPENDIX I

G. H. Hopkins 1892–1896
#W. F. Brook 1893–1913
#R. C. Elsworth 1896–1919
C. L. Isaac 1913–1944
W. L. Griffiths 1913–1935
H. W. Gabe 1919–1948
W. H. O. Woods 1926–1945
W. Maclean 1946–★
C. J. Cellan-Jones 1946–★

Assistant Surgeons:

A. F. B. Richards 1906–1909
Edgar Reid 1906–1912
#A. W. Cameron 1910–1946
C. L. Isaac 1912–1913
Trevor Evans 1913–1935
W. Maclean 1928–1946
C. J. Cellan-Jones 1928–1946
I. Q. Evans 1946–★
J. G. Bowen 1946–★
C. H. Tanner 1947–★
L. W. Hefferman 1943–★
H. Elwyn James (temporary) 1943

Gynaecologists:

Edgar Reid 1911–1924
#J. Lloyd Davies 1924–1946
Vyvyan Davies 1946–★

Assistant Gynaecologists:

Vyvyan Davies 1943–1946
I. J. Thomas 1946–★

Ophthalmic Surgeons:

T. D. Griffiths 1880–1885
W. T. F. Davies 1885–1888
#Jabez Thomas 1890–1900
Alex D. Davidson 1890–1900
#Frank G. Thomas 1900–1924
H. E. Quick 1911–1947
E. K. Roy Thomas 1947–★

Assistant Ophthalmic Surgeons:

E. K. Roy Thomas 1924–1947
F. G. Hibbert 1947–★

Orthopaedic Surgeons:

W. H. O. Woods 1927–1945
G. D. Rowley 1947–★

Throat, Nose and Ear Surgeons:

W. F. Brook 1893–1893
R. C. Elsworth 1894–1896
A. F. B. Richards 1896–1913
Alban Evans 1913–1932
C. P. Robinson 1932–★

Assistant Throat, Nose and Ear Surgeons:

C. P. Robinson 1928–1932
J. Crowther 1932–★

Pathologists and Anaesthetists:

James K. Couch 1889–1892
E. le Cronier Lancaster 1892–1892
R. C. Elsworth 1893–1894
James K. Couch 1894–1894
A. Lucas Morgan 1894–1897
Edgar Reid 1897–1899
Daniel E. Evans 1899–1903
A. W. Cameron 1904–1906

Pathologists:

Daniel E. Evans 1903–1904
A. W. Cameron 1904–1906
D. R. Edwards 1906–1919
A. F. Sladden (first full-time pathologist) 1919–★

Radiologists and Electro-therapeutists:

#D. R. Edwards 1906–1932
Iwan Davies 1932–★

Assistants:

Iwan Davies 1923–1932
W. P. G. Williams 1923–1932
Howell Davies 1932–1946
Glyn Jones 1946–★

APPENDIX I

Radiotherapist:

K. Mendl (full-time)	1946–★

Psychiatrists:

Ian Skottowe	1932–1934
Norman Moulson	1934–★

Vaccine Therapist:

A. Clarke Begg	1911–1920

Anaesthetists:

A. W. Cameron	1903–1904
D. R. Edwards	1904–1906
C. L. Isaac	1906–1908
W. L. Griffiths	1908–1912
Alban Evans	1909–1913
A. Clarke Begg	1910–1911
Trevor Evans	1911–1913
J. B. Dawson	1912–1912
Urban Marks	1912–1913
H. W. Gabe	1914–1919
T. Lewis Jones	1914–1923
D. B. Chiles Evans	1914–1917
W. Macdonald	1919–1927
E. Morgan	1923–1926
J. S. Lewis Roberts	1921–1923
Joseph Lloyd	1921–1923
J. Lloyd Davies	1923–1924
E. Morgan	1923–1926
Haydn Peters	1923–★
H. Spencer Davies	1925–1935
F. M. Lloyd Jones	1925–★
D. Rhys Lewis	1925–1930
W. H. O. Woods	1925–1926
Rhys T. Lewis	1926–1928
P. Oswald Davies	1926–1936
T. Ben Thomas	1927–★
Iorwerth H. Jones	1928–★
F. H. Kingston Knight	1928–★
Vyvyan Davies	1930–1943
D. Vaughan Davies (Deputy)	1931–1932
W. V. Howells (Deputy)	1931–1935
W. H. Thomas (Deputy)	1932–★
W. V. Howells	1935–★
G. A. Madel (Deputy)	1935–★

Claude Davies	1939–★
Glyn Howell	1943–?
W. Havard Jones	1943–★
D. S. Jones	1945–★

Surgeon Dentists:

F. J. Clouston Scott	1869–1890
H. J. Thomas	1891–1919
T. B. Tustian	1920–1938
S. J. St Helier Tweney	1920–1933

Medical Officers for Outdoor Patients:

Andrew Davies	1863–1864
T. D. Griffiths	1863–1865
Griffith R. Thomas	1864–1870
Jabez Thomas	1865–1876
George Mowat	1869–1878
J. A. Rawlings	1870–1881
H. A. Latimer	1875–1881
J. Farrant Fry	1878–1889
A. O. H. Phillips	1881–1881
D. A. Davies	1881–1881
Alex D. Davidson	1883–1894
W. C. Humphreys	1884–1890
Richard Nelson Jones	1889–1891
F. Knight	1890–1892
G. H. Hopkins	1891–1892
J. S. H. Roberts	1892–1897
E. le Cronier Lancaster	1892–1903
A. Lucas Morgan	1897–1899
James K. Couch	1894–1906
Edgar Reid	1899–1912
Daniel E. Evans	1904–1908
A. W. Cameron	1906–1946
C. L. Isaac	1908–1913
W. L. Griffiths	1911–1913
Alban Evans	1912–1913
Trevor Evans	1913–1935
Urban Marks	1913–1945
W. Macdonald	1924–1928
Rhys T. Lewis	1927–1933
P. Milligan (Deputy Asst.)	1928–1930
W. Esmond Rees	1930–1934
D. Rhys Lewis	1934–1938
T. J. Evans (Deputy Asst.)	1934–1938
H. W. Howell (Deputy Asst.)	1938–1943

Paid staff

Assistant Pathologists:

Miss C. I. Fox	1920–1921
Miss M. V. Grant	1921–1923
Miss M. K. Semple	1923–1924
P. Milligan	1924–1930
V. Magee	1927–1927
Anne Gibson	1930–1931
Miss A. M. Bodoano	1931–1938
Miss J. C. Drury	1938–1947
M. G. Pearson	1944–?

Assistant Bacteriologist:

Miss Florence Price	1908–1908

Matrons:[2]

Margaret Morris	1822–?
Anne Couch	?1840–1841
Margaret Smith	1841–1851
Mrs Howe	1851–1854
Miss Jones	1854–1858
Miss Cox	1858–1865
Mrs Tate	1865–1866
Miss Markham	1866–1869
Mrs MacVey	1869–1871
Anne John	1871–1882
Miss Bann	1882–1884
Mrs Foulkes	1884–1889
Miss Bellars	1889–1893
Miss Sykes	1893–1898
Miss Rigney	1898–1899
Miss Bridges	1899–1902
Miss Crispin	1902–1906
Miss Musson	1906–1908
Miss Scovell	1909–1932
Miss Duncan	1932–1938
Miss White	1938–1941
Miss E. A. Smith	1941–*

Secretaries:

William Stroud	1817–1823
J. J. Williams	1823–1831
G. T. Stroud	1831–1866
E. J. Morris	1866–1868
J. W. Morris	1868–1898
W. D. Hughes (Asst.)	1894–1898
W. D. Hughes	1898–1927
O. C. Howells (Asst.)	1913–1927
O. C. Howells	1927–*

Note: [1] Where there were minor inaccuracies in the Hospital Register, these have been corrected by the author.

[2] Matrons' names were not included in the original Hospital Register.

Appendix II

Menu for the Public Luncheon on the occasion of the laying of the foundation stone of the new hospital on 4 March 1867

Pickled salmon and cucumber	Galenas
Lamb and mint sauce	Collard Hean
Boiled Fowls, in Bechamel Sauce	Raised Pies
Roast Turkeys	Perigord Pies
Roast Fowls	Veal and Ham Pies
Rounds of Beef	Chicken and Pigeon Pies
Roast Beef	Eel Pies
Beef à la mode	Veal Cakes
Hams and Tongues, Ornamented	Dishes of plain Lobster
Gelantines of Veal	Lobster Salad
Roast Pig	Dressed Crabs
Boar's Head	Plain Salads

Lobster in Aspec (*sic*)

Pastry:

Mince Pies	Tipsey Cakes
Cheese Cakes	Cream Apple Tarts
Raspberry, Apricot, Greengage and Strawberry Tarts	Custards
Pastry Sandwiches	Cherry, Gooseberry and Rhubarb Tarts

Sweets:

Orange and Calf's-foot Jellies	Lemon, Strawberry and Apricot Cream
Blanc Manges	Charlotte à la Russe

Gateau à la Millefleur

The Cambrian (8/3/1867) described the tables as having:

> groaned with the weight of the feast ... The repast consisted of substantial joints and the most tempting delicacies, the wines were excellent, and what was rather unusual upon such occasions, the waiting was really first-rate.

Diet Table of the Swansea Hospital

Full Diet
Breakfast – One pint of Oatmeal Gruel
Dinner   – 12 oz meat   1 lb Potatoes
Supper   – 1 Pint Broth (from Dinner)
             $\frac{3}{4}$ lb Bread in the Day

Half Diet
Breakfast and Supper same as full Diet
Dinner   – $\frac{1}{2}$ lb Meat   1 lb Potatoes
             $\frac{1}{2}$ lb Bread in the Day

Low Diet
Breakfast – 1 Pint Tea
Dinner   – 1 Pint Broth
Supper   – 1 Pint Oatmeal Gruel
           Leeks, Parsley for the Broth

Tea might be substituted for Broth at the discretion of the Medical Officers.

All extras must be distinctly specified on the Ticket by the Attending Physician or Surgeon.

Memd^m
  Received pr Dr Lloyd
    July 29 1873

Appendix III Operations performed in the year ending 3 July 1874

A boy from the Hafod	Partial amputation of foot	Cured
A man from Swansea	Operation of fistula	Cured
A man from Llangyfelach	Operation of fistula	Cured
A man from Swansea	Secondary apputation (*sic*) of thigh	Died
A man from Swansea	Removal of tumour from arm	Cured
A girl from Swansea	Operation for deformed hand	Improved
A woman from Llandeilo	Amputation of thigh for disease	Cured
A boy from Landore	Lithotomy	Cured
A man from Llanelly	Removal of tongue for cancer	Relieved
A woman from Mumbles	Operation for strangulated hernia	Died
A man from Swansea	Operation for fistula	Cured
A man from Llansamlet	Double operation for cataract	Relieved
A woman from Swansea	Operation for haemorrhoids	Cured
A man from Swansea	Amputation of forearm	Cured
A man from Swansea	Operation for fistula	Cured
A woman from Swansea	Removal of axillary tumour	Cured
A woman from Mumbles	Removal of cranial [blank]	Cured
A boy from Swansea	Lithotomy	Cured
A woman from Cwmafon	Operation for necrosis of humerus	Cured
A boy from Swansea	Partial amputation of hand	Cured
A girl from Swansea	Removal of orbital tumour	Cured
A man from Swansea	Amputation of hand	Cured
A boy from Swansea	Amputation of four fingers	Cured
A man from Swansea	Lithotomy	Cured
A man from Swansea	Extipation (*sic*) of eyeball	Cured
A man from Gower	Removal of tumour from jaw	Cured
A boy from Swansea	Amputation of leg	Cured
A man from Swansea	Amputation of leg	Cured
A woman from Brecon	Excision of breast	Relieved
A man from Neath	Extirpation of eyeball	Cured
A man from Swansea	Extirpation of eyeball	Cured
A woman from Swansea	Amputation of leg	Cured
A woman from Aberdare	Operation for fistula	Cured
A woman from Swansea	Excision of cervix uteri	Cured
A girl from Swansea	Double operation for strabismus	Cured

This extract from the Medical Staff Report for 1874 showed that during the previous twelve months, Dr Grossett Collins, the Resident Medical Officer, had attended 798 patients at their own homes with a total of 4,693 visits.

(H, 3 July 1874).

Appendix IV

A. *A comparison of work undertaken in the Swansea Hospital in 1817/18 with that in 1947*

	18/7/1817–13/7/1818	1947
Number of in-patients treated	18	4877
Number of out-patients treated:		
New[a]		33411
Old[b]		7079
Total	1740[c]	40490
Out-patient attendances		140310
X-rays taken		33292
Surgical operations performed		5674

B. *A comparison of costs of the Swansea Hospital in 1817/18 with those in 1947*

	18/7/1817–13/7/1818	1947
Total income	£320 18s. 8d.	£182,234 3s. 5d.
Total expenditure	£379 18s. 1d.[d]	£181,713 18s. 9d.
Cost of medicines	£ 40 3s. 1d.	£ 9,592 16s. 0d. (as drugs and dressings)
Coal, soap and candles	£ 13 16s. 9d.	£ 6,055 6s. 1d. (as fuel and lighting)
Printing	£ 21 0s. 0d.	£ 745 10s. 11d.
Salaries and wages	£ 91 14s. 0d.	£ 84,606 18s. 0d.
Average cost per in-patient per week		£ 9 16s. 4d.
Average cost of each out-patient attendance		£ 5s. 4.75d.
Average total cost of each out-patient		£ 1 2s. 8.9d.

[a] Of the new out-patients dealt with in 1947, nearly 41% were casualties, more than 23% were referred for X-ray examinations, 5.6% to the general medical clinics, 4.8% to the eye department, 4.7% to the surgical clinics and 3.4% to the VD Department.
[b] Of the old patients dealt with in 1947, nearly 43% were referred for X-rays.
[c] This figure excludes patients who were vaccinated at the Infirmary.
[d] This figure excludes £100 invested in Parish Bonds in the course of the year.

Appendix V   Dedication Wards at the Swansea Hospital by 1947

There were 14 dedication wards:

Ward	Named after
Llewellyn	Griffith Llewellyn, Baglan Hall.
Patti	Adelina Patti, Baroness Cederstrom.
Dyer	Mr and Mrs John Dyer, Richmond Villas.
Talbot	C. R. M. Talbot, Margam Abbey.
Studt	Henry Studt.
Penllergaer	John Dillwyn Llewelyn, Penllergaer.
Beck	Roger Beck, Langland Bay.
Graham Vivian	W. Graham Vivian, Clyne Castle.
E. Martin Player	Mr and Mrs John Player.
Henry Folland	Henry Folland, Llwynderw.
Griffith Thomas	Sir Griffith Thomas, Court Herbert, Neath.
William Edwards	William Edwards, Haresfield, Langland.
Martha Davies	Mrs D. W. Davies, Ystalyfera.
Evans and Powell	Sir S. T. Evans and his sister Mrs Powell: named in accordance with the will of Mrs Sarah Powell, Skewen.

The Eye Hospital, both operating theatres, the D. W. Davies Block (with its 36 beds) and the Beck Laboratory (with its Brook and Lancaster Rooms) were also endowed and there were 48 dedication beds (the plaques commemorating many of those beds have been preserved at Singleton Hospital).

Notes and References

Chapter One
1. E. A. Dillwyn, *The Rebecca Rioters: a story of Killay life* (London, 1880), pp. 34–5.
2. William Buckland, *Reliquiae Diluvianae* ... (London, 1823), pp. 84, 86; I am grateful to Mr George Boon, Keeper of the Department of Archaeology at the National Museum of Wales for emphasizing that not too much reliance should be placed on Buckland's ability to diagnose either ankylosis (fusion of bones) or evidence of a blow.
3. John Cule, 'Some early hospitals in Wales and the Border', *National Library of Wales Journal*, 20, 2 (1977) p. 105.
4. George Grant Francis, 'A brief memoir of Henry de Gower', *Archaeologia Cambrensis*, VII (1876), pp. 11–12.
5. Edmund Gibson, *Codex Juris Ecclesiastici Anglicanii* ..., Volume the Second (Oxford, 1761).
6. Thomas Richards, *Wales under the Penal Code (1662–1687)* (London, 1925), p. 168.
7. NLW, Church in Wales Records, 'Bishops' Transcripts', SD/DB 152.
8. Ibid., 141.
9. Ibid., 147.
10. Ibid., 88, 143.
11. NLW, Church in Wales Records, 'Bishops' Visitation Returns', 1705.
12. *Archaeologia Cambrensis*, IV, 5 (1887), pp. 53–4.
13. Rees Price ac Evan Griffiths, *Y Llysieu-lyfr Teuluaidd* (Abertawy, 1849).
14. Thomas Richards, op. cit., p. 169.
15. D. Rhys Phillips, *The History of the Vale of Neath* (Swansea, 1925), p. 606.
16. *Y Bywgraffiadur Cymreig hyd at 1940* (Llundain, 1954). p. 615.
17. *The Cambrian*, 26/7/1806.
18. William Llewellyn, *Mode of treatment of spasmodic cholera* (s.l., 1832), Glamorgan Record Office, D/DX mt.
19. G. T. Clark, *Report to the General Board of Health* (London, 1849), p. 15.
20. James Rogers, *The Cholera Epidemic at Ystalyfera* (Swansea, 1867).
21. James Rogers, *Sanitary Reform* (Swansea, 1873).

Chapter Two
1. John Bradshaw (ed.), *The Letters of Philip Dormer Stanhope, Earl of Chesterfield*, Vol. III (London, 1892), p. 1371.
2. Ibid., Vol. I, p. xxiii.
3. James Stonehouse, *A Friendly Letter to a Patient just admitted into an Infirmary* (London, 1748).
4. T. McKeown and R. G. Brown, 'Medical evidence related to English population changes in the eighteenth century', *Population Studies*, 9 (1955), pp. 119–41.
5. E. M. Sigsworth, 'Gateways to death? Medicine, hospitals and mortality 1700–1850', *Science and Society 1600–1900*, ed. Peter Mathias (Cambridge, 1972), pp. 97–110.

NOTES AND REFERENCES 245

6   *The Cambrian*, 6/11/1813.
7   M. Phillips, *Memoir of the Life of Richard Phillips* (London, 1840), p. 140.
8   *The Cambrian*, 11/1/1812.
9   Henry Sockett, *A Concise Account of the Origin of the House of Industry* (Swansea, 1834), p. 4. Henry Sockett's main interest, as visitor to the Poor House, was with the House of Industry, not with the Infirmary.
10 *The Cambrian*, 28/12/1816.
11 *The Cambrian*, 28/6/1817.
12 *The Cambrian*, 26/7/1817.
13 J. Evans, *Letters written during a Tour through South Wales* (London, 1804), p. 171.

Chapter Three
1   William Osler, *Aequanimitas* (New York, 1963), p. 33.
2   Quoted in *The Cambrian*, 13/6/1818.
3   NLW, Lewis Weston Dillwyn, 'Diary', 18/1/1818, 20/1/1818.
4   John Ingman, 'The early days of the Caernarvonshire and Anglesey Hospital', *Caernarfonshire Historical Society Transactions*, 11 (1950), p. 72.
5   H, 13/7/1821. This was the opinion of the Medical Board.
6   H, 16/9/1817. Subsequent quotations from Mr Edwards are taken from the same source on various dates in September and October 1817.
7   *The Cambrian*, 13/12/1817.
8   NLW, Lewis Weston Dillwyn, 'Diary', 16/12/1817.
9   H, 12/10/1824.
10 H, 15/6/1825.
11 H, 6/7/1824.
12 H, 30/12/1817: 'A catalogue of simple and compound medicines in use in Swansea Hospital . . ., Professor J. Gwyn Griffiths points out that the word 'Nasaconii' presents difficulties in translation.
13 H, 15/10/1822.
14 Henry Sockett, *The Substance of Three Reports* . . . (London, 1821), pp. 34–5.
15 Florence Nightingale, letter dated 19/1/1867, quoted in Brian Abel-Smith, *A History of the Nursing Profession* (London, 1960), p. 5.
16 Edward Osler, *The Life of Admiral Viscount Exmouth* (1835).
17 *The Cambrian*, 27/6/1835, 4/7/1835.
18 *The Cambrian*, 1/8/1835.

Chapter Four
1   *Provincial Medical and Surgical Association Journal*, 11/7/1842.
2   H, 2/7/1841.
3   Sidney and Beatrice Webb, *English Poor Law History*, Vol. 1 (London, 1929), pp. 316–7; *Twenty-second Annual Report of the Poor Law Board, 1869–70* (London, 1870), p. 98.
4   *The Cambrian*, 10/8/1866.
5   *The Cambrian*, 14/7/1854.
6   *Report of the Commissioners of Inquiry for South Wales* (London, 1844), p. 459.
7   H, 3/7/1857; *The Cambrian*, 21/8/1857.
8   H, 2/7/1852.

9. Glamorgan Record Office, P/S S/BO 1/2: 2/2/1850.
10. Cecil Woodham-Smith, *Florence Nightingale 1820–1910* (London, 1950), p. 340.
11. H, D/DHS 38.
12. *The Cambrian*, 24/2/1838.
13. H, 26/1/1854.
14. *The Cambrian*, 30/6/1854.
15. *The Lancet*, 25/1/1847, p. 156.
16. *The Cambrian*, 15/1/1847.
17. *The Cambrian*, 26/2/1847.
18. *The Cambrian*, 17/12/1847.
19. *The Cambrian*, 23/6/1848.
20. George Gwynne Bird, *An Address* . . . (Swansea, 1852).
21. *The Cambrian*, 8/7/1858.
22. J. E. Thomas, 'The Poor Law in West Glamorgan 1834–1930', *Morgannwg*, XVIII (1974), pp. 45–69.
23. The statement was made by the Health of Towns Association, quoted in Asa Briggs, *The Age of Improvement 1783–1867* (London, 1966), p. 334.
24. J. W. Gutch, 'On the medical topography, statistics, climatology and natural history of Swansea', *Provincial Medical and Surgical Association Journal* (1839), p. 256.
25. H, 1/7/1864.
26. London Record Office, H1/ST/NC2/V3–21/64.
27. For details of Mr Graham's life history, see *The Builder*, 16/2/1912, p. 194.
28. London Record Office, op. cit.
29. London Record Office, op. cit.
30. London Record Office, op. cit.
31. London Record Office, op. cit. Florence Nightingale had promised a donation in 1864. She delayed sending the money for quite some time—probably until she was certain that her views had been accepted.
32. *British Medical Journal*, 7/10/1865, p. 384.
33. *The Cambrian*, 8/3/1867 for the following description of the luncheon.
34. In December 1868, Miss Markham wrote to Mrs Wardroper, (matron at St Thomas's Hospital), asking for permission to apply for the post at Hereford. Mrs Wardroper in turn wrote to Henry Bonham-Carter saying that she had refused to give permission unless Miss Markham was able to give three months' notice.

Chapter Five
1. *The Cambrian*, 29/10/1869.
2. Reverend C. W. Ireland Jones, *Poems* . . . (Oxford, 1840), p. 41.
3. H, 7/7/1871.
4. H, 27/10/1869.
5. H, 2/7/1886.
6. H, 27/11/1884.
7. H, 29/6/1882.
8. *The Cambrian*, 19/1/1883.
9. H, 10/7/1879.
10. *The Lancet*, 16/10/1875, p. 565.
11. H, 23/3/1876.
12. H, 23/3/1876.
13. H, 17/7/1879.
14. *The Cambrian*, 12/7/1879.
15. H, 25/1/1872.

16 *The Cambrian*, 17/7/1885.
17 J.C.E., *The History of District Nursing in Swansea* (Swansea, 1909).
18 *The Times*, 7/1/1888, correspondence columns: letter from the Duke of Westminster, Sir James Paget and Sir Rutherford Alcock concerning the Jubilee Fund; ibid., 23/1/1888.
19 H, 23/5/1878, 10/7/1879.
20 H, 30/5/1878.
21 *The Cambrian*, 10/5/1878, 19/7/1878, 1/11/1878, 12/7/1879, 28/1/1887, 7/6/1887.
22 *The Cambrian*, 12/9/1879.
23 *The Cambrian*, 1/11/1878.
24 Quoted in H, 4/11/1880.
25 *British Medical Journal*, 1/5/1880, p. 674; *The Cambrian*, 2/7/1880.
26 *The Cambrian*, 29/5/1885.
27 H, 16/12/1886.
28 Quoted in H, 3/8/1866.
29 Quoted in H, 20/1/1887.
30 H, 11/8/1881; *The Cambrian*, 19/8/1881.
31 *The Cambrian*, 26/8/1881.
32 Quoted in H, 23/9/1881.
33 *The Lancet*, 9/10/1847, p. 394.
34 H, 16/9/1882.
35 *The Cambrian*, 12/9/1884, 26/3/1886; H, 15/7/1886, 1/7/1887.
36 *The Times*, 23/1/1888.
37 H, 23/3/1871ff. No information has been preserved about the nurses from St Mary's Hospital, London.
38 H, 27/12/1888.
39 *The Cambrian*, 6/1/1882.
40 *Proposed College for South Wales: Memorial of the Corporation of Swansea* (London, 1882).
41 *The Cambrian*, 27/1/1882.
42 H, 13/9/1888.
43 *The Cambrian*, 14/4/1838.

Chapter Six
1 *The Cambrian*, 5/3/1890.
2 H, 24/7/1890.
3 *The Cambrian*, 22/8/1890.
4 Quoted in *The Cambrian*, 24/10/1890.
5 H, 20/7/1893.
6 H, 16/3/1893.
7 H, 24/1/1907.
8 H, 24/1/1907; Glamorgan Record Office, D/D BMA, 9/1/1907.
9 Robert Pinker, *English Hospital Statistics 1861–1938* (London, 1966), p. 52.
10 Quoted in H, 13/7/1894.
11 H, 6/8/1896.
12 H, 14/9/1898. On the rare occasions when Dr Ebenezer Davies, still a faithful supporter of the hospital, made known his differences with his medical colleagues, it usually concerned the Ophthalmic Department. Having never quite lost the sense of annoyance which he had developed ten years earlier over the way in which his son was treated, it was he who led the opposition against the eye surgeons.

13 H, 8/9/1898.
14 H, 4/11/1897. I am grateful to the Librarian of the Royal Institute of British Architects for information about Mr Glendinning Moxham (see *Who's Who in Architecture* (1926), p. 213) and Mr J. B. Wilson (see *The Builder*, 79 (1900), p. 547).
15 H, 8/9/1898. Sir William McCormac was an old friend of Mr Brook's. Later that day, he lectured to local doctors on the topic 'Surgery—a retrospect and forecast'.
16 H, 6/11/1901. Colonel W. Llewellyn Morgan was born at St Helen's House where his family had lived for generations. He retired from the army in 1887 and was keenly interested in archaeology. (*South Wales Daily Post*, 13/7/1906.)
17 Mr John Dyer of Swansea was the Chairman of Thomas and Evans Ltd and of John Dyer, Millers and Corn Merchants. *Who's Who in Wales* (Cardiff, 1921), p. 103.
18 H, 12/9/1878.
19 H, 16/3/1904.
20 *The Cambrian*, 24/2/1893.
21 Glamorgan Record Office, D/DHS, 130, 131.; A. A. Hoehling, *Edith Cavell* (London, 1958).
22 House of Commons Parliamentary Papers, *Select Committee on the Registration of Nurses*, Vol. VII, Appendix 6 (1905), 6/6/1905, p. 182.
23 For details of Miss Musson (later Dame Ellen Mary Musson, DBE, Ll.D., see Gerald Bowman, *The Lamp and the Book* (London, 1967), p. 191.
24 *The Cambrian*, 24/2/1893.
25 *British Medical Journal*, 22/8/1903, p. 436.
26 Glamorgan Record Office, D/D BMA, 27/2/1908.
27 Ibid., 14/11/1907.
28 Ibid., 14/11/1907, 2/4/1909.
29 Ibid., 9/2/1911.
30 Dr Silas Weir Mitchell (1829–1914) was a Philadelphia physician—see John D. Spillane, *The Doctrine of the Nerves* (Oxford, 1981); for an account of the treatment referred to in the text, see *The Family Physician*, Vol. IV (London, n.d.), pp. 279–80.
31 H, 20/8/1906; F. S. Stewart, *Bigger's Handbook of Bacteriology* (London, 1962), p. 149.
32 Mr and Mrs Frank Thomas's sons were both doctors. Mr Trevelyan Thomas of Bournemouth represents the third generation of ophthalmologists in his family.
33 Dr Clarke Begg was appointed Vaccine Therapist in May 1911 (H, 11/5/1911).

Chapter Seven
1 Sidney and Beatrice Webb, *English Poor Law Policy* (London, 1910), p. 319.
2 A. J. P. Taylor, *The First World War* (Harmondsworth, 1981), p. 22.
3 D. Lloyd George, *Better Times* (London, 1910), p. 53.
4 H, 31/5/1911.
5 Harry Roberts, 'The Nation and the Athenaeum', *Proceedings of the Royal Society of Medicine*, 1/6/1935.
6 *The Times*, 3/1/1912.
7 Urban Marks, *A Varied Life: Memoirs of a Swansea General Practitioner* (London, 1984), pp. 46–7. Having been an Assistant Physician at the hospital since 1913, Dr Marks had hoped to become a full Honorary Physician. He was barred from this because he did not have the necessary postgraduate qualifications. (H, 30/8/1928.) It seems possible that his failure to persuade the committee to change

the rules accounts for his later caustic remarks about some aspects of life at the hospital.
8 H, 2/10/1912; the only newspaper account that can be traced probably refers to another patient. (*South Wales Daily Post*, 25/9/1912.)
9 Hansard, Parliamentary Debates, 29, 298, 1/8/1911.
10 *The Hospital*, LIV, 10/5/1913, p. 187; 17/5/1913, p. 213; 21/6/1913, pp. 550–51.
11 *Nursing Times*, 10/4/1915, p. 247.
12 The Sketty Red Cross Hospital was housed at Parc Wern in 1917.
13 Urban Marks, op. cit., pp. 48–9.
14 The first nurses named as having had Certificates of Training from the hospital were Elizabeth Stephens, Amelia Davies, Florence G. Howard and Edith G. Thomas (H, 7/3/1906.)
15 Salvarsan is a compound of arsenic which was first used in the treatment of patients by Ehrlich in 1909. It remained the most effective treatment for syphilis until the advent of penicillin.
16 The Welsh National Fund referred to was possibly the King Edward VII Welsh National Memorial Association although their work was concerned with the treatment of tuberculosis.

Chapter Eight
1 Dr John S. Billings, at the opening of the Johns Hopkins Hospital, Baltimore, in 1889.
2 In March 1914, there were 130 patients' names on the waiting list and by June 1818, that number had increased to 243. In May 1914, the debt was £6,125. 15s. 6d., and by July 1918, it was £7,311. 14s. 8d.
3 Parc Wern was formerly the home of Sir H. H. Vivian MP (who became the first Lord Swansea) before he inherited the Singleton estate. (Thomas Nicholas, *The History and Antiquities of Glamorganshire* . . . (London, 1874), p. 188.)
4 The term Ear, Nose and Throat Department was used for the first time in the hospital in 1919.
5 Mr Roger Beck moved to Swansea in 1872 as a partner in the Elba Steel Works, Gowerton, which was eventually amalgamated with the firm of Baldwins, of which he was a director. He also had other industrial interests (*Who's Who in Wales* (Cardiff, 1921), p. 18). He was a cousin twice removed of Lord Lister and his brother Marcus was Professor of Surgery at University College Hospital, London (D'Arcy Power et al, *Plarr's Lives of the Fellows of the Royal College of Surgeons of England* (London, 1930), pp. 75–7).
6 H, 11/1/1922.
7 During the Egg Week held in 1927, a local woman was arrested for selling eggs collected 'ostensibly for the hospital' (H, 28/4/1927).
8 Swansea City Archives, TC5/Health 3, 4/10/1921; TC5/Health 4, 29/5/1923.
9 H, 17/6/1925.
10 Dr A. F. S. Sladden was an Oxford graduate who had been Pathologist and Registrar to the Metropolitan Hospital and an army pathologist before moving to Swansea. (*Medical Directory* (London, 1938), p. 1544.)
11 In June 1920, Mr Beck asked that the 'further liability' associated with the appointment of an Assistant Pathologist should be borne by him, but the committee insisted that the hospital should share the expense.
12 A. Clarke Begg, *Insulin in General Practice* (London, 1924).
13 From 1869, the Surgeon-Dentist was required to be a Licentiate in Dental Surgery (LDS) unless he had been in practice before 1860 (H, 24/11/1869.)

14. *The Hospital*, LXVI, 23/8/1919, p. 516.
15. Brian Abel-Smith, *A History*, pp. 74–96, 107, 112.
16. H, 13/7/1921.
17. H, 19/12/1923, 17/4/1925ff.
18. The use of Parc Beck as a Nurses' Home dated from 1925.
19. H, 9/5/1923.
20. H, 13/2/1929.

Chapter Nine
1. *The Times*, 9/11/1936.
2. H, 6/11/1929.
3. Swansea City Archives, A 64, 4/6/1932, 20/10/1932; *Development and Co-ordination of Health Services*, 9964, December 1934.
4. *British Medical Journal*, 23/11/1935, p. 1015.
5. T. G. Davies, *A History of Cefn Coed Hospital* (Swansea, 1982), p. 14.
6. *British Medical Journal*, 8/5/1937, pp. 984–6.
7. *The Times*, 30/9/1937.
8. *The Lancet*, 20/2/1932, p. 409.
9. *British Medical Journal*, 20/11/1937, p. 1027.
10. H, 11/9/1935ff.
11. The new hospital, had it been built, would have housed 180 male surgical and 70 gynaecology beds (H, 6/9/1935.) The County Council did develop the site at Penrhiwtyn as the West Glamorgan County Hospital which was later renamed the Neath General Hospital. It is now one of the three large district general hospitals that serve the population of West Glamorgan.
12. *British Medical Journal*, 29/2/1936, editorial column, p. 419.
13. Hansard, Parliamentary Debates, 1936–7, 323, 6/5/1937, 1235.
14. *British Medical Journal*, 30/4/1938 (Supplement).
15. *The Times*, 30/9/1937.
16. T. G. Davies, op. cit., p. 16.
17. H, 5/11/1930.
18. Quoted in H, 5/4/1939.

Chapter Ten
1. *Swansea Hospital Annual Report for 1939*.
2. Glamorgan Record Office, D/D BMA, 16/2/1939.
3. *British Medical Journal*, 30/1/1937, Supplement, p. 53.
4. Ibid., 16/9/1939, p. 627.
5. T. G. Davies, op. cit., pp. 22, 25.
6. *British Medical Journal*, 18/10/1941, p. 565.
7. Ibid., 18/10/1941, p. 565.
8. Ibid., 8/11/1941, p. 657.
9. Ibid., 6/12/1941, p. 820.
10. Ibid., 10/6/1939, p. 1193.
11. *Evening Post*, 17/2/1943.
12. *Swansea Hospital Annual Report for 1943*.
13. H, 29/4/1943.
14. H, 10/3/1943.
15. *Medical World*, 8/1/1943, p. 507.
16. *Swansea Hospital Annual Report for 1944*.

Chapter Eleven

1. B. J. Boughton, 'Personal View', *British Medical Journal*, 24/5/1986, p. 1391.
2. *British Medical Journal*, 22/8/1942, Supplement, p. 17.
3. Labour Party, *A National Service for Health, The Labour Party's Post-war Policy* (London, 1943).
4. Hansard, Parliamentary Debates, 1943–4, 398, 16–17/3/1944, 427–654. At the conclusion of that debate, it was resolved 'That this House welcomes the intention ... to establish a Comprehensive National Health Service.' It was a later government, elected in July 1945, that brought about the passing of the National Health Service Act of 1946.
5. Glamorgan Record Office, D/D BMA, 23/3/1944.
6. *Swansea Hospital Annual Report for 1942*.
7. *Hospital Survey* (London, 1945), pp. ii, 5. One of the authors of this survey, which had been commissioned by the Welsh Board of Health, was Dr A. Trevor Jones who had previously worked at the hospital and who later became the Senior Administrative Medical Officer to the new Welsh Regional Hospital Board and after that the Provost of the Welsh National School of Medicine.
8. H, 23/8/1945.
9. *British Medical Journal*, 2/9/1944, p. 317.
10. Hansard, Parliamentary Debates, 1945–6), 416, 8/11/1945, 1455–6.
11. H, 9/1/1946.
12. Quoted in H, 14/1/1948.
13. Swansea City Archives, TC55, 30/12/1946, minute 1251.
14. H, 24/3/1948.
15. *Glantawe Hospital Management Committee, First Annual Report* (1949). Mr Lloyd Davies (Gynaecologist) and Alderman Richard Gronow (Chairman of the Cefn Coed Hospital Management Committee) were also members of the Welsh Regional Hospital Board at its inception (H, 2/7/1947.) At the time of the introduction of the National Health Service, psychiatric hospitals had their own separately administered Hospital Management Committees.
16. H, 30/6/1948.

Select Bibliography

Abel-Smith, Brian, *A History of the Nursing Profession* (London, 1960).
Alban, J. R., 'Preparations for air raid precautions in Swansea 1935–9', *Morgannwg*, XXVIII (1984).
Allen, David, *A Short History of the Hospital Service in England and Wales* (Manchester, 1976).
Allin, W. E., 'Poor Law Administration in Glamorganshire...', University of Wales M.A. thesis (Cardiff, 1936).
Bromhan, Ivor J., 'Ann of Swansea', *Glamorgan Historian*, 7, ed. Stewart Williams (Cowbridge, 1971).
Brown, P. S., 'Medicines advertised in Eighteenth Century Bath Newspapers', *Medical History*, 20 (1976).
Clark, G. T., *Report to the General Board of Health* (London, 1849).
Clarke-Kennedy, A. E., *The London: a study in the voluntary hospital system*, Vol. 2 (London, 1963).
Cope, Zachary, 'The origin of the general practitioner', *History of Medicine*, 5 (1973).
Davies, H. R. J., 'The Industrial Revolution', *Swansea and its Region*, ed. W. G. V. Balchin (Swansea, 1971).
Davies, T. G., 'Datblygiad seiciatreg yng Nghymru yn y bedwaredd ganrif ar bymtheg', *Tradodion Anrhydeddus Gymdeithas y Cymmrodorion* (1980).
  'Cymdeithasau Meddygol Tref Abertawe hyd at 1903', *Cennad* 6, (1985), (2).
  'Dau Iachawr o Abertawe: Y Baron Spolasco a James Rogers', *National Library of Wales Journal*, XXV (1987), 1.
de la Beche, H., *Reports...* (Swansea, 1845).
J. C. E., *The History of District Nursing in Swansea* (Swansea, 1909).
Encyclopaedia Britannica, Vols. 2, 15 (Chicago, 1980).
Evans, A. D. and Howard, L. G. Redmond, *The Romance of the British Voluntary Hospital Movement* (London, 1932).
Evans, D. Emrys, *The University of Wales: a Historical Sketch* (Cardiff, 1953).
Evans, Neil, 'The First Charity in Wales', *Welsh History Review*, 9, (1978–9).
Finer, S. E., *The Life and Times of Sir Edwin Chadwick* (London, 1952).
Forsythe-Jauch, W. E. I., *The Medical Victoria Crosses* (Aldershot, 1983).
Gebhard, Bruno, 'The historical relationship between scientific and lay medicine', *Bulletin of the History of Medicine*, 32, (1958).
General Medical Council Annual Report for 1982 (London, 1983).
Glamorgan Record Office, D/DHS 249/1, (*n.d.*, anon.).
Griffiths, Ralph A., 'The Boroughs of the Lordship of Glamorgan', *Glamorgan County History*, Vol. III, ed. T. B. Pugh (Cardiff, 1971).

Harris, José, *William Beveridge: A Biography* (Oxford, 1977).
Harrison, T. R., Adams, R. D., et al., *Principles of Internal Medicine*, 5th edition (New York, 1966).
Hart, Harold W., 'Some notes on the sponsoring of patients for hospital treatment under the voluntary system', *Medical History*, 24, (1980).
Hughes, Amy, *The Story of District Nursing* (Swansea, 1909).
Ingman, John, 'The early days of the Caernarvonshire and Anglesey Hospital', *Caernarfonshire Historical Society Transactions*, 11, (1950).
John, Arthur H., 'Glamorgan 1700–1750', *Glamorgan County History*, Vol. V, ed. Arthur H. John and Glanmor Williams (Cardiff, 1980).
Jones, Emyr Wyn, 'Addysg Feddygol i Ferched', *National Library of Wales Journal*, XIX, 3, (1976).
Jones, Glynne R., 'The King Edward VII Welsh National Memorial Association', in *Wales and Medicine*, ed. John Cule (Llandysul, 1975).
Law Reports... (London, 1875).
Lee, Charles E., *The Swansea and Mumbles Railway* (Surrey, 1954).
Leriche, René, 'The Listerian Idea in the year 1939', *British Medical Journal*, 15/4/1939.
Local Government Act 1929 (19 Geo. V).
MacLeod, R. M., 'Law, Medicine and Public Opinion: The Resistance to Compulsory Health Legislation 1870–1907', *Public Law* (1967).
Major, Ralph H., *A History of Medicine*, Vol. 2 (Oxford, 1954).
McConaghy, R. S., 'Early attempts to control medical practice', *Proceedings of the Royal Society of Medicine*, 60, (1967).
McMenemey, W. H., 'The Hospital Movement of the eighteenth century and its development', in *The Evolution of Hospitals in Britain*, ed. F. N. Poynter (London, 1964).
Medical Register for the year 1780 (London, 1780).
Morgan, Kenneth O., *Wales in British Politics 1868–1922* (Cardiff, 1970).
Phillips, D. Rhys, *The History of the Vale of Neath* (Swansea, 1925).
Philosophical Transactions, XXXII, (1723).
Pinker, Robert, *English Hospital Statistics 1861–1938* (London, 1966).
Roberts, R. O., 'Cangen-Fanc Abertawe 1826–1859', *Trafodion Economaidd a Chymdeithasol* (1956–63).
Robinson, W. R. B., 'The Church in Gower before the Reformation', *Morgannwg*, 12, (1968).
Shryock, Richard H., 'Nineteenth Century Medicine: Scientific Aspects', *Journal of World History*, 3, (1957).
Sockett, Henry, *The Substance of Three Reports*... (London, 1821).
Soulsby, Ian, *The Towns of Medieval Wales* (Chichester, 1983).
Swansea and District Workmen's Journal (June 1901).
The Dictionary of National Biography, Vol. XIV (London, 1895).
The Dictionary of National Biography 1922–30 (Oxford, 1937).
The Swansea Guide (Swansea, 1802).
Tithe Map Apportionment, P/123/18/2, (1841).
Thomas, J. E., 'The Poor Law in West Glamorgan, 1834–1930', *Morgannwg*, XVIII, (1974).
Thomas, Norman, *Western Mail*, 8/1/1979.

Thomas, W. S. K., 'Tudor and Jacobean Swansea . . .' *Morgannwg*, V, (1961).
Twenty-Second Annual Report of the Poor Law Board, 1869–70 (London, 1870).
Vaughan, Paul, *Doctors' Commons* (London, 1959).
Watkin, Brian, *Documents on Health and Social Services 1834 to the Present Day* (London, 1975).
Williams, Glanmor, 'Neath Abbey', in *Neath and District: A Symposium*, ed. Elis Jenkins (Neath, 1974).
Williams, Moelwyn I., 'Observations on the population changes in Glamorgan 1800–1900', in *Glamorgan Historian*, Vol. 1, ed. Stewart Williams (Cardiff, 1963).
Williams, W. Samlet, *Hanes a Hynafiaethau Llansamlet* (Dolgellau, 1908).
Woodham-Smith, Cecil, *Florence Nightingale 1820–1910* (London, 1950).
Woodward, John, *To do the sick no harm* (London, 1974).
Y Bywgraffiadur Cymreig hyd at 1940 (London, 1953).
Y Llusern, 3, (1860).
Youngson, A. J., *The Scientific Revolution in Victorian Medicine* (London, 1979).

Index

after-care, 61, 78, 199
  see also ladies' committee
air-raid precautions, 208ff, 214ff
air raids, 210ff
alcohol allowance for staff, 52, 74
alleged abuse of facilities, 112–13, 115–16, 147, 177, 193, 196
  by government bodies, 110, 116–17, 118
anaesthetics, 55–7, 82, 106, 122, 138–9, 214, 228
antiseptic and aseptic surgery, 79–81
Apothecaries' Act of 1815, 22
Approved Societies, surplus funds, 167–8
architects, 63ff, 121, 123, 248n
Aubrey, Richard, forms a night asylum, 42
autopsies, 106

bacteriology, see pathology
Bann, Miss (Matron), 102
Bathing House, 17, 18, 19
baths, used in treatment, 7–8, 25, 64, 73, 97, 98
Beck, Roger, 115, 146, 158, 249n
  buys Parc Wern, 165
  Laboratory, 146, 174
  opens Preliminary Training School, 183
Begg, Dr Clarke, 154, 160, 175, 194, 248n
Bellars, Miss (Matron), 102, 127
Beveridge Report, 223
Bird, Dr George Gwynne, 10, 36, 43, 52–4, 57, 67, 139
blood transfusions, 176, 204, 211
BMA, 57, 115, 116, 139–40, 144, 150ff, 190, 201, 207, 208, 214, 217, 219, 220, 223, 232
  Dr Bird as President, 57
  Dr Griffiths as President, 139
  meetings held at the hospital, 139–40

Bowdler, Dr Thomas, 30, 31
Bridges, Miss (Matron), 131, 133
British Hospitals Association, 100–1, 107–8, 127, 148ff, 190, 195, 221, 224, 233
Brook, Mr W.F. (surgeon), 114, 116, 127, 134, 135, 146, 153, 173, 174, 180–1, 248n
Buckland, Dean, 1, 244n
Burdett, Sir Henry, 101, 107–8, 119, 130, 142

casualty work, 29, 43, 60, 73, 124, 145, 153, 160
Cavell, Edith, 131
Cellan-Jones, Mr C.J. (surgeon), 178, 233–4
chaplaincy, 61–2, 78
charity sermons, 22, 44, 45
chiropody, 6
cholera, 10, 28, 54, 58
clinical records, 81, 138, 178
College of Nursing, 191
  formation, 180–1
  opposition by Mr Brook, 180–1
Collins, Dr J.C., 8–9, 15, 21, 31, 33
complaints, 82, 101, 108–9, 110–11
Convalescent Home, 124–6, 199
Couch, Dr James, 47, 55, 106
Couch, Dr James Kynaston, 55, 106
Couch, Mrs (Matron), 46, 47, 55
Cox, Miss (Matron), 48, 49–50
  instructed to leave, 50
Crispin, Miss (Matron), 133

Davidson, Dr Alexander, 89, 94, 120–1
Davies, Mr Andrew (surgeon), 66
Davies, Dr Ebenezer (Medical Officer of Health), 84ff, 92, 93, 133, 140, 247n
Davies, D.W., Ystalyfera, 206
debt, 73, 74, 76, 97, 100, 110, 152, 157, 166, 168, 169, 213, 216, 230, 249n
dentistry, 6, 37, 157, 177, 233, 249n

INDEX

Dillwyn, Elizabeth Amy, 1, 124ff, 132
Dillwyn, Lewis Llewelyn, 43, 61, 73, 78, 92–3
Dillwyn, Lewis Weston, 15, 22, 25, 28, 31
dispensaries, early, 12–13, 14, 46
dispenser, 17, 48–9, 50, 59, 74, 87, 163, 227–8
drugs, early use of, 28, 31–2, 245n
drunkenness among staff, 50
Dunvant Railway Bill, 62–3
Dyer, Mr and Mrs John, 123, 165, 248n

Eaton, Robert (banker), 38, 64–5
Edwards, Dr William, 19, 21, 22, 24, 25–6, 30, 31, 35
   gifts to the hospital, 39
Edwards-Vaughan, Nash Vaughan, Rheola, 65
Elsworth, Mr R.C. (surgeon), 132, 135, 159, 163
Emergency Hospital Medical Service, 210, 213, 214, 219ff, 229, 230
Evans, Dr Daniel, 138
Evans, Dr Thomas (Medical Officer of Health), 175, 188ff
Evans, Mr William Price (surgeon), 9–10, 13
Eye Department, 124, 138, 154, 160, 165, 247n
Eye Dispensary, 88ff

financial crisis of 1825–6, 38
folk medicine, 4ff
Foulkes, Miss (Matron), 102, 103
Francis, George Grant, 68–9, 72
Friendly Societies, 3, 69, 76–7, 87, 117, 118, 147, 151–2, 167
Future Policy Subcommittee, 232

Gabe, Mr Howell (surgeon), 157, 208
General Medical Council, 57
Glamorgan County Council, 160, 170, 188, 197, 199, 206–7, 212, 229, 232, 250n
   Penrhiwtyn (Neath) Infirmary, 188, 193, 197, 206, 212, 250n
   Hospital Association, 193, 199, 200
Glantawe Hospital Management Committee, 233, 251n
Graham, Alexander (architect), 64ff
   uses the pseudonym 'Omega', 65
Griffiths, Dr T.D., 66–7, 83–4, 90–1, 96, 127, 134, 135, 139
   accusations against medical staff, 66
   calls for his resignation, 66
   complaints made by him, 82, 97–8
   invitation to the Prince of Wales, 98–9

Hall, Mr James Griffith (surgeon), 59, 107, 122
healing wells, 4
Hobbes, Dr Thomas, 6, 15, 21
honorary medical staff, 15, 36–7, 59, 203, 207, 209, 212, 217, 220, 230, 232, 245n
   disputes with, 21, 32, 43–4, 151–3, 217ff
   visiting staff fund, 193, 196, 200, 201–2
Hospital of the Blessed St David, 2
Hospital Saturday, 110
Hospital Sunday, 44, 110
   see also charity sermons
house surgeon, domestic duties of, 31, 34
Howe, Mrs (Matron), 48
Howell, Dr Edward, 35, 43, 44, 54, 56
Howells, O.C. (Secretary-Superintendent), 224, 230, 233
Hughes, T.W. (first workingmen's representative), 113, 117

infections, 8–9, 23ff, 57–8, 67, 68, 79–81, 104, 140–1, 142, 155, 160, 161, 175
   Cray Isolation Hospital and, 123, 145
insulin, use of by Dr Clarke Begg, 175
   payment for by patients, 175, 193
Isaac, Mr C.L. (surgeon), 154, 206
isolation hospital, 24–5, 81, 84, 123, 141ff, 154, 155, 164
infirmaries, other early, 12ff, 17, 46

John, Ann (Matron), 101
Jones, Mr Joseph, Llanelli (surgeon), 18, 22

ladies' committee, 43, 61, 66, 78, 102, 124, 186, 199, 204, 206
Lady Almoner, appointment of first, 193, 199, 200
Lancaster, Dr le Cronier, 142, 143, 153, 173, 174, 182
Langland Bay Annexe, 210, 211, 215, 220, 221, 226
Latimer, Mr H.A. (surgeon), 90, 96, 102, 105

INDEX

legal actions, 159, 177–8
licensing of doctors by bishops, 2–3
linen guild, *see* ladies' committee
Llewellyn family of Baglan Hall, 74, 85, 96, 122
Llewellyn, William, Baglan (surgeon), 9
Llewelyn, John, Penllergaer, 15
Llewelyn, John Dillwyn, 73, 124
Llewelyn, Sir John Talbot Dillwyn, 107, 164
Local Government Act of 1929, 187, 188, 190, 207
Long, Mr William Harris (surgeon), 33, 43, 56
Llwynderw, 226

Maes-y-gwernen (Morriston) hospital, 214, 216, 219, 225, 229, 230
Markham, Miss (Matron), 51–2, 70, 246n
MacVey, Mrs (Matron), 101
medical apprentices, 22–3, 35, 37
medical students, 104, 138, 156, 172, 174, 209, 227, 228
medical education, first mention of, 28
medical school, attempts to form, 57, 74, 104, 105, 157, 174, 227, 228
Ministry of Health, 166, 182, 183, 187ff, 198, 202–3, 206, 209, 210, 213, 220, 226, 227, 232, 233
see also Welsh Board of Health
Ministry of Pensions, 161, 171, 172
Moggridge, Matthew, 43, 44, 64–5
Morgan, Colonel W.Ll., 109ff, 122, 123, 126, 128–9, 132, 134, 141, 143, 154, 159, 248n
Morgan, Reverend Thomas, Blaengwrach, as vaccinator, 7
Morris, Margaret, first use of title of Matron, 34
Morris J.W. (Secretary), 72
Mount Pleasant Hospital, *see* Tawe Lodge Hospital
Mowatt, Mr George (House Surgeon), 75, 79
Musson, Miss (Matron), 133, 248n

National Health Service, 190, 223ff, 228, 229, 230, 233, 234, 251n
Neath Abbey, 2
Nicol, Dr and the marriage contract of Edward II, 4

Nightingale, Florence, 34, 50–1, 63ff, 246n
nurses,
 complaints about, 34, 47ff, 51–2, 101, 102, 128ff
 examinations, 158, 191
 first male appointed, 46–7, 160
 first probationer appointed, 101
 patients used to help, 102
 paupers used as, 24, 34, 46
 plans for training, 86, 101, 102, 126ff, 132, 158, 180ff, 219, 249n
 sickness among, 68, 104, 184
nursing institutes and associations, 84–6, 104, 132, 164, 167

obstetrics and gynaecology, 108–9, 134, 135, 144, 182–3, 189, 190, 204–5, 225
orthopaedics, 60, 171, 203, 228, 229, 232, 233
Osler, Dr Edward, 31, 36ff

Paddon, Dr John, 66, 83
Padley, Dr George, 82, 99, 107
Parc Beck, *see* Parc Wern
Parc Wern, 164–5, 168, 189, 197ff, 206, 227, 249n, 250n
pathologist and anaesthetist, 106
pathologist and chloroformist, *see* pathologist and anaesthetist
pathology, 140, 142ff, 174–5, 176, 228, 249n
 and Dr Sladden, 174, 249n
patients, paying, 18, 109, 112, 115, 167, 188, 191
Patti, Adelina, 99, 119, 120, 122
pernicious anaemia, 204
pharmacist, *see* dispenser
penicillin, 227–8
Phillips, Richard, founder of dispensary, 14–15
Poor Law Amendment Act of 1834, 41
post-war planning, 212ff, 223ff
prehistoric evidence of disease, 1–2
Price, Dr Florence, 137, 138, 142–3, 156, 160, 173
 first woman doctor appointed, 138
 marriage to Mr Frank Thomas, 143
Providential Dispensary, 86–8, 118, 119
psychiatry, 6–7, 38, 140, 141, 204, 212, 230, 251n

INDEX

radiotherapy, 215–16, 226, 229, 232
see also radium *and* radon
radium, 159, 176, 203, 214–15
radon, 206, 215
Rawlings, Dr J.A., 84, 91, 96–7, 102, 105, 109, 129, 134, 135
   reports on organization of medical services, 91, 105, 135
Red Cross Hospital at Sketty, 154, 249n
registration of doctors, 3, 7
Rigney, Miss (Matron), 130, 131
rules, revision of, 38, 49, 78–9, 90, 91, 103, 105, 162
Roman medicine, 1, 2
Rowlands, Dr William, 23, 52, 54

Samaritan Fund, *see* ladies' committee
Scovell, Miss (Matron), 133, 157, 173, 190
smaller local hospitals, 73, 85, 166, 168–9, 170, 183, 189, 195ff, 203, 209, 216, 219
Smith, Miss E.A. (Matron), 219, 231
Smith, Mrs (Matron), summons issued against, 47–8
smallpox, 3–4, 7, 8, 15, 26, 28, 59, 83, 139, 140–1
Sockett, Henry, Visitor to the House of Industry, 17, 24–5, 32, 33, 36–7, 110, 245n
staff insurance and pensions scheme, 131–2, 204
Stroud, George Turton (Secretary), 50
Stroud, William (Secretary), 19
Studt, Mr, arranges annual fêtes, 120, 122
surgery man, 46, 48
Swansea Board of Health, 58, 68, 83
Swansea Corporation and Public Health Committee, 19, 38, 123, 139, 142, 144ff, 160, 169, 170ff, 175, 187ff, 196ff, 202–3, 205ff, 209, 215, 216, 225ff
Swansea Dispensary, 14–18
Swansea Hospital,
   amalgamation with Eye Hospital, 93–6, 107
   increase in number of beds, 73, 77, 119, 123, 197, 205
   laying of foundation stone, 68–9
   opening of new building, 72–3
   St Helen's site, 63, 64, 67ff, 86
Swansea Infirmary,
   attendance of outsiders at operations, 56
   building, disposal of, 69, 70
   committee, 19, 43, 44
   fever wards at, 24–5, 84
   formation of, 17–18
   patients, 18, 25, 29–30, 38, 41, 53, 57, 60, 61
      disciplinary action against, 29–30, 61
      religious differences, 61–2
   plans for new building, 38, 46, 62–5
   surgery, early, 25–6, 28, 37, 38, 52–3, 55–7, 59, 60
Swansea Medical Society, 84, 104
Swansea Medico-Chirurgical Society, 23
Swansea Poor House and House of Industry, 15, 19, 21, 32ff, 42, 63
Swansea Poor Law Authority and Board of Guardians, 19, 29, 32, 44, 46, 58, 88, 108ff, 115, 136, 160, 183, 188
Sykes, Miss (Matron), 127ff
Sylvester, Dr H.T., 79
Sylvester, Mr (surgeon), 14, 15, 35, 79

Talbot, C.R.M. (High Sheriff), 69, 73
Tate, Mrs (Matron), 51
Tawe Lodge Hospital, 189, 199, 202, 203, 225
Thomas, Mr Frank (ophthalmologist), 118, 136, 137, 143, 160, 180
Thomas, Dr Jabez, 67, 88ff, 95, 100, 107, 120, 121, 126, 131, 134ff, 163–4
   complaints against, 82
   convener of first medical subcommittee, 103
   meeting with Friendly Societies, 77
   opens eye dispensary, 88ff
   praise for, 90, 92
   seeks permission to open eye clinic, 67, 88
Throat and Ear Hospital, an attempt to form, 134–5, 249n
tuberculosis, treatment of, 26, 62, 97, 104, 142, 189, 219, 249n
Turton, Dr William, 7–8
typhoid fever, 23, 83–4
typhus, 8–9, 23–4

unqualified doctors, 6, 57
University College, attempt to establish, 105
   request to teach science to nurses, 182

vaccination, 3–4, 7, 8, 15, 26, 28

venereal diseases, 38, 140, 160, 171, 205, 249n
Vivian family, 64, 164–5, 249n
Voluntary Hospitals Association, 170, 190, 202
Voss, John (Treasurer), 15, 17, 19

war,
   compensation for damage, 216, 221
   preparations for, 153ff, 208ff
Wardroper, Mrs, Matron of St Thomas's Hospital, London, 51, 246n
Wasdell, Mr (House Surgeon), 31, 34
Weir Mitchell treatment, 140, 248n
Welsh Board of Health, 189, 197, 201, 207, 212, 214ff, 220, 221, 225, 226, 229, 230, 232
   survey, 225, 251n
   see also Ministry of Health
Welsh Hospital Board, 233, 251n
Wiglesworth, Mr (surgeon), 55–6
Williams, Dr Thomas, FRS, 54, 57, 63ff, 66

Williams, Mr O.G. (surgeon), 58
Williams, Mr Thomas (surgeon), 3–4
women doctors, refusal to appoint, 136, 142
   see also Price, Dr Florence
Woods, Mr W.H.O. (orthopaedic surgeon), 165
workingmen's clubs, *see* Friendly Societies
workmen,
   contributions, 68, 75ff, 111ff, 115, 151ff, 161–2, 166, 188, 191ff, 200ff, 230
   contributory schemes, 111–12, 166, 168, 191, 194, 195, 197, 200, 202ff, 207, 209, 213, 224
   representatives, 72, 110ff, 148, 166, 169, 194, 196, 200ff, 210, 213

X-rays, 145, 164, 176–7, 193, 203, 205, 206, 215, 232
   injuries to staff from the use of, 176–7, 205